WESTERN NEVADA COLL

S0-ALD-023

3 1439 00083 5127

WITHDRAWN
LIBRARY & MEDIA SERVICES
WESTERN NEVADA COLLEGE
2201 WEST COLLEGE PARKWAY
CARSON CITY, NV 89703

MISS BLYTHE BULMER
128 Ralston Street
Reno, Nevada

F. B. BULMER
⌐ Ralston Street
Reno, Nevada

THE SIERRA

Other books by W. STORRS LEE

Canal Across a Continent
God Bless Our Queer Old Dean
The Strength to Move a Mountain
Yankees of Connecticut
Green Mountains of Vermont
Town Father
Bread Loaf Anthology (EDITOR)
Footpath in the Wilderness (EDITOR)
Stagecoach North
Father Went to College

THE SIERRA

by

W. STORRS LEE

ILLUSTRATIONS BY
EDWARD SANBORN

WNC
F
868
.S5
L44
1962
AP 08 '76

Bridgeport

Mono Lake

Tioga Pass

Mono Pass · Bishop

Big Pine

Kings Canyon
National Park   Independence

Sequoia
National Park   Lone Pine

isalia   Mt. Whitney

Porterville

Los Angeles Aqueduct

Nevada
California

Death Valley

Mojave Desert

Kern R.

Walker Pass

kersfield

Tehachani Pass

G. P. PUTNAM'S SONS
NEW YORK

© *1962 by W. STORRS LEE*

All rights reserved. This book, or parts thereof, must not be reproduced in any form without permission. Published simultaneously in the Dominion of Canada by Longmans, Green & Company, Toronto.

Library of Congress Catalog
Card Number: 61-12735

MANUFACTURED IN THE UNITED STATES OF AMERICA

To the Sierra Club

whose members for almost three quarters of a century have served as guardians of the Sierra Nevada wilderness, as pioneers in developing its recreational resources and as champions in the conquest of its heights.

CONTENTS

THE SIERRA

I

THE EARTH HEAVED
AND TOSSED

The first stunning shock of the Sierra earthquake of March 26th, 1872, came at twenty minutes past two in the morning. Under the impact, the whole chain of mountains trembled.

To an imperturbable old miner at Angels Camp the rumbling sounded like a train running deep underground directly beneath his shanty. At Visalia, ranch hands fancied they heard a shuddering bombardment far up in the Kings River and Kern Canyon country. Tehama neighbors compared notes and agreed that the noise was like that of a thousand stampeding cattle thundering over a wooden bridge.

Passengers at a stage post in Merced listened in awe to rocks and uprooted trees crashing down the Sierra slopes, and decided not to proceed farther. At the foot of Mount Whitney citizens soberly described a subterranean assault of heavy artillery—booming explosions that continued in close succession for hours, each followed by a jolting earth tremor that vibrated along the mountain range until lost in the distance.

"There was a peculiar throbbing motion," testified a jittery housewife. "Sometimes the house acted as though it were set on stiff, jouncing springs; again as if struck underneath by a monster, cushioned sledge hammer; at other times the sensation was like tossing about on a stormy ocean, and suddenly being dragged over a submerged rock."

One tremor rumbling under the city of Sacramento was enough to send the populace scurrying into the streets in their night clothes. As they ran, shock after shock grumbled under them with increasing intensity. Each jolt brought a rising crescendo of murmurs among the knots of onlookers anxiously listening to the ominous creak of buildings and an occasional crash of china inside. With a yell of terror a man, still hardly awake, leaped from the top story of a hotel, landed on the roof of an outhouse and sent forth yells of agony until silenced by police.

Even the oldest residents of Sacramento, and the proudest, agreed that the ramshackle metropolis had never been visited by anything like this. It was a humbling thing. The capital had maintained a superior attitude toward earthquakes. Tremors were supposed to be centered around that rival city of sin and sand dunes on the Bay—San Francisco. Sacramento liked to boast of its immunity.

Lights in the offices of the *Daily Bee* had been aglow all night. As the shocks continued, the presses came to a halt and an unsteady legman sauntered away from the building toward the milling crowds, in search of a story. He had felt real earthquakes in San Francisco and wasn't inclined to be impressed by the valley variety. He elbowed his way through the throng, took a constitutional down a few side streets and concluded that the worst was over. By his standards, the city had suffered little damage—except to its pride.

While the pressmen cooled their heels and the city calmed down, the *Bee* journalist collectedly scrawled his story. He gave it the light touch. According to his observations, the rumbling had indeed been "awful," but its distance from Sacramento was great. He referred to "troublous times in the bowels of the earth," expressed fears for what might have befallen the Bay region, deplored the hysteria of, and showed little sympathy for, the one casualty—the gentleman who had jumped from the hotel window.

Then with the effects of the earthquake dismissed and space still to fill, he launched into a frivolous review of Sacramento's night attire, describing in some detail the scant clothing in which female alarmists had made their debut for the evening's excitement. It was nothing short of scandalous, more shocking than the quake. He had witnessed the unmentionable. "Ladies made their appearance in public in a manner that would have put to the blush a corps of ballet girls," he alleged. For future earthquakes he warmly endorsed garments of more adequate modesty.

The Sacramento press did not encourage its readers to take the visitation too seriously; the city had every right to retain its superior attitude toward the shakes. But as newsmonger for the capital city of the State of California, the *Bee* next day did assume the responsibility for locating the likely center of a disturbance that must surely have raised havoc somewhere.

In a note of disguised disappointment, San Francisco soon had to be eliminated. Within twenty-four hours sleuths had pinpointed Visalia as the spot on the map where "the main force of the earth shock seems to have been expended." Brick buildings there had been badly cracked and one moved a full inch on its foundation. Moreover, great destruction was reported in the Sierra Nevada, directly east of Visalia. An editorial gave the enlightening explanation that "the shock was severest in the valleys where the deep alluviums propagate the waves of disturbance more vigorously than they would be propagated on the isolated and rocky peninsula upon which San Francisco is built."

But on the 29th all this had to be retracted and the focal point transferred to Owens Valley, east of the mountains, and "the little county of Inyo high in the Sierras." By telegram came a disturbing report that Independence had suffered gravely. Alas, that must be the center. The courthouse and the Exchange Hotel were destroyed, several brick residences flattened, the splendid store of Harris and Rhines was in ruins, and the Wells, Fargo express buried in them. In fact, there was not a brick or adobe building or chimney left standing in the forty-mile stretch between Bishop and Independence.

An enormous fissure, asserted the telegram, a fissure fifty to two-hundred feet wide and up to thirty-feet deep extended along the base of the Sierra. Springs that had never been known to fail were dry. Everywhere the earth was cracked and fragmented. Roads were blocked by huge boulders which had plummeted from mountain heights. Terrible snow slides had occurred at higher altitudes. There were countless injuries and one death from falling debris at Independence, but the greatest fears were felt for the isolated town of Lone Pine to the south.

Not until the first of April, six days after the earthquake, did the Sacramento editors learn the truth about Lone Pine and finally fix the center. And then it came second hand. San Francisco's *Examiner* had ignominiously scooped the *Bee*.

Colonel Whipple had extracted himself from the ruins of his home in Lone Pine, surveyed the general disaster about him for two days and hurried to San Francisco with the news and a call for help. "At Lone Pine at about half past two o'clock last Tuesday morning," Whipple reported, "the whole town was toppled over." Over fifty buildings lay in ruins. Twenty-seven people were dead, and many more grievously injured.

With him the Colonel brought a copy of his county newspaper, the Inyo *Independent,* which gave the stark details, and incidentally flaunted one of the most astonishing displays of typesetter's virtuosity ever to appear in a news journal. The earthquake had pied practically every case of type in the *Independent* office, but out of the rummage had been sorted enough Bodoni, Caslon, Goudy and Manuscript Gothic to create 72-point headlines running halfway down the front page in thirteen banks:

HORRORS!

APPALLING TIMES!

EARTHQUAKES!

AWFUL LOSS OF LIFE!

25 PERSONS KILLED!

EARTH OPENS!

HOUSES PROSTRATED!

LONE PINE!

ITS TERRIBLE CONDITION!

MOST HEART-RENDING SCENES!

MIRACULOUS ESCAPES!

INDIVIDUAL HEROISM!

A DEMORALIZED PRINTING OFFICE!

"No words of ours can begin to portray the terrors of that great moment," admitted the editor, "nor the great horror that fell upon every living thing. The solid earth was loosened from its foundations, and heaved and tossed as if in the throes of a terrible agony. The Mighty Power beneath it threw it up and down, hither and yon, as a strong man might toss a helpless babe.

"Men whose cheeks would never blanch in ordinary dangers cried out in a very agony of terror. Women screamed as they clasped their crying little ones. Cattle lowed, horses broke from their fastenings and huddled together, dogs howled, chickens left their roosts and staggered about in the darkness. Strong wooden houses bounded up and down and rolled to and fro like ships in a heavy seaway. Crockery smashed, and furniture danced about the floors. Chimneys dropped instantly to the ground; stone and adobe houses crumbled and went to earth like piles of sand, burying the miserable occupants in the ruins, and the whole world appeared to be in its last convulsions!"

In Lone Pine, directly at the foot of the highest mountain in the United States, had occurred such earth distortions as had seldom been known before on the continent. Altogether there were hundreds of shocks; though no one had neglected the nursing of his personal fears long enough to do any actual counting. Everywhere the surface was marked with cracks and seams. Down the valley for thirty-five miles, according to the report, stretched a yawning chasm from a few inches to four feet wide, and the level plain on which Lone Pine had been laid out was now broken by a scarp where the ground had lifted on one side and settled on the other, leaving a clean wall eight to ten feet high and three miles long.

Nature had gone on a rampage at the village. In the darkness of Tuesday night, people watched cascades of rock roaring down the mountains in monstrous avalanches, throwing out such brilliant trails of sparks that they were assumed to be flows of lava. Rumor after rumor of widespread volcanic eruption poured in.

At the height of the detonations from the quake, both the Kern and Owens Rivers had reversed their courses and run upstream until the beds were completely drained. Then suddenly the water turned and came rushing back in a small tidal wave. At Tibbets Ranch a plot of forty acres had sunk seven feet. Big Owens Lake had risen four feet to a new high-water mark, while another lake to the south had entirely disappeared. Owens River first overran its banks, depositing quantities of fish along the shores, then receded to a fraction of its normal flow; and across what had been a parched plain, a brand new creek was now cutting a meandering channel.

Sinners and pillars of virtue alike were sure that the end of the world was upon them. The continuous underground explosions could only mean that an avenue to hell was about to open up. In the midst of all the disturbance, a band of Indians quickly broke camp and disappeared. Not that they were concerned about the fire and brimstone of nether regions—they had been frightened out of their wits by the tales of a wise old chief who reminded them of another spasm of nature in forgotten past ages, when a chain of hills hugging the Sierra had settled into Owens Valley. No telling, claimed the Indians, California might be facing a similar upset. They had no hankering to stay around for it.

In time, agents of science arrived on the scene to survey the area more philosophically than had either Colonel Whipple or the Indian chief. They pared down the statistics of *Bee* chroniclers, but no one denied that the survivors of the frightful Sierra earthquake had seen and heard an earth disruption of staggering magnitude. Shocks radiating from the range had shaken up most of California and Nevada—a total area of no less than 150,000 square miles.

But what the people of Lone Pine had actually witnessed was little more than a trivial encore to a major terrestrial drama that had started almost three-quarters of a million years before. Far back in geologic time, Owens Valley was part of the High Sierra, perched at a lofty height of 9,000 feet, and the range itself a vast arch extending much farther to the east. But near the eastern crest, running north and south for many miles, a great fracture in the arch occurred.

Along the fault line the whole east flank of the Sierra gave way in a marvelous spectacle of crashing rock, fiery lava flows and quakes that must have shuddered across the continent. The jagged peaks held in place, while inch by inch the gigantic block that was to form Owens Valley slumped down and down; granite crushing against granite, crumbling and cleaving with explosive force. Over the years it dropped more than five thousand feet. The shocks that Lone Pine experienced in March, 1872, were only a belated repercussion from that ancient cataclysm.

It was the collapse of the eastern wall that finally left the Sierra with the general form and profile it still retains—a vast barrier stretching down the continent for 430 miles, reaching from the depression just south of a volcanic peak known as Lassen to the southern end of a pass called Tehachapi. In width the range varied from forty to eighty miles, all a single uptilted block of the earth's crust, large enough to carry on its spine a whole system of linear ranges.

On the west side was a gradual slope comprising 90 per cent of the total area of the range; on the east, along the old fault line, the heights fell off precipitously to form one of the boldest escarpments on the relief map of the globe. The great plains, of which the Sierra had once been a part, remained virtually unchanged, and the mountains stood out as a bold oasis surrounded by dry lowlands.

The canyon contours and the very bulk of the range itself were created in an infinitely slow process of earth forces—upheaval, subsidence, recurrent upheaval; the interminable, undramatic action of glacier, frost and stream wearing away at the surface. But spectacle was always present; ostentatious spectacle, violence, pageantry, magnificent dimension characterized the range during its millions of years of geologic history, and the character has not changed during the brief association with human history.

The mountains are so spectacular that they seem to call out for action and incident on the grand scale. Here are the greatest continuous mountain block and the highest peak in the United States, south of Alaska; here are the largest trees in the world, some of the deepest and most beautiful valleys, the rarest collection of leaping waterfalls; and here lies the most formidable natural obstruction between the Atlantic and Pacific coasts, a challenge to be met in spectacular feats of human endurance by a procession of pioneers, explorers and mountaineers. They are exciting mountains echoing to the roar of waterfalls and the rush of rivers, the surge of storms and the thunder of avalanche. Even in their quiescent moods, the mountains retain their air of suspense. They never seem to be completely at rest.

Time and again, in past ages, the monotony of the low

building up and wearing away of the Sierra was interrupted by overwhelming phenomena of nature—such indelible highlights in geologic history that the details can still be clearly read in the rocks. Four times stupendous icecaps blanketed the range, except the highest peaks, and over long periods gigantic glaciers inched their way far down the slopes to gouge out valleys like Yosemite and the Grand Canyon of Tuolumne. Faults and fragmentation occurred repeatedly high in the mountains, leaving souvenirs like the sheer scarp which rises to a height of 400 feet near the mouth of Kern River Canyon. Terrible and grand were the periodic floods that washed down the western slopes with ever-increasing velocity as the range was slowly uptilted.

But no cataclysms were more prodigious than the frequent volcanic eruptions. The black façades of Mount Ritter and Banner Peak, "The King and Queen of the Sierra," and the Minarets, standing in stark contrast to neighboring giants of granite, recite their story of early volcanic origin. High in the basin of the Middle Fork of the San Joaquin River rises the Devil's Post Pile, a monumental cliff of basalt lava columns, sixty feet high, prisms of four, five and six sides so perfectly honeycombed together that they appear to have been carved and stacked by superhuman hands. And two miles south, Rainbow Fall leaps 140 vertical feet over a similar cliff. Those marvelous "posts" were formed from billowing streams of red-hot lava that poured from an earth vent at Mammoth Pass and rolled for six miles down the mountainside.

Once the whole northern third of the range was all but buried under successive floods of volcanic mud and blankets of cinders ejected from craters along the crest. All the original northern mountain contours, except the highest peaks, were obliterated under thousand-foot layers of igneous debris; and had the devastating eruptions extended fifty miles farther south, the site of Yosemite Valley would have been despoiled too.

The line of Mono volcanoes extending for twelve miles south of Mono Lake, bubbling hot springs spotted here and there in the mountains, disintegrating drifts of pumice, cinder cones and trails of ancient lava flows, all bear witness to past episodes of spectacular volcanic activity.

But it has been a long time since the last violent eruption occurred in the range. It is necessary to look to Mount Lassen, nearest mountain neighbor of the northern Sierra, for recent incidents that demonstrate the kind of disruption to which the range was subjected in prehistoric times.

Unwitnessed by white men, a cinder cone ten miles north of Lassen Peak blew its top in the early 1800's and belched forth a deep body of lava. In a stream four miles long and two wide, it snaked across the valley, setting aflame the fields and forests, temporarily turning a lake in its path into a boiling caldron and then permanently dividing it into halves. When first identified it was thought to be the only lava eruption of modern history in the continental United States, and discovery of the huge extrusion raised questions among geologists as to just how dormant the mountain was.

The questions were answered on May 30th, 1914: Lassen Peak suddenly awoke from a sleep of centuries, and in a grim display began emitting tons of rock and ash under an imposing plume of steam and smoke. It was a momentous event—exciting news to valley residents who still liked to believe that Lassen belonged to the Sierra rather than the Cascade Range, and stirring news to a nation that didn't know it had an active volcano—though scientists referred to it derogatively as a "gigantic plug cone."

Intermittently for days new explosions and blacker eruptions occurred. Between them, rangers climbed the 10,466-foot mountain and brought back reports that another crater had indeed formed. The top of the mountain was strewn with rock debris, its snowcap littered and discolored with ashes. Sightseers and tourists thronged to the base of the peak for a look.

To please the curious, enterprising promoters arranged a stage lift as far as Manzanita Lake, four miles by trail from the crest, and started talk of giving Lassen its deserved status as a national park. Then for a few days the mountain became disappointingly quiet; the excitement seemed to have ended.

On June 13th a group of ten local gadabouts got together and decided they had seen enough from below. They wanted a more intimate view. Assembling at Manzanita Lake, they spent the night there, and early the next morning set out for the top.

The scene that greeted them from the edge of the crater was anything but glamorous. It was just as the rangers had reported—dirty snow, lots of broken rock strewn around; altogether a very dull show as a reward for so stiff a climb.

But they weren't given much time to air their dissatisfaction. Suddenly, without an instant's warning, as they stood on the lip of the steaming maw, everything before them exploded. In the deafening noise of a thunderclap the crater blew up. Clouds of black ash turned the top of the mountain into midnight darkness. The ten men became mere shadows to each other.

Stunned by the explosion and half suffocated by the smoke, they stumbled over the loose rock, hurriedly retreating from the crater—every man for himself. Worse than the blinding ash and the Stygian gloom was the gas; gagging sulphur fumes. Draping coats over their heads for masks and cushions, they struggled over the rough footing on the run.

Chips of hot rock that had been catapulted high into the air rained down on them like flying shrapnel. They bounced, shattered and sizzled on the moist ground. The men groped for some refuge, but there was none on the exposed summit. Pelted by the debris, they scrambled for the nearest incline, shouting at one another to keep together.

Six did manage to remain together; the other four vanished in the darkness. Explosion after explosion burst behind them, each adding to the torrent of lava fragments and the blinding shroud of ash. Still there was no shelter from the smoking barrage.

Once off the shoulder of the summit, the six fugitives found the going easier. Bruised and battered, they plunged down the mountainside through the fields of deep snow, and at last began to get out of range of the falling rock. With coats wrapped around their heads, they buried themselves in snow to escape the suffocating gases. All six were beaten, winded and shaken, but lucky to be alive.

For four hours they lay in the snow, as the eruption continued. They had a strong compulsion to make a dash for safer ground, but they had lost four of their company on the summit and couldn't leave before at least attempting a search. By the middle of the afternoon the explosions began to diminish; then they ceased abruptly. The air cleared. Cautiously the six dug themselves out of their snow caches and with very little enthusiasm started for the top.

Through the day the magnificent eruption had been closely watched in the valley. It was the most violent one that had yet occurred. The plume of black smoke darkened the sun, and the thunder of the explosions had an ominous sound. Word quickly passed that ten men were presumably on the summit at the time of the first outburst, and no one gave them a remote chance of survival. It was too late to organize a search party. No point in risking more lives, they argued. The bodies could be found just as well next day, after the volcano let up.

But late in the afternoon the coroner in Redding received a phone call from Manzanita Lake. Seven of the ten had survived, he learned; six, after spending most of the afternoon in a snowbank, had returned to the summit, found one man completely demented by the ordeal—a raving lunatic who had to be forcibly restrained; another was found buried in lava dust, horribly mangled, with his chest torn open and a shoulder almost severed—dead; and the remaining two had probably met a similar fate, for no trace of them could be found. At Manzanita Lake official instructions were wanted on what to do with the body.

"Go on back to the top and bring the corpse down," advised the coroner inconsiderately. He'd start for the lake at once and would meet the survivors there.

It was long past nightfall when a second call came from Manzanita Lake. Now the story was entirely different. The two lost men had turned up uninjured; the maniac had shaken off his delirium; and miracle of miracles, when the leg-weary scouts reached the summit, the corpse had shown signs of life. Despite his desperate injuries, his exposure at a freezing altitude for half a day, first smothered by lava ashes and then chilled in a snow bank, the man was alive—"Call off the coroner and send a doctor quick!"

All ten of the fire-eaters outlived the harrowing day—the only mortals ever known to have a volcano blow up in their faces and survive to brag of it. Like the people of Lone Pine, they had seen firsthand, and at all too close range, some suggestion of the spectacular violence which the California mountains had weathered in their younger years.

The Lassen and Lone Pine disturbances were hardly more than dying gasps and quivers of a long-recumbent range. Belonging to the geologic past are the great volcanic eruptions and lava flows, the major upheavals and depressions. Mountain disfigurations are mostly superficial now, the surface etchings of fire, glacier, avalanche and tempestuous storm. But even these forces are fierce enough to rack the heights catastrophically, and of these fire is the most savage.

Forest conflagrations raging out of control over thousands of mountain acres bring destruction that can be roughly estimated in terms of dollars and board feet of lumber lost, but there is no way to calculate the scenic loss, the despoiling of water resources, and the devastation from erosion that inevitably follows. Fire and its consequences can alter the appearance of a mountain almost as radically as the most virulent commotion from the earth's interior.

Native Indian hunters burned the forests methodically to flush game and to clear low growth for broader visibility. Back in 1910 when the scars from these burnings were more evident, a conservationist estimated that the Indians had reduced the original virgin stands of timber by 35 per cent, and converted 2,000,000 acres of priceless woodland into unproductive wastes.

Nor can the early conflagrations all be blamed on the aborigines. Fires caused by lightning were fully as destructive. The top of a sequoia, ignited by a bolt, burns furiously for days; a colossal torch two hundred feet above ground, showering the surroundings with wind-blown sparks. Early explorers probing deep into the Sierra wilderness, where there were neither Indians nor white men, would sometimes see several distant forest fires simultaneously sweeping across a wide landscape.

In a confusion of debris the remains of a great sugar pine, five feet in diameter and 175 feet high, were once found in Kern Canyon. It had been struck by a deadly bolt of lightning at the tip and its bark stripped in a perfect spiral to the base of the crown. There the charge had exploded a six-foot segment of the trunk as though it were packed with dynamite, casting charred splinters about the forest in all directions. Released in mid-air, twenty tons of crown had come crashing down. The splintered stump had driven four feet into the ground, then the crown had toppled over to scatter fragments of smoldering wood for 150 feet. Rain had doused the embers and preserved a story of the majestic death of a pine, yet all too commonly in the electric storms of the High Sierra there is no accompanying downpour to extinguish the blazes they kindle.

In the last century hordes of campers, tourists, mountaineers, lumbermen and sheepherders have joined the conspiracy against the mountains and inadvertently set off fires in their favorite haunts. The Lake Tahoe region, with its expanse of sapphire water, its frame of sheer cliffs and white-topped mountains, is a notable example.

At an elevation of over 6,000 feet Tahoe ranks among the world's three greatest Alpine lakes; its crystal depths and magnificent setting make it one of the nation's scenic wonders. Mark Twain called it "the fairest picture the whole earth affords." Yet time and again the surroundings have been recklessly ravaged by human incendiaries—and Twain is not the least of the offenders.

On a camping trip there in 1870, like many another woods vagabond, he too let his fire get out of hand one evening. It spread along the carpet of needles, flared up in a pocket of paper-dry cones, caught onto low-hanging branches and was off. Trapped on the wrong side, Twain's campmate Johnny dashed through the flames to the shore. The two hastily made for their rowboat and shoved out into the lake where they had a stunning view of the pyrotechnics.

"The ground was deeply carpeted with dry pine needles, and the fire touched them off as if they were gunpowder," Twain narrated graphically. "It was wonderful to see with what fierce speed the tall sheet of flame traveled! In a minute and a half the fire seized upon a dense growth of manzanita chaparral six to eight feet high, and then the roaring and popping and crackling was something terrific.

"Within half an hour all before us was a tossing, blinding tempest of flame! It went surging up adjacent ridges—surmounted them and disappeared in the canyons beyond—burst into view upon higher and farther ridges presently—shed a grander illumination abroad, and dove again—flamed out again, directly, higher and still higher up the mountainside—threw out skirmishing parties of fire here and there, and sent them trailing their crimson spirals away among remote ramparts and ribs and gorges, till as far as eye could reach, the lofty mountain fronts were webbed, as it were, with a tangled network of red lava streams. Away across the water the crags and domes were lit up with a ruddy glare, and the firmament above was a reflected hell!

"Every feature of the spectacle was repeated in the glowing mirror of the lake. Both pictures were sublime, both were beautiful; but that in the lake had a bewildering richness about it that enchanted the eye. We sat absorbed and motionless through four long hours. By eleven o'clock the conflagration had traveled beyond our range of vision, and then darkness stole down upon the landscape."

To a modern Sierran, finding aesthetic entertainment in such a blaze would be like acclaiming the glory of a burning cathedral. Mark Twain bemoaned the loss of his possessions and the blackening of his camp site, but if his conscience was pricked with contrition for what he had started, he wasn't inclined to express it. Not a shovel was lifted to fight the conflagration. No sirens came screaming up the highway. No roving reporter flashed the news of a fire storm racing into the Sierra.

It was very different a century later when a similar holocaust swept across the mountains at the end of the hot, dry summer of 1960. TAHOE AREA HIT BY RAGING FIRES, trumpeted banner headlines in the West. FOUR STATES SEND HELP. THREE MILLION IN TIMBER DESTROYED. Nor was the fire of purely local concern. Newspapers three thousand miles away from the smoke and flames spread the alarm.

"I saw the charred carcass of a cow that died running from the flames," wrote a spot reporter working in the smudge hanging over Forest Hill village. "A bewildered deer leaps through the blackened, smoky forest. An old man surveys the smoldering ruins of his barn. Rotten logs and old trees glow and flame amid the black tree trunks rising from the gray forest floor. A cloud of smoke billows 8,090 feet into the summer sky. Cars and trucks line the streets loaded with family belongings, in case the evacuation order should come. The town's memorial park is the base of 1,200 fire fighters.

"It is like the Army. Chow lines form beside open-air kitchens and the weapons of the fire fighters are stacked in neat rows on the bandstand. Trucks bring in new provisions and equipment. Trucks move out carrying fire fighters to a new hot spot or break in the fireline. The General—a State forest ranger—works in a trailer headquarters. Orders come and go through a mobile radio station furnished by the California Disaster Office. Farmer Russell Powell was still cutting a firebreak around his home when he was ordered to evacuate . . ."

This was no ordinary fire. Three of them were raging simultaneously a few miles back from Lake Tahoe. The one at Forest Hill was a real fire storm, blistering through the trees at incredible speed. Thirty thousand acres had been blackened by the explosive blaze in a few hours. The entire village of Bath was gone, and a dozen homes in Michigan Bluff and Baker Ranch destroyed. Scores of mountain hamlets were evacuated. Over fifteen hundred men were on the fire line and re-enforcements were on their way from Montana, Washington, Oregon and Idaho.

A few miles to the north in the heart of the old gold rush country, sprinkled with names like "Bullards Bar," "French Corral" and "Rough and Ready," a second fire exploded. Overnight its expanse broadened from 1,500 acres to 7,000. The town of North San Juan was imperiled, but fighters were gaining in the battle. They hoped to save the town.

Worst of all was the third fire near Donner Lake, over the mountain crest north of Tahoe. It hadn't appeared too serious at first, and there was some prospect of confining it to a seven-thousand acre zone. But then forty-mile-an-hour winds had swooped across it and sent crackling flames over an area more than three times as large. Route 40 over Donner Pass was closed, except for local and emergency traffic. The fire had traveled seventeen miles in twenty-four hours. It was within five miles of the Nevada border and the border was less than ten from the outskirts of Reno.

Along Donner Ridge, fires had melted miles of power line that fed electricity to a territory of 15,000 square miles, with a population of 90,000. Filling stations were closed because electric pumps were dead, and hundreds of motorists were stranded with empty gas tanks.

The Reno gambling citadel was in turmoil—almost entirely blacked out. Burglar alarms were off. Nevada sheriffs and highway-patrol cars could no longer communicate with headquarters. Restaurants were serving cold meals by candlelight. Three hundred cars were trapped in a pigeonhole garage when the electric elevator ceased to operate. Marilyn Monroe and a host of Hollywood celebrities were in town for the world première of *Let's Make Love*. The show had to be canceled for lack of power to run the film. A heavyweight fight was called off.

Only the gambling casinos seemed to have Diesel power, and business there was booming in a dim light. Clouds of smothering smoke had settled over the city, penetrating every street and enclosure with their stale odor.

Around Lake Tahoe the situation was the same—no electricity, no power, water shortage, gasoline shortage. Only a fringe of the lake could be seen, for the pall of yellow smoke limited visibility to a few hundred yards.

Armies of men were on the fire lines and larger armies were assembling at strategic points. Volunteers by the truckload poured in from surrounding towns and cities. Experienced fighters were now being rallied in eight states. Marines and navy personnel were arriving by plane from Alameda and Oakland. Eight hundred air-force men had been mobilized— from Hamilton Base at Marin, Travis near Fairfield, McClellan at Sacramento, Stead at Reno. Trained Apaches, Navahos and Zuñis, in tin hats and combat regalia, were being flown from Albuquerque. All available forest-service men—federal, state and local—were on duty.

The infantry was backed by all the heavy equipment that could be rounded up. Thirty bulldozers roared and coughed along Donner Ridge, carving breaks and tearing into the forest floor; thirty-six battled the fire at Forest Hill. Power shovels and graders worked with them. Scores of trucks hauled men and supplies up logging roads. A dozen helicopters whirred through the smoke making surveys, dropping supplies and chemicals. Ancient bombers, flying low, dropped tankloads of borate.

Plane and helicopter pilots were having a rough time. The smoke camouflaged the fire. Dense black clouds rolled up to heights of 9,000 feet. The whole Tahoe region was under a black blanket. Even the men on the ground weren't sure where the worst of the blaze was. Swept by spotty winds of forty and fifty miles per hour, fingers of fire raced ahead in minutes, or flying embers touched off isolated blazes a half mile beyond the known line.

The assault began on Saturday, August 20th. Into Sunday

the fires continued to scud across the mountains, under control only in a few areas where concentrations of men and equipment were massed. By late Sunday the line was holding at Forest Hill. North San Juan had been saved. A finger reaching toward Verdi and Reno was in check. In a few key sectors rampant blazes were stopped by bulldozed breaks, borate bombing and the frantic work of men on foot.

By Monday afternoon officials began to issue announcements with an occasional optimistic phrase. Reports of fronts 40 per cent under control, 50 per cent, 70 per cent were released. A change in weather brought relief. Winds subsided and temperatures dropped. Working in the heat of ankle-deep ashes and smoking rubble, linesmen repaired the collapsed power lines. Reno and Lake Tahoe once more had electricity, and traffic could start moving.

But fresh outbreaks of fire continued to occur in deep canyons and on remote mountain slopes. The margins were now the danger zones. They had to be guarded constantly against ember blazes started by wind eddies and underground smudges that could burst into flame yards outside a break. Every foot of the boundary line had to be patrolled, and it was a long way around. The seven-mile rim of the Donner fire was considered rather formidable on Sunday; two days later the perimeter was stretched to fifty-five miles.

Not until Friday, nearly a week after the first smoke had been reported, would anyone venture a declaration that the fires were completely licked. By then a total of 75,000 acres had been ravaged, 150,000,000 board feet of timber destroyed —enough timber to build a city of 9,000 homes. And exclusive of the lumber loss, the fires had run up an estimated expenditure of $2,000,000 in fire-fighting costs and miscellaneous damage. Countless hundreds of stricken deer and other game littered the blackened Sierra. Although a realistic figure to represent the over-all destruction could never be computed, someone made a guess at $5,500,000.

Yet before the fire fighters had left the scene, conservationists were already planning reforestation; planes and helicopters were dropping mustard and rye grass seed, with the hope that a ground cover would sprout before autumn rains brought floods and erosion. In another hundred years the fire site would be hard to find.

Scarred areas like those of the Lake Tahoe region dot the length and breadth of the Sierra Nevada, but so vast is the range that it can absorb a multitude of local disasters and still retain the sum of its splendor: the spectacle of scenic grandeur easily surpasses the spectacle of catastrophe that recurrently visits the slopes.

And spectacle it is—the towering summit of Mount Whitney, highest point in the land, overlooking the lowest point 14,777 feet below; the valleys, falls and mile-high cliffs of Yosemite; Lake Tahoe, "the fairest picture the whole earth affords"; the highland wilderness of Kings Canyon; the groves of giant sequoias; flower-banked mountain meadows; titanic glaciers grinding away at the upper heights; the Pacific storms riding the mountain crests.

There is the spectacle of human drama, too—drama created by men trying to conquer the passes and summits, borrow wealth from the rugged flanks and cope with the moods and mysteries of the mountains. The range is the noblest backdrop in America for the drama of contrast: violence against beauty, struggle against repose, tragedy against fortune.

"This is the morning of creation, the whole thing is beginning now. The mountains are singing together," cried John Muir with a patriarchal gesture one morning, from a granite ledge overlooking the magnificence of Vernal and Nevada Falls in Yosemite. Many thousands have experienced similar moments in the Sierra. The trials of time and nature have engraved deep character lines on the face of the mountains. They are old and they have known torment, but their morning is still young. The whole thing is just beginning.

II

WHO OPENED THE GATES
TO THE WEST?

Neither Captain John Smith nor King James I knew it, but Virginia was granted prior territorial claim to the Sierra Nevada. Under a charter of 1609, the colony was to extend "from sea to sea"—from Atlantic to Pacific—the lower boundary following a transcontinental parallel of latitude that cut across California well south of Tehachapi, the upper rigged at a northwesterly angle that had to take in the northern extremities of the Sierra, with Mounts Lassen and Shasta thrown in for good measure.

By royal retraction the bounds were later liberally reduced, and Virginia, like other early colonies, eventually ceded its western lands to the Union. Nevertheless, those magnanimous grants did serve a purpose. From the beginning they stirred colonists with a curiosity to explore their broad back yards, While Virginia still held title to the land, pioneers pushed westward over the Appalachians. They investigated their holdings all the way to the Mississippi, established a county called Kentucky, promoted settlements of promise in Ohio. An enterprising young Virginian, George Washington, served his first military and political apprenticeship in trying to preserve western extraterritorial claims.

Nor were the sense of land covetousness and the determined urge to explore dampened even after the property was nationalized. Virginia took the lead in exploring the terrain it had relinquished. Trailhound Daniel Boone, a fringe Virginian by virtue of his Kentucky residence, went on the prowl. Thomas Jefferson, most ardent of advocates for finding a path to the Pacific, released his own secretary, Meriwether Lewis, and sent him on a momentous venture with William Clark all the way to the mouth of the Columbia. Although the Lewis and Clark expedition was made in the interests of a nation, the leadership and most of the recruits for it came from the oldest of the thirteen original states.

By default of statesmen and scientists, the first significant penetration of the West came through commercial exploitation—the reconnoitering of fur dealers; and here still another Virginian, William Henry Ashley, of the Rocky Mountain Fur Company, stole the leading role as he pushed his rowdy squads of trappers into the Rockies, beyond them and toward the Sierra.

Ashley did things in a big way. He recruited his boys by the hundreds—restless fellows, social outcasts, ruffians handy with guns, impenitent outlaws. He packed them off to St. Louis and from there to remote outposts in search of beaver. After the Blackfoot Indians made things too hot for him in the headwaters of the Missouri, he shifted his men to the upper reaches of the Yellowstone, the Columbia, the Colorado or wherever their lust for the hunt might lead them. They were gradually moving in on the Sierra.

The Indians had long held annual summer-trading fairs at which friendly tribes gathered to swap furs and horses for European trinkets, beads, riding gear and blankets brought in from Mexico. Ashley borrowed the idea and organized the first trappers' rendezvous in the summer of 1825 on the Green River in Utah. From St. Louis, which had become the emporium of the fur trade, he imported impressive displays of wares and cheap whiskies. The Indians came in throngs, brought their squaws, their wigwams and their pelts. They loved it, and so did the ruffian whites just in from the far frontiers. It was a whirlwind blowout for Ashley's men, and a splashing festival for the Indians.

The second rendezvous, in 1826, was so successful that Ashley could retire on the fortune he had made. He sold the business to a trio of his trappers, and Jedediah Smith was one of the three. It was this transaction that led to the first crossing of the Sierra, and seemed to signal the end of Virginia's predominance in Western reconnaissance. The Yankees and Yorkers took over.

Smith was a six-foot, Bible-reading Northerner from western New York, and such an ardent student of the Ashley school of trapping that he outstripped the master. Still only in his middle twenties, he had already scouted the West from St. Louis to Montana and the Canadian border, explored the Salt Lake country and knew more about the wilds of Wyoming, Colorado and Utah than any living man. He had haggled with the Arikari Indians in the Dakotas, the Mandans and Flatheads of Montana, the Iroquois working for Hudson's Bay Company in the far northwest and the Blackfeet above Yellowstone. A

superb rifleman and as canny as a fox in wriggling out of
trouble, he was regarded as the wariest frontiersman working out of St. Louis or Salt Lake.

Ashley had been a big operator; Smith intended to be a
bigger one. His first step in meeting that objective was to move
southwest almost in an opposite direction from the general trapping traffic. He wanted to size up an entirely new, virgin area.
With fifteen veterans picked from a wealth of candidates at the
1826 rendezvous, he set out from Great Salt Lake, and a few
weeks later was scouting Southern Utah for signs of beaver.

But the usual Jedediah luck had played out. Beaver were
scarce on the Green River, scarcer on the Sevier. Every kind of
game seemed to have disappeared from the headwaters of the
Virgin River. Smith's supplies were getting low and the horses
were failing, still they kept going, counting on a change in
luck.

Exhausted and discouraged, they wandered into a Mohave
village where they managed to postpone the threat of starvation with the corn and pumpkins the Indians were willing to
share. Their situation looked hopeless to the Mohaves. "Why
not appeal to your white brothers for help?" proposed an Indian who had picked up a few words of Spanish; "the missions are not far away."

Smith had heard of those missions in Mexican California,
and he had heard of a long range of mountains some two hundred miles inland from the Pacific which might be good beaver
country. It could prove disastrous to turn back; California
might bring a shift in their fortunes. The Indian's proposal
made good sense.

A disconsolate Smith once more became the enterprising
Smith, brimming with large ideas, and playing with a vague
conception of western geography. On the spot he changed his
whole winter itinerary; he would get fresh supplies from the
missions, follow one of the California rivers to its source in the
high mountains, collect his beaver, then cross the mountains
by a short route to Great Salt Lake.

Smith and his cohorts continued on down the Colorado,

suffered their way over the parched Mohave Desert and on November 27th, 1826, checked in at Mission San Gabriel—on the outskirts of present-day Los Angeles. They had made the first overland trip to California.

Father José Bernado Sánchez, head of the mission, was a man of worldly sophistication as well as of Catholic sophistry; he realized at once that these tousled, travel-drugged trappers had made history, but they were foreigners without passports, and he wasn't at all sure how the Governor General at San Diego might react to the invasion. The unpredictable Governor might take it into his head to honor them with stately ceremony; he was just as likely to rank them as spies and toss them into prison. So Fray José played safe. He welcomed them with Christian charity, graciously invited them to surrender their arms, ushered Smith to the guest room reserved for distinguished visitors in his own mansion, and saw that the seventeen subordinates were well housed.

At the polite hour of ten o'clock all were summoned to drinks and dinner. Over the bottles and viands the reserve of the friars disappeared; priests and ragged explorers struck up an exchange in broken English and broken Spanish. "I was introduced to the two priests over a glass of good old whisky," gloated Rogers, the company clerk, "and found them to be very jovial, friendly gentlemen. Supper consisted of a number of different dishes, served different from any table I ever was at. There was great feasting among the men, as they was pretty hungry, not having had any good meat for some time. Plenty of good wine during supper, and before the cloth was removed segars was introduced. . . . They all appear and treat us well; although they are Catholics by profession, they allow us the liberty of conscience, and treat us as they do their own countrymen or brethren. Everything went on in style, with the priests being pretty merry. They all appear to be gentlemen of the first class, both in manner and habits."

The next day brought more of the same—tea, bread and cheese served at sunrise, gin cocktails before lunch. The visitors were taken on an inspection tour of the mission, and again Rogers offered nothing but uncompromising praise of the establishment: "The four rows of houses forming a complete square, where there is all kinds of macanicks at work; the church faces the east and the guardhouse the west; the north and south line composes the workshops. They have large vineyards, apple and peach orchards, and some orrange and some fig trees. They manufacture blankets, and sundry other articles; they distill whisky and grind their own grain, having a water mill of a tolerable quality; they have upwards of one thousand persons employed, men, women and children, Indians of different nations. The situation is very handsome, pretty streams of water running through from all quarters, some thousands of acres of rich and fertile land as level as a die in view, and a part under cultivation, surrounded on the north with a high and lofty mountain, handsomely timbered with pine and cedar, and on the south with low mountains covered with grass. Cattle—the mission has upwards of thirty thousand head, and horses, sheep, hogs, etc. in proportion. They slaughter at this place from two thousand to three thousand head of cattle at a time; the mission lives on the profits."

But the impatient Jedediah was in search of beaver; he wasn't going to be taken in by the peaches, pork and prime ribs. A few days of this hospitality would see his men getting soft and fat. He wanted to get on with his business. All he desired from the priests were a few supplies and their blessings on an expedition to the north. "Ah," confided the good friar, "permission to travel in the province can come only from the Governor General in San Diego, and he has already been informed of your wishes."

To speed up the processes of Mexican administration, Smith himself drafted a letter to the Governor and was shortly ordered to appear for a formal audience. But the trapper's reception in San Diego was far from cordial. He was relieved of his diary, placed under surveillance and generally caught up in the toils of a tedious bureaucracy. Finally in desperation he sent off an appeal to the United States' Plenipotentiary in Mexico.

"I wrote to the Governor General requesting permission to pass through the country to the Bay of San Francisco," Smith summarized. "I wished to follow up one of the largest rivers that emptied into the Bay, cross the mountain at its head and from thence to our Deposit on the waters of the Salt Lake. After waiting for an answer 9 days (during which time my self and men were verry hospitably treated by the Reverend Father and obliging little Commandant) I received an order to go to the Governor at Sandiego, a distance of 50 leagues. Here I have been questioned and cross-examined three different times by the Governor (who appears to be much of a Gentleman, but very Suspicious). I have endeavored to convince him of the truth that I was only a hunter and that dire necessity had driven me here. I am to call next tuesday for to know whether I can pass or be detained here for three months for an answer from Mexico . . . He seems to be detaining me until he ascertains that I am no spy—which will deprive me of making a valuable spring hunt."

Meantime back at Mission San Gabriel, Smith's men were having the time of their lives. There were Indian women as well as ample stores of liquor to keep them happy. Though there were lapses of conduct, the ribald, unkempt trappers did everything they could to ingratiate themselves with the Holy Fathers. They attended services regularly, volunteered to do little chores, went hunting with the padres, roamed freely about the Indian shops, helped break in wild horses, showed the mission blacksmith how they made their bear traps and constructed one in which to catch natives who were stealing oranges. They swapped pelts for new clothes, presented Fray José with eight of their finest beaverskins as facing for his ceremonial robes, made good use of their time in putting equipment in order, shoeing their horses—and kept their night life to themselves.

"My situation is a delicate one," confessed Rogers, sorely embarrassed over his limited wardrobe. "I have to be amongst the grandees of the country every day; and make a grotesque appearance when seated at table next the dandys with their ruffles, silks and broadcloths."

Rogers was more selective in his feminine companionship than some of his associates. "The women here are very unchaste," he alleged. "All that I have seen and heard speak, appear very vulgar in their conversation and manners. They think it an honnour to ask a white man to sleep with them; one came to my lodgings last night and asked me to make her a blanco Pickanina, which, being interpreted, is to get her a white child, and I must say, for the first time I was ashamed, and did not gratify her or comply with her request. Seeing her so forward, I had no propensity to tech her."

Smith, far removed from the gallivanting at San Gabriel, finally got his reply from the Governor. The appeal to the American diplomat had been futile. In a brusque edict, the trappers were ordered to leave the province promptly. They would not be permitted to go to San Francisco, but must leave at once by the same route over which they had come.

The order was accepted without dispute. It was final. Smith returned to Mission San Gabriel, where "the Reverend Father and obliging little Commandant" were better disposed toward him than the government. He spent a few more weeks cultivating the good will of Fray José, succeeded in purchasing forty-one new horses, took on supplies of corn, peas, flour, cheese and dried meat—mostly as presents. By the middle of February they were ready to take leave of Fray José. "I ever shall hold him a man of God, taking us in when in distress, feeding and clothing us, and may God prosper him and all such men," Rogers offered as a benediction.

The merry padres bade farewell to their guests, now outfitted with a train of sixty-eight horses, but no sooner was Smith out of sight of San Gabriel than he quit the trail on which he had been granted permission to travel, and turned north. The friars had verified the information about a long range of mountains they called the Sierra Nevada, and Smith was going there as quickly as possible, regardless of the Governor's command.

Staying clear of the chain of Spanish missions by a safe 150 miles, the eighteen men guided their horses up the San Joaquin Valley, over a route parallel to the Sierra—trapping and hunting as they went. Repeatedly they encountered bands of friendly Indians, notable chiefly for their nakedness, their short-cropped hair and their diet of acorns, roots and grass; but the grass-eating Indians had few pelts to barter.

Finally they set up camp along the upper waters of the San Joaquin River, and from there Smith decided to attempt a crossing of the mountains to Salt Lake. The valleys were green and hot; the snow in the high country would surely be melting; they had to get on their way to Salt Lake and the summer rendezvous.

It was springtime in the valley, but the mountaineers soon learned that winter still held the highlands in a fierce grip. Snow in the canyons was up to the bellies of the horses, and nowhere was there a suggestion of browse for the animals. They floundered around in the drifts for days, while the horses turned into angular distortions of skin and skeleton, and the men, so recently fattened on Fray José's beef, grew lean and despondent. One after another, five starved horses had to be abandoned in the snowdrifts. It was clear to Smith that he would soon be abandoning men as well as horses if he persisted in his attempt to force a way into still greater heights. He turned back, admitting crisply, "I could not cross my horses."

That first failure of white men in the Sierra was an augury of the many disasters to follow. Smith was wise enough to know when he was beaten. He returned to the valley. There was nothing to do but wait for the snow to melt, and meantime look for a less formidable pass over the range.

Continuing their trapping, the party slowly worked farther north—probably as far as the Stanislaus River. Other reconnaissance trips were made into the mountains in search of a trail. They were all as unsuccessful as the first. Early in May they set out with determination, and a few days later came back utterly frustrated and with scarcely half their horses.

Their greatest problems were in numbers and shortage of

provisions. There were too many of them. In the repeated as-
saults on the mountains they had worn their clothing to shreds,
used up the last of the food from San Gabriel, depleted the
string of pack animals. If the crossing were going to be made—
if they were to get their pelts to the summer rendezvous—the
company would have to be cut. Smith could not hazard the
lives of all of his fifteen men. He made a crucial decision: thirteen would be left behind; he would take the risk himself with
two men.

At that point a new element was added to their predicament.
Through the Indians, word of their presence in the valley
leaked to Mission San José, and the Fathers there wanted to
know what they were doing. Did they have a proper passport?

On May 19th Smith penned a tactful letter to Fray Narciso
Durán at the mission, explaining exactly who they were, noting
that they had called on the Governor in San Diego and had
been entertained bountifully at Mission San Gabriel. He
avoided mentioning that he was *persona non grata* in California or that he had received orders to leave the province by
a specific route.

"I have made several efforts to cross the mountains," he continued, "but the snows being so deep, I could not succeed in
getting over. I returned to this place (it being the only point
to kill meat) to wait a few weeks until the snow melts so that I
can go on; the Indians here also being friendly, I consider it
the most safe point for me to remain until such time as I can
cross the mountains with my horses; having lost a great many
in attempting to cross ten or fifteen days since. I am a long way
from home, and am anxious to get there as soon as the nature
of the case will admit. Our situation is quite unpleasant, being
destitute of clothing and most necessities of life, wild meat being our principal subsistence. I am, Reverend Father, your
strange, but real friend and Christian brother, J. S. SMITH."

Considering the circumstances, no letter could have been
more disarming, better calculated to win sympathy and less
likely to incur further inquiry. Early the next morning Smith
and two of his best men took leave of the other thirteen and

headed into the mountains, equipped with seven horses bearing the winter's catch of pelts and two mules piled high with hay. He dared not wait for a reply from Fray Narciso. The men were being left in a delicate situation, but the best hope for all of them lay in his getting back to Salt Lake quickly and returning as soon as possible to rescue those left behind.

A week later the three had crossed the divide and were plunging down the east slope of the Sierra. In the high pass they encountered snow as deep as eight feet, but it was crusted and so firmly compacted that even the horses could walk on it. To be sure, they lost horses—two of them, as well as a mule—but consumption of the hay allowed for redistribution of the cargo of furs, and the horse meat from the casualties richly augmented the lean rations of the men.

After all the false starts and previous unsuccessful tries, that first crossing of the High Sierra went so easily that historians and mountaineers have been trying ever since to retrace the route—and have not yet been able to agree on it.

Smith was back at Salt Lake by the middle of July with the remnants of his winter beaver catch. He attended the summer rendezvous and immediately set out for California to rescue the thirteen he had left behind. Although the return trip was more arduous than the first, the trappers in the western foothills of the Sierra welcomed him into camp before mid-September.

The tireless promoter of Rocky Mountain Fur interests led his men on to more perilous and more profitable ventures, until they parted company four years later. It was then that he met a savage end in the hands of Comanche Indians on the Cimarron River. But in one decade of uninterrupted exciting exploits, Jedediah Smith had won for himself the title of "the man who had opened the gate through which passed the American builders of the West." He ranks as the first conqueror of the Sierra.

The experiences of Smith and his cohorts set a kind of standard in grim ordeals for a long procession of men and women no less determined to cross the range. They, too, were to discover that the precipices were sheer, the heights formidable, the snow overwhelming. They, too, would learn to relish horse meat, mule meat, dog meat when floundering lost, bewildered and aching with fatigue on the barren, frozen summits.

Years later John-of-the-Mountains Muir maintained that nearly every notch between the peaks is a pass: "The free mountaineer with a sack of bread on his shoulders and an ax to cut steps in ice and frozen snow can make his way across the range almost anywhere, at any time of year when the weather is calm." But the early frontiersmen didn't find it as simple as that. To them there was no unobstructed route over the Sierra. It was a range without passes, in terms of popularly accepted geography. Other mountain chains offered gaps where the heights made halfway compromise with valley levels; in the Sierra there were no such gaps. Regardless of the point at which the mountains were attacked, streams had to be forded, cliffs ascended and the confusing miles of summit wilderness penetrated.

In 1833, Joseph Reddeford Walker, famed throughout the West as an intrepid Indian fighter, trapper and guide, tried an approach from the east. His was another expedition in the general interest of the fur trade, with a company of some fifty mounted veterans and a long supply train of pack animals. And to make sure that there would be no ambiguity in the records of the expedition, an official scribe went along, in the person of Zenas Leonard.

It was already late in the season—the middle of October—and supplies were all but exhausted, when the company halted at the foot of the mountains just north of Mono Lake to survey the heights. A scouting party, sent ahead to search for a possible route, located an old Indian trail, and early on October 15th the column started up it. Before midmorning the trail was lost on the steep slopes of loose rocks and the horses were finding the going hard; by midafternoon they were in deep snow. They camped for the night on a wind-swept plateau with nothing to eat but a few wild juniper berries and handfuls of preserved insect larvae, purchased on the previous day from the valley Indians. The horses went unfed.

On the second day prodigious quantities of snow blocked their way—depths of as much as a hundred feet in sheltered hollows. In it the horses would sink out of sight. Exhausted men became the servants of their own beasts, beating a trail for them and dragging the terrified animals over it. Men mutinied and insisted on turning back, until Walker gave them leave with the understanding that they would go without arms, ammunition or equipment.

The first two emaciated horses had to be slaughtered that night. "Some of the men had fasted so long," noted Leonard for the record, "and were so much in want of nourishment, that they did not know when they had satisfied the demands of nature, and eat as much and as eagerly of this black, tough, lean horseflesh, as if it had been the choisest of beefsteak. But it gave fresh courage, and we went to bed this night in better spirits than we had done for a long time."

The fresh courage and better spirits, however, did not last long as day followed day with nothing but hills, rocks, deep snow and another cut of horseflesh for supper. On the first night they assumed they had reached the summit of the mountain, but the summit went on and on. Parties were sent ahead to search for another pass and to look for game. They returned without finding either.

"The prospect at this time began to grow somewhat gloomy and to threaten us with hard times," wrote Leonard in shrewd understatement. "We were at a complete stand. No one was acquainted with the country, nor no person knew how wide the summit of the mountain was. We had traveled for five days since we arrived at what we supposed to be the summit—were now still surrounded with snow and rugged peaks—the vigor of every man almost exhausted—nothing to give our poor horses, which were no longer any assistance to us in traveling, but a burthen, for we had to help the most of them along as we would an old and feeble man."

Even the scribe seemed to lose track of time after that. Every new day was like the last, but they were at least aware of the fact that they were making a slow descent. Patches of dried grass appeared through the snow for the horses to nibble on, and on the edge of a little lake a stretch of green pasture. Each night two or three more horses were sacrificed and the meat kept the men alive. Optimism returned when it was realized that the depth of snow was diminishing at the lower altitude.

Leonard stood at the top of a high cliff one morning and gloomily contemplated "streams which would shoot out from under high snowbanks, and after running a short distance in deep chasms, precipitate themselves from one lofty precipice to another until they were exhausted in rain below." He conjectured that some of the precipices were more than a mile high. Leonard did not know that he and his bewildered companions were the first white men ever to see the grandeur of Yosemite Valley, and nothing could have interested them less.

The worst of their tribulations were over. Within a day they were overlooking a green valley stretching as far as eye could see. Scouts jubilantly returned from a hunt with the plump carcasses of two black-tailed deer and a bear, another with the report of a possible trail down the vertical side of the mountain. Spirits perked up as appetites were satisfied with barbecued venison and bear steak.

But the report about the trail was unduly optimistic. Before they were halfway down the mountain, they were faced with another impasse, and could neither go forward nor return. The only way out of the predicament was to hoist the horses down over the cliff, one by one, with improvised block and tackle.

On the 30th of October they descended the last foothills. The men had all survived, but Zenas Leonard had on his conscience the dead horses that had made survival possible during the fifteen-day crossing. Twenty-four animals had given out, and seventeen of them had been eaten. "It seemed to me the greatest cruelty," he concluded, "to take your rifle when your horse sinks to the ground from starvation, but still manifests a desire and willingness to follow you, to shoot him in the head and then cut him up. It was not such meat as a dog would feed on, but we were driven to extremes and had either to do this or die. It was the most unwholesome as well as the most unpleasant food I ever eat, or ever expect to eat—and I hope that no other person will ever be compelled to go through the same."

Leonard expressed his hope in vain. A few years later John Charles Frémont, another Southerner with a Virginia family background, made a crossing under conditions even worse, for he attempted it in the dead of winter. Frémont's expedition was important and official. He was a lieutenant in the United States Topographical Engineers, charged with making a scientific survey of the country between the Rockies and the Pacific.

By the time he and his corps of forty reached the eastern slopes of the Sierra on the last day of January in 1844, they had already completed a safari of three thousand miles—from St. Louis to Fort Vancouver and back south through the Oregon Territory. As with those before him, Frémont's provisions were gone, except for a little sugar, coffee and pea meal which he was secretly hoarding for a dire emergency. Their horses were gaunt, the men haggard.

A wagonload of expensive scientific equipment, with which they had left St. Louis, had been abandoned piecemeal along the way; but a cumbersome mascot in the form of a French mountain howitzer, Frémont would not give up. It had been dragged, pushed and portaged for three thousand miles, and though it had been fired only for signal or celebration in all that distance, the lieutenant had formed such a sentimental attachment to it that now he insisted on lugging it up the mountain.

With a train of sixty-seven horses, burdened with such impedimenta as the cannon, bulky culinary equipment including a huge iron kettle, bundles of plants collected on their travels, blankets and bolts of red cloth to catch the eyes of Indians, guns and countless rounds of ammunition and a miscellany of trading goods—yet without staple food of any kind, without so much as a shaker of salt—the party prepared to cross the Sierra.

Amiable Indians pleaded with Frémont not to make the attempt. They pointed to the snow on the mountains, drew their hands across their necks and raised them over their heads to illustrate the depth of the snow. They explained that the trip was "six sleeps" in the summertime; in the winter it was impossible. In simple sign language an old Indian portrayed rock on rock, snow on snow and explained that even if they did get across the top, the horses could never descend the precipices on the other side. Out of sympathy they implored and wept. Frémont's answer was an order to proceed.

In the weeks that followed, the lieutenant had occasion many times to reconsider the counsel of the Indians. The howitzer was soon abandoned and bundles of equipment littered the length of their route. They were deserted by the Indian guide who had been taken in by the gorgeous apparel with which he had been bribed to accompany them. At best they could flounder through the snow only a few miles a day, once only a few hundred yards.

Snow was so deep in ravines and hollows that the expedition had to take to the steep slopes, make long circuits and ascend the highest, most exposed ridges. Ten horses and riders were first assigned trail-breaking duty; each one wallowed forward a few yards, then moved aside to let the next in line take the lead. But even that slow, toilsome procedure exhausted the men.

The procession was halted, and men tried packing mushy snow during the middle of the day, and traveling on the frozen path at night or early in the morning. Repeatedly horses lost their footing, and in spectacular plunges rolled down the mountainside heels over saddle into places where they could not be recovered. They slipped off precipices. When the horses gave out, mauls and shovels were fashioned and men pounded and dug a path. On icy slopes every foot of the way had to be chopped with axes.

Almost incessantly they were plagued with high winds. Intermittent sleet squalls turned into blinding blizzards that blotted out the landscape, destroyed all sense of direction and filled trails that had been so laboriously mauled, shoveled and hacked before the main body could use them. For an entire day the company could be trapped and held immobile by a raging storm, while the men lay shivering in their blankets, sought shelter in hollow trees or squatted in the lee of rocks.

Then when the sun came out, they were painfully afflicted with snow blindness. From the stores of trading goods Frémont produced wads of silk scarves and distributed them to use as veils. They improvised snowshoes like those worn by the Indians. They improvised sledges for drawing supplies and the sick.

Rarely could they find level ground where the snow was less than five feet deep, and more frequently it was twenty. In it a horse or mule that slipped off the beaten trail plunged about in wild violence, as if in water without buoyancy, until rescued or shot. A valuable horse pitched over a cliff carrying the bundles of botanical specimens they had been nurturing preciously for a thousand miles.

Night after night the men had to camp in the open in sub-zero temperatures, and at altitudes of seven, eight and nine thousand feet. Their only food was horse meat and mule meat, mule meat and horse meat, with perhaps a handful of pine nuts. In desperation Frémont dipped into his meager reserves at the end of a particularly harrowing day and brought out the last of the pea meal. Their pet dog Tlamath was shot and butchered, and that night they banqueted on pea soup, mule meat and dog meat. But for another occasion the only item on the menu was soup made from the head of a mule, boiled in that awkward iron kettle they still carried.

Men turned distressingly ill from the unpalatable food. One, crazed by hunger, fatigue and fear, went completely out of his mind. A famished straggler wandered off by himself as they reached a lower elevation, became lost, and when he finally caught up with the main body reported that the only food he had eaten in four days was a few wild onions, acorns, small frogs swallowed raw and a nest of big black ants.

But despite the starvation diet, the snow, the frostbite and the agonies of fatigue, Frémont did what the more practical Indians maintained no man could do—and without a fatality among his men. It took more than a month, but on March 8th he hailed Captain John A. Sutter in the lush Sacramento Valley and proudly introduced his company as they straggled in, "each man weakened and emaciated—leading a horse or mule as weak and emaciated as himself."

Of the sixty-seven animals with which the Sierra climb was started, thirty-three survived the trials of the trail and the hunger of their riders. Yet the whole expedition was regarded at the moment as a failure. Its primary purpose had been to locate fabulous Mary's Lake and Buenaventura River, and neither had been found—for the ironical reason that they did not exist.

Frémont lost no time in getting back to Washington to publish a report on his ventures. He spun out the details of their sufferings, as well as the glories of California, and the catalogue of tribulations alone should have been enough to discourage anyone from wanting to head west.

The report had the opposite effect. It was a sensation. Every land-hungry, itchy-footed Easterner who read it wanted to set out for golden California, regardless of the impenetrable barrier standing in the way. More than any other American, it was John Charles Frémont who set in motion the tidal wave of westward migration that would soon follow.

Near Council Bluffs, Iowa, on his way back East, Frémont passed the first caravan of covered wagons headed for the Sierra and California, and in that caravan was a seventeen-year-old named Moses Shallenberger, destined to spend the following winter snowed in at Donner Lake while guarding the abandoned belongings of other members of the party who couldn't get their wagons over the mountains. In a doorless log cabin that he helped build, he kept alive the tradition for scant Sierra sustenance which Jedediah Smith, Joseph Walker and Frémont had established, though trapped fox and wolf were his *pièces des résistances.*

The next winter a few survivors of the ill-fated Donner party moved into the cabin, and before their ordeal was over they had consumed all other food and were resorting to cannibalism.

In half a decade the scattering of eager, misguided immigrants trekking across the plains and into the Sierra swelled into a procession. Then came the War with Mexico. The bear flag of the Republic of California was raised at Sonoma. A month later it was hauled down and replaced by the Stars and Stripes, and within a year and a half word leaked out that gold had been discovered on the American River. The Sierra Nevada was suddenly on the map.

III

TITANS HAVE BEEN
AT WORK HERE

Not until May 29th, 1848, did Monterey pick up the first
wild rumors about a discovery of gold four months earlier near
Sutter's Fort on the American River. To be sure, Sutter's Fort
was two hundred miles away, and Monterey was no longer
the important city it had been as capital of Alta California, but

if there were any truth to such incredible tidings, certainly the city would have been let in on the secret at once.

Nobody was taken in by the gossip, including the new American magistrate or *alcalde,* a conservative Vermonter and Navy Chaplain, the Reverend Walter Colton. The reluctance to give credence to the rumor was partly a matter of pride among the Mexican populace. They had just lost control of California, but if gold had been lying loose around the province, they wouldn't have left it for the gringos to appropriate.

Nevertheless, the rumor invoked hopeful illusions among the water-front loungers and market-place magpies, and one old sibyl admitted that for several nights the moon had appeared scarcely more than a cable's length from the earth, a white raven had been seen playing with an infant and an owl had rung the church bells. Something was doing. Perhaps the information shouldn't be discredited entirely.

A week later everyone was again set on edge as more details filtered in. A fellow named James Marshall, the rumor ran, had been digging a tailrace for a new sawmill in the Sierra foothills forty-five miles from Sutter's Fort, and when the water was turned into the channel it washed off the silt, leaving the bed fairly sparkling with yellow chips. Nor could the story be a complete American fabrication, for an honest Sonoran who had spent most of his life in the Mexican mines had examined the flecks and declared them the genuine article. Gossip in Monterey became a little more animated, yet it was all too fantastic to take very seriously.

The Yankee *alcalde,* however, saw that excitement was building up. The whole town was going to be in suspense until the rumor was spiked, so after thinking it over for a night, he dispatched a messenger to Sutter's to get at the facts. It was a long trip, sure to be fruitless, but such services tended to win popular sympathy for his regime and demonstrate the efficiency of the American authorities. Besides, he was right curious himself.

The messenger went off on June 6th. On June 12th a straggler drifted into Monterey displaying a glob of ore from the

American River, weighing a full ounce. The entire town circled him. For half an afternoon he was a sensation. The natives wanted to heft the glob, to rub it, to melt it, to hammer it, to smell it. The ore was demonstrably compared to a gold ring. A gentleman balanced the specimen on top of his gold-headed cane, held it aloft and challenged anyone to detect the difference.

But generally the reaction was a collective exclamation of *Humbug!* It was impossible that gold within easy reach could have been sitting in the dust all these years waiting for intruding Yankees to gather. They were trying to make the long-time occupants of California look stupid. The whole thing was a ruse, invented to justify the American occupation. The Mexicans weren't going to be deceived.

The *alcalde's* messenger returned on June 20th. Here at last was the man whose word could be trusted. He was one of them. A sea of upturned faces, grinning with suspicion, tense with mixed hope and doubt, silently watched him dismount. Leisurely he drew the evidence from his pocket and passed the yellow lumps around. The truth slowly sank in.

Doubt vanished. The crowd vanished. Within the hour every family in Monterey was feverishly sorting tools and supplies, saddling pack animals, trying to appear unhurried lest a neighbor jump to the conclusion that they were anxious to get a head start. The straggling procession of prospectors—fathers and sons, uncles and hired hands, even whole families—started on the long journey to Sutter's and the Sierra. Monterey was all but evacuated.

From one end of California to the other, everywhere in the West, and a good distance to the east, the scene was the same; men by the thousands were scurrying to the Sierra. The gold rush had started. "The blacksmith dropped his hammer," reported *Alcalde* Colton, "the carpenter dropped his plane, the mason his trowel, the farmer his sickle, the baker his loaf and the tapster his bottle. All were off for the mines; some on horses, some in carts, some on crutches, and one went in a litter. An American woman who had recently established a boarding house pulled up stakes and was off before her lodgers even had time to pay their bills. Debtors ran, of course. I have only a community of women left, and a gang of prisoners, with here and there a soldier who will give his captain the slip at the first chance. I don't blame the fellow a whit; seven dollars a month, while others are making two or three hundred a day!"

Colton even lost his landlord and landlady. Both answered the summons from the headwaters of the American River, and no sooner were they out of sight than the servants followed, and the *alcalde*—along with a general of the United States Army and the commander of a warship—found themselves alone in a kitchen frying their own fish, grinding coffee and peeling their own onions.

By the middle of August, a few of the Monterey Argonauts were beginning to straggle home. A group of four citizens, who had been at the diggings on the Feather River for exactly seven weeks and three days, were dividing $76,854. Back from the Yuba River came a respected friend who had cleared $5,356 in sixty-four days; from the North Fork another townsman with $4,534 after fifty-seven days; from the Mokelumne a fourteen-year-old boy with $3,467; a Mexican woman, who had put in forty-six days in the dry diggings, with $2,125.

Week by week the amounts increased. On September 16th a local scoundrel turned up in patched buckskins toting a sack of yellow dust worth $15,000. This was too much for the alcalde. Regardless of his religious scruples and his responsibilities to the United States Government, he had to see the diggings and do a little panning for himself.

Within four days the Reverend Colton temporarily deserted his post and was on the road, accompanied by a trio of adventurers and equipped with the necessary tools, light provisions and blankets. Before the end of the month he was in the heart of the Sierra gold diggings, where he jumped from his horse, took up a pick and in five minutes held up a piece of gold large enough for a signet ring.

But as a gospel minister and a public servant, Colton made at least a pretense of being as much interested in sociology as in digging. To get the feel of the business, he slogged about in bogs and knee-deep mud for flakes and nuggets; with a crowbar and pick he chiseled away at slate, traprock and quartz. He rocked cribs for other miners, whirled and pitched his own pan until his muscles were tied in knots, and from the effort he made a good thing of it financially. But much of his time was spent in wandering from gulch to ravine, from eddy to mud flat watching the crowd, and he soon acquired a reputation as an "amateur gold hunter, very much given to splitting rocks and digging in unproductive places."

He was fascinated by the way every miner kept track of the movements of his neighbors. In all the milling about, no matter how rich the diggings were, if a notably lucky panner suddenly departed for a new spot, fifty competitors followed. The quiet disappearance of a wise old Midas for a day or two would throw a camp into panic, while searching parties struck out in all directions to catch up with him. Often the disappearance was merely a calculated maneuver to disperse a crowded camp, and when the searchers returned from their foray, Midas was quietly sifting the wealth they had deserted. Even if he packed up his equipment and took formal leave for home, he would be followed for miles.

Camps were in a constant state of flux and confusion. The arrival of a rumor that a big strike had been made on the Feather River or the Stanislaus, forty miles away, was a signal for every last man to bolt. Usually they returned disgruntled and empty-handed a few days later.

"Some fifty thousand persons are drifting up and down these slopes of the great Sierra," Colton estimated, "persons of every hue, language and clime; tumultuous and confused as a flock of wild geese taking wing at the crack of a gun. All are in quest of gold; with eyes dilated to the circle of the moon, they rush this way and that, as some new discovery or fictitious tale of success may suggest. Some are with tents and some without; some have provisions and some are on their last ration; some are carrying crowbars, some pickaxes and spades, some washbowls and cradles, some hammers and drills and powder enough to blow up the Rock of Gibraltar. Such a mixed and motley crowd —such a restless, roving, rummaging, ragged multitude never before roared in the rookeries of man."

Colton himself ran out of provisions and found that he had to pay $400 for a barrel of flour that would cost twenty in Stockton, four dollars for a pound of soft brown sugar or for a pound of coffee beans. He sold his twenty-dollar brace of pistols to a Mexican for a pound of raw gold worth $250. A physician whom he had befriended wanted to transfer his equipment and himself a few miles upstream and asked a teamster going in that direction to give him a lift. The horseman was agreeable enough, and on arrival at his destination, the physician politely inquired whether he might pay for the accommodation.

"Sure," replied the teamster, "a hundred dollars would be about right."

The doctor winced and handed over the bills without audible complaint. But two days later the teamster was back with a bad case of colic. The doctor offered relief in the form of a couple of pills.

"Your fee?" asked the patient.

The doctor made a feint at scribbling and adding figures on a scrap of paper. "Charge comes to exactly a hundred dollars," he replied—and got the money.

In six weeks Colton had his fill and was ready to return to the quiet, unremunerative life of Monterey. "I have walked on the roaring verge of Niagara," the globe-trotting *alcalde* recounted, "I have strolled through the grumbling parks of Londone, on the laughing boulevards of Paris, among the majestic ruins of Rome, around the flaming crater of Vesuvius, among the monumental remains of Athens, and beneath the barbaric splendors of Constantinople; but none of these, nor all combined, have left in my memory a page graven with more significant and indelible characters than the gold diggers of California."

The Westerners had the gold country to themselves only for a few months. On the last day of February, 1849, the first rip-roaring shipload of eastern diggers disembarked at San Francisco. More steamers were on the way, and the traffic across the plains was building up. Never in history had there been such a stampede of raw humanity into one place as this rush to the Sierra foothills.

Tens of thousands swarmed over virgin slopes where civilized men had never appeared before. In three days they could convert a secluded, pristine river canyon into a hideous chaos of broken trees, trampled ground and mud-splashed litter. They set up camps in the thick of the squalor—tents, lean-tos, unsightly, jerry-built huts—or merely dumped their pots, pans, blankets and digging gear alongside a tethered burro and went to work as if they had already been cheated by those who had arrived before them. There were hordes from every part of the nation—Yankees, Mormons, Southerners, Mexicans, Midwesterners—all united in their compulsion to tear into the Sierra hills.

"Titans have been at work here," exclaimed Lawyer C. H. Shinn, an Easterner who had come to make an early appraisal of the free-for-all. "The land for miles is like a battlefield where primal forces and giant passions have wrestled. Rivers have been turned aside; mountains hurled into chasms or stripped to the bedrock in naked disarray. Side by side in the same gulch, working in claims of eight paces square are fishermen from Cape Ann, loggers from the Penobscot, farmers from the Genesee Valley, physicians from the prairies of Iowa, lawyers from Maryland and Louisiana, college graduates from Yale, Harvard and the University of Virginia."

Then came the foreigners—Italians, Frenchmen, Chinese, Irishmen, Australians, countless Hawaiians, delegations of Latin Americans and South Americans all lumped carelessly under the heading of "Chileans."

The rush brought a boom to the shipping and transport industries; it brought Wells, Fargo and Company to the hinterland; it brought self-imposed law where there was no one to enforce established law; it brought a kind of economy that jumped the eastern retail price of a stove from $8 to $170, the one-way fare on a river boat from San Francisco to Sacramento to an extortionate $150—half as much as a second-class passage all the way from New Orleans to the Golden Gate.

To the Sierra it brought scores of mushroom camps and towns with the most plebeian assortment of names that ever littered a map:

> Boneyard Meadow, Hangman's Bridge,
> Picture Gallery, Jawbone Ridge,
> Nigger Slide, Sonora, Baker,
> Poker Flat, Couts, Hell's Half Acre,
> Henpeck City, Hottentot,
> Grizzly Gulch, Gwin, Wyandotte,
> Hawkeye, Red Dog, Calaveras,
> Shirttail Canyon, San Andreas,
> Cuteye Fosters, Cherokee,
> Shotgun, Hell's Hills, Trinity,
> Slaughter Bar, Louisiana,
> Montezuma, Lancha Plana,
> Pine Knot Village, Red Cloud Mine,
> Brandy City, Porcupine,
> New Chicago, You Bet, Sattley,
> Dog Town, Shaver Crossing, Mattley,
> Gold Hill, Fiddletown, North Branch,
> Rough and Ready, Quartz, Burnt Ranch,
> Yankee Jim's, Condemned, Mount Bullion,
> Rawhide, Devil's Nose, Slumgullion,
> Priest, Exchequer, Hazel Green,
> Penon Blanco, Hawk Ravine,
> Groundhog's Glory, Gold Run Wonder,
> Bedbug, Bumpass, Bogus Thunder,
> Whisky Flat, Volcanoville,
> Wood's Dry Diggings, Jackass Hill.

The rapidity with which these towns sprouted from the bush was phenomenal. Nothing quite like it had ever occurred in America or on any other continent. Within six months after James Marshall's discovery on the American River, a group of Mexican prospectors was exploring one of the northern tributaries of the Tuolumne, far back in the wilderness toward

Yosemite. They made a strike of startling richness—so big that they could afford to share the news with friends. They were quickly joined by throngs of their countrymen. Most of them were from the Mexican state of Sonora, so they dubbed the site "Sonora Camp."

When the first nuggets were picked up early in the summer of 1848, the place was a tenantless wild; before the end of the year Sonora ranked in size and prosperity with the biggest settlements on the Sierra slopes. The seven hills that gave it geographical distinction were already half stripped of their timber and crowded with tents and hovels. Main Street wound through the valley for more than a mile.

The diggings were paying off handsomely, but there was only a trail from the outside world into Sonora. The nearest supply town was Stockton, seventy miles away. All the wealth of Sonora couldn't purchase a decent breakfast. By November, half the population was rotting with scurvy. If the village was to survive, provision had to be made at once for the care of the ailing. There was no government organization, so the town was incorporated for the purpose of erecting a hospital. In its wards victims were treated with a diet of raw potatoes at $1.50 a pound and lime juice at $5 a bottle.

Word of the scurvy scare spread abroad, but word of the inexhaustible store of gold in the hills spread faster and farther. The diggings at Sonora became California's greatest sensation. The Americans had no intention of letting the Mexicans be the only ones to clean up on the find. Mobs of Yankees headed for Sonora. During the spring and summer of 1849, the procession of miners increased until the seventy-mile route from Stockton could be traced at night by the glow of their trailside campfires.

Interspersed with the migrant miners were long strings of mules, loaded high with everything from hinges and hoes to sugar and sausage. The merchants of Stockton were also getting in on the deal, packing in two hundred tons of freight a week—every ounce of it on muleback.

The trail soon widened into a road. Wagons took the place

of pack trains. Local government expanded its interest beyond the operation of a hospital. New retail stores lined the streets as fast as supplies could be brought in for the counters. Before the end of 1849 the hillsides sheltered the largest mining camp in the West. The population was 5,000 and still going up.

Mexicans were crowded into the background. An American *alcalde* temporarily took over the government until a mayor and council were elected in November. Sonora shortly became a city, duly incorporated, the supply center for a dozen other mining villages springing up around it and a transportation center with coaches and express stages making daily runs to Stockton in less than nine hours.

Meantime the placers were yielding fortunes. Surface claims only ten feet square produced chips and chinkers worth $10,000. San Francisco newspapers spread the intelligence that a hundred chunks of solid gold averaging twelve pounds apiece had been brought in for assay. Eight boulders of pure gold, each weighing over twenty pounds, made bigger news; one tipped the honest scales of Wells, Fargo at exactly twenty-eight pounds—and it was worth eighteen dollars an ounce.

But that same year a new law calling for a tax of twenty dollars on every foreigner engaged in gold mining went into effect. It threw Sonora into tumult. Mexicans had pioneered this bonanza; they had rights to it and refused to submit to any such gringo treachery. Chileans and Europeans sided with the Mexicans. They brought out their arms. War was imminent.

Under threat of rebellion and attack, the Americans rose to the defense of law and order, as they defined it. They organized en masse under the Stars and Stripes and, preceded by a fife-and-drum corps, with flags waving and shotguns booming, marched against the foreign camp.

The Mexicans heard them coming in time to make a getaway. Most of the rebels were over the hill before the defenders of Yankee law came within sight, and the last of the foreigners were frantically pulling up stakes and packing their mules, ready to move on to other diggings where the new statute was likely to be less rigidly enforced. The battle was called off, and when the excitement had died down, the Americans had things their own way—and Sonora had a fifth of its former population.

On July 4th, a few days after the rebellion, the depleted town made more news—by producing a newspaper. To many a California editor, the arrival of the Sonora *Herald* in the mails, along with other exchanges, was the first intimation that the town itself existed. But in addition to the newspaper, Sonora soon had schools, churches, half a dozen hotels, the inevitable theatre, a bull ring and seven saloons to every block.

Eliminate the Mexicans, change the setting, and the saga of Downieville, a hundred miles to the north, was of the same pattern. It, too, sprang from a remote, uninhabited gully into a booming community of thousands within a few months, complete even to a theatre—where Edwin Booth, dancer Lola Montez and child prodigy Lotta Crabtree played to audiences of bewhiskered denizens who showered them with gold-dust pokes worth a queen's ransom.

Downieville, however, had a disadvantage in its location that Sonora was spared. It was high in the Sierra, surrounded by a wall of mountainsides. Winter came early and stayed long, as the town's founder, Major William Downie, learned at the price of almost freezing and starving to death, during his first winter there.

With a motley following of assistant prospectors—an Irishman, an Indian, a Kanaka named Jim Crow, and ten Negro sailors—the Major paused one night along the North Fork of the Yuba River, late in November, 1849. At sunrise the next morning he saw the gold he was looking for magnified by the ice that had formed over the stream. He went to work immediately, and the first pannings made it clear that they had struck it rich.

There was a threat of snow in the air, so they quit prospecting long enough to throw together a rude hut, and by the time it was finished the ground was deep in white. Nevertheless, the Major kept his men busy for days, tormenting them with instruction on how to sift snow, as well as gravel and gold in the freezing river. When the ice was too much to cope with, they moved to the banks, dug through the drifts and into crevices, to come up each day with nuggets worth a few hundred dollars.

Then food supplies began to get low. Eight of the men, with Jim Crow as guide, were dispatched to the lowlands for provisions. The men had suffered enough punishment. Only Jim came back, and he didn't show up until spring. The Kanaka returned just in time to save the Major and his five faithful servants from starvation.

During the long winter in the valley, Jim Crow, of course, had not been able to keep his mouth shut, so he was tailed back to camp by an eager mob armed with shovels, picks, pans and hammers. They spread out over the foothills, pushed up the river canyons and explored the countless upstream tributaries. Camps sprang up on every bar and flat. The rewards at Tin Cup Diggings were typical: if a man couldn't fill his drinking cup with gold in a day, he was wasting his time.

A blizzard of rumors about the stupendous strikes at the Yuba headwaters swept through the Sierra. Anyone had to be doing very well indeed to resist the invitation of Downieville. In March, 1850, the only habitation had been Major Downie's shack; by June it was a city of five thousand.

All that summer and fall the average yield per man was two pounds of gold a day. The next year a single chunk valued at $8,000 was unearthed; four men made an average of $1,250 a day for eleven consecutive days on a claim six by ten feet. From Durgan's Flat across the river $80,000 worth of gold was produced in six months, and miners at dozens of other spots in the immediate vicinity bragged of similar findings.

Like Sonora, Downieville became an important trading center. A Washington hand press was freighted into town and the *Mountain Messenger* was born. Besides a theatre, the usual shops and a wide choice of saloons, Downieville had its St. Charles hotel, a church, a school, a courthouse and a mill for crushing granite.

Two of its most prominent citizens brought the town notoriety by fighting a famous duel with shotguns at close range— the Lippincott-Tevis duel, which only Lippincott survived. The erection of a gallows at the foot of Piety Hill and the institution of public flogging gave the town an air and a reputation, but the one incident that really put Downieville on the map was the lynching of Juanita, a Spanish adventuress on July 5th, 1851.

Juanita had stabbed a popular gambling hero named John Cannon, so she was strung up from the Downieville bridge by a mob. For this affair condemnation was heaped upon the town by newspapers up and down California, across the nation and even on the other side of the Atlantic by the London *Times*.

The scores of mining camps and towns distributed through the Sierra foothills and into the mountains were all in character with Sonora and Downieville; and the sins and social transgressions of the inhabitants varied little in type. "In California are the elite of the most desperate and consummate scoundrels from every part of the world," warned a distinguished British artist, J. D. Borthwick, after an inspection of the gold fields. He gathered the impression that almost as many were there to make money off the gold diggers as to participate in the actual drudgery.

"The unsettled state of the country, the wandering habits of the mining population, carrying an amount of gold on their persons inconvenient from its very weight, together with the isolated condition of many individuals, strangers to everyone around them, and who, if put out of the way, would never be missed—all these things," explained Borthwick, "render the country one where ruffians have ample room to practice their villainy."

It was primarily a man's society during the first three hectic years of the rush. Here and there the presence of vigorous, honest, moral citizens was felt, but there were not enough such citizens to control the throng of irresponsible hoodlums and misanthropes. The influence of the hoodlums was far greater than that of sober guardians of the law.

"I knew I couldn't carry my religion with me through California," explained the typical miner from the East, "so when I left home in Missouri I hung my religious cloak on my gatepost until I should return." Very many, added a roving pastor, left at home their character, scruples and codes of conduct too.

Murder, robbery, grand-scale extortion were commonplace. Gambling and voluminous drinking were the chief sources of entertainment. The raping of squaws, Mexican and Chilean women was an accepted sport until the daughters of joy from the East began to arrive in numbers. No form of vice seemed to escape the indulgence of the miners. Even men of fortitude starved for entertainment, for the sight of a woman, for any symbol that reminded them of home.

It was a topsy-turvy world. After two years in the gold fields, youngsters were known to tramp for thirty miles merely to get a glimpse of a mother reported to have arrived in a remote cabin. Rough-and-tumble men with tattered clothes and beard-shrouded faces joined regularly in Saturday night dances, round and square, choosing partners from their own stag lines. When troupers arrived from San Francisco to put on a show of any kind—melodrama, bawdy vaudeville or opera, it didn't matter—the artists were met at the stage and carried through the streets like national heroes; they were showered with gold and the theatres mobbed. Even a transient parson could usually manage to assemble an attentive audience, though most preached on far too lofty a plane to reach their listeners.

"Plume your wing for heaven," declaimed the Reverend Colton, as if anyone fresh from the ditches was concerned about either plumage or heaven. "What multitudes are leaving their distant homes for glittering treasure. Let the wrecks of those who have perished speak: let the broken hearts and hopes of thousands utter their admonition. Their voices come

surging over the pines, breaking from these cliffs, sighing in
the winds and kneeling from the clouds. Your treasures you
must resign at the dark portal of the grave; there the glittering
heap and the strong arms which wrenched it from the mine lie
down together. Plume your wing for heaven ere it droops in
the death-dew of its dissolving strength."

But many a minister and missionary did exert a sobering influence on the mining communities. Protestant pastors had
been vitrually unknown in California until the Americans took
over. For political and business reasons, the earliest immigrants had accepted tacit association with the Catholic
church and the Spanish padres. But most of the Argonauts
were Protestant, at least in name, and the Methodist, Baptist
and Congregational Churches of the East were quick to realize that there was a new field to harvest on the rough Sierra
slopes.

Preachers came by ship with the immigrants. Not infre-
quently one accompanied an overland party, and the ministers
were not above taking on two jobs—digging for gold on week-
days and expounding on Sundays. Intent on sharing a few
worldly goods, the Reverend James Wood piloted a group of
miners—mostly converted Mexicans—from San Francisco, and
promoted the most orderly encampment in all the diggings.
Like an Old Testament prophet, he thundered his denun-
ciation upon tipplers, gamblers and blasphemers, and cast
them out. The Sabbath was dedicated to the service of the
Lord among Wood's disciples at Jamestown. The combination
of prayer, self-restraint and tireless digging netted them a respectable fortune; and incidentally left Wood's name attached to a variety of gulches in the area. For miles around,
everyone knew and respected the "hollerin' preacher of Jim-
town."

Transient preachers weren't always as successful. After organizing the first Methodist-Episcopal Society in San Francisco, the Reverend William Taylor took to the hills to survey
the fields. He complained bitterly about the moral condition of
the miners, their intemperance, their Sabbath-breaking and

profanity, and maintained that he could travel through the diggings for a week at a time without encountering a Christian.

One Sunday morning he put it on the line to a surprisingly large congregation gathered under a pine tree at Long Bar. He sang, prayed and preached, getting such a warm response that he announced another service for the afternoon, certain that he could draw an even larger audience. But to his mortification, less than two dozen showed up for the second sermon. It puzzled him, so immediately after the benediction he set about making inquiries, only to learn that the morning congregation was busy drowning the doleful effect he had created. In fact, the whole population by midafternoon on any Sunday was much too drunk to find its way to a church service. "Such a variety of antics as they displayed beat anything I ever witnessed," the pastor acknowledged.

Taylor moved on to Hangtown—Placerville, where he set up a packing-box pulpit at the stage depot and let an empty coach take the place of pews. A multitude gathered and the stagecoach was crowded far beyond its capacity. He wanted to convince this audience of its unfitness for heaven in an unregenerated state.

"If God should dispatch a rail-car train to the city of Placerville this afternoon, to convey passengers direct to heaven, the conductor might whistle till the setting of the sun and not get a single passenger," he defiantly charged. "Heaven has no attractions for you. It is a place to which you don't want to go. Why, if the flaming steeds of Elijah's chariot of fire were hitched to that stagecoach, and the driver cracked his whip for the heavenly country, ever fellow in it would jump out."

Instantly, claimed Taylor, every last man in the coach leaped for the street, "in an apparent fright from the apprehension that perhaps Elijah's horses might be hitched to the stage, and they taken off to glory."

A red-blooded Congregationalist, the Reverend Sherlock Bristol, had much better luck. Bristol was brought up in the school of hard knocks. A Connecticut Yankee, kicked out of Phillips Andover Academy for unseemly behavior, only to make good later at Oberlin, he had held several difficult pastorates in New York, Massachusetts and Ohio, and run up against a great many adversaries.

It was on the Ohio frontier that he had been confronted with his strongest opposition. There he was threatened with both shotgun and ax if he dared come near one stubborn pioneer. His answer was to go directly to the home of the would-be assailant and call his bluff. While his host ranted, waved his loaded gun and kept an ax handy, Bristol kneeled at the hearth and prayed as he had never prayed, expecting any moment that the death-dealing ax would be raised above his head. But Bristol admitted that he cheated a little; he kept one eye half open, "contrary to his custom," while he prayed. He and God won the contest.

The young reverend was as wiry and fit as any miner when he arrived at the diggings on the outskirts of Downieville and, as seemed to be his lot, fresh adversaries at once gathered about him

"Hear ye! Hear ye!" called a contemptuous harrier the moment Bristol identified himself. "Every man quit work! Hurry here! There's fun ahead! Big fun! Come one! Come all!"

The six-foot bruiser intended to beat up the minister on the spot and send him packing, but he wanted an audience to witness the demonstration. Instantly the pans and rockers up and down the river ceased their rattle, miners dropped their picks and came on the run. In five minutes a circle of fifty men, spoiling for the excitement of a few rounds regardless of the qualifications of the underdog, formed about them. Bristol toyed with the idea of taking to his heels, but he resisted it, and probably prayed as usual.

"Put him through! Put him through!" taunted the crowd.

To begin the fun, the challenger seized the parson's collar and gave it a violent jerk.

"A strange spasm of impulsive energy, giving me twice my ordinary energy, came over me," the Reverend recalled. A powerful right came up to connect squarely with a bearded jaw, sending the overconfident pugilist sprawling backside down into a puddle. The crowd roared its approval. Angrily the assailant came back for more, and while the men yelled their heads off, Bristol downed him again and again. Finally the amazing little pastor seized the braggart by his collar and pants, lifted him bodily and prepared to heave him into the river. At that point the challenger announced his willingness to capitulate.

Bristol became the hero of the hour. Miners vied with one another in extending invitations to chow. They wanted to give the champion assistance in setting up his camp, to lead him to the best claim or take him on as a partner. If he would stay on at the bar and preach on Sundays, they promised to turn out en masse and help with the singing.

"Within two days," Bristol confided, "I had bought a claim for over three thousand dollars, two thousand of which was loaned me by these same miners, without interest and with no security. The following Sunday I preached to quite a congregation. As no house could hold us, our meeting was held outdoors, and I preached to them literally standing on a rock. Better order or closer attention no man could wish to have, and so it was for the following four months, till my claim was worked out and I went elsewhere."

Clergymen, roving journalists and sight-seeing politicians unanimously agreed that what the forty-niners most needed was more such religious fare, along with the influence of wives and good women. They were soon getting all three. Even the maladroit Pastor Taylor felt compelled to concede that the semimonthly arrival of families did more to stabilize Sierra society than his packing-box oratory.

"For a couple of years after the gold discovery," he wrote, "few of the great mass of California adventurers had any thought of a permanent settlement in the country. They had generally given themselves two years in which to make their 'pile' and return home, but after that sojourn, very many began seriously to contemplate a permanent settlement. They were delighted with the climate and became deeply interested in the development of the immense resources of the country—

agricultural, mineral and commercial—and in the growing greatness of the young giant State. Some went in person for their families; many more sent for them; a great many young men requested my mediation to try and secure for them good wives."

But the transformation didn't come with any suddenness, for new strikes kept up the turmoil of excitement. As diggings on the western slopes dwindled, miners moved to new bonanzas on the Nevada side of the Sierra. Professor William H. Brewer of the Sheffield Scientific School in New Haven, Connecticut, made a tour of the mining country, and eyed with particular interest the Nevada border town of Aurora. It ranked then as the second city in importance on the east side of the mountains. At first view he thought it "picturesque," but the more he saw of the community the less he liked what he saw. The hills were as barren as a desert, scattered with scrubby pines and cedar—"no grass, no anything to attract man except the precious metals." Aurora had grown up entirely in two years, had a population of five thousand and could claim scarcely more than one woman for every hundred men.

"Thousands of prospectors come here poor as rats," he calculated, "and expect to grow immensely rich in a few months—but alas! most of them either die here or leave still poorer." He pictured the center of the city with a few hastily built wooden and brick buildings, surrounded by hundreds of brush shelters, tents, stone huts or canvas-covered holes in the hillsides serving as homes. There were hideous, comfortless lodging houses where a dozen men were crowded into a single room; but no hotel and no accommodations at all for a full fourth of the population.

"Saloons—saloons—saloons, liquor everywhere," he moaned. "At home in the cheerless, lonesome hovels and huts? No, in the saloons where lights are bright and where there is the hum of many voices and the excitement of gambling. Here come men to make money—make it quick—no matter how, so long as the law doesn't call it robbery. There are no home ties or social checks, no churches, no religion—here one sees gambling and vice in all their horrible realities. Here are tables with gold and silver piled upon them by hundreds and even thousands of dollars. Here, too, are women—for nowhere else does one see prostitutes as he sees them in a new mining town. All combine to excite and ruin. No wonder one sees sad faces, haggard countenances and wretched looks."

Although great fortunes continued to be made, the big rush was beginning to peter out by 1854. Hundreds of millions in gold had been dug out of the flanks of the Sierra. But of far greater worth than all these millions was an unexpected human by-product. Mining had turned men's heads. Sudden wealth made weaklings into drifters, delinquents and libertines for life. But it tested the souls and character of others, enlarged their horizons, brought out hidden virtues.

Young men who would have remained on farms back East, behind counters or lost in factories if they had not answered the call of adventure and the gold rush, were given a chance to size up their capabilities against the limitations of lesser men. They stood taller after their experiences in the gold fields, and a few became giants.

A farm youngster named Phillip Armour got wind of the rush in Stockbridge, New York, and talked it over with a group of other boys from neighboring farms. Together they headed West, walking most of the way. The trip to the Sierra took six months. After a year in the diggings, his companions turned homeward with their earnings, but Phillip stayed on. He had made enough to build a flume for supplying water to other miners. That led to investments in similar mining enterprises, all of which brought amazing profits. Still only twenty-four when he finally went back East, he had lost his enthusiasm for farming, and went on instead to organize the nation's greatest meat-packing industry.

News of California gold caught up with the son of another New York farmer, Leland Stanford, in Wisconsin, where Leland had recently started a modest law practice. By a twist of fate, he suddenly lost his law library in a fire. Instead of purchasing a new one, he answered the call of California, opened a general store in Michigan Bluff, made a good start in the gold country and then turned to bigger business and politics. He became the first Republican Governor of California and a close friend of Abraham Lincoln. He struck the first blow for the construction of the Central Pacific in 1861, and as president of the company, drove the last gold spike for the line on May 20th, 1869. Stanford University bears witness to the kind of memorial in which he saw fit to invest his fortune.

For ten years George F. Hearst, a young man from Missouri, endured all the hardships of mining and gained few of the rewards, but he stuck with it. He moved to the Comstock Lode, invested in the Ophir mine and in five years was a millionaire. On returns from the gold fields, he founded the San Francisco *Examiner,* the forerunner of a twenty-six-paper chain under his son William Randolph.

In 1849, at a little store in Hornitos, Domingo Ghirardelli, an immigrant from Italy by way of Peru, started building his fortune as a merchant selling groceries, liquors and spices to Mexican and Chinese prospectors. He left Hornitos to become the "Chocolate King" of the West.

A New Jersey lad, John B. Stetson, destined to become a world-famed hat manufacturer and founder of Stetson University, served a rewarding apprenticeship at the diggings of Shaws Flat; and an eighteen-year-old youngster from Illinois, James G. Fair, led an expedition across the plains to the Sierra, tried his hand first at surface excavation, then at tunnel operation. None of his associates at the time would have guessed that he had the makings of a notable senator and one of the nation's leading financiers.

John G. Studebaker, from Pennsylvania, turned out miners' wheelbarrows by the thousands in his California factory, then went back East to give zest to the Studebaker dynasty, as a manufacturer of carriages and cars.

Mark Hopkins had been drifting from one occupation to another in New York and New England—clerking, selling plows, studying law, bookkeeping. As soon as he got wind of the gold discovery, he organized the New England Trading and Mining Company and, with his partners, set sail for San Francisco. The two shares of company stock, for which he invested $2,000, were eventually worth $20,000,000 and their owner was treasurer of the Central Pacific.

Even the arts and the humanities drew profitable dividends from the gold fields. Philosopher of American philosophers, Josiah Royce, born and brought up in the disorder of Grass Valley during the height of the rush, went forth to expand his conviction that the natural order of the world must also be a moral order.

Bret Harte, son of an Albany, New York, professor, sought his fortune in the Sierra and found it in literature rather than in gold. And when a variety of other get-rich-quick schemes failed, Missourian Mark Twain took to the seclusion of a cabin on Jackass Hill and wrote "The Celebrated Jumping Frog of Calaveras County"—the first yarn to bring fame to the humorist.

All were alumni from the gold school of the Sierra, and there were many more. Combine the family fortunes of only a few of them and the capital would far exceed the millions that came from the dirt and the quartz. Add the benefits accrued from their philanthropies and their creativity, and the total comprises one of the monumental contributions to the structure of a nation.

And the like of John C. Frémont should not be omitted, for not all of the fortunes paid lasting dividends. The man more responsible than any other for starting the Westward march purchased a vast tract known as the Mariposa Estate, and through a little chicanery and some major adjustment of boundaries, had the estate pushed back into the rich gold fields. He became one of California's most honored citizens, a political leader and senator. In 1856 he won the popular vote in the country for the Presidency of the United States, only to lose the plurality in electoral ballots. But financial reverse followed political reverse, one compounded on another, until tortured by creditors and an unsympathetic public, he remarked in irony, "When I came to California, I hadn't a cent: now I owe two million dollars."

IV

NIGH IMPOSSIBLE TO
KEEP THE TRAIL

The gold rush came too soon: California wasn't ready for
it; the country wasn't ready for it. Quite aside from all the
other deficiencies in preparedness, the lack of a highway across
the desert and over the Sierra was enough to forecast calamity
for uninitiated adventurers. If there had only been a road, everything else would have been relatively easy. But there wasn't

even a dependable track in 1849; nor a reliable map. Any responsible American west of the Rockies readily admitted that the crying need of California was a road over the mountains, yet no one did much about it.

"Hire a guide, if you can possibly find one," was the advice of those who had lived through the nightmare of struggling over the Sierra. "Hire a guide! Hire a guide and don't take chances." Immigrants heard the advice, but in the hurry to get to the gold fields, seldom heeded it. Besides, guides were hard to come by; they were all at the diggings—except perhaps Caleb Greenwood. This old-timer was always available, if he could be found and wasn't otherwise engaged. He didn't give a rap about gold.

Though Caleb could pass for a weathered codger not a day over fifty, he was well into his eighties—a rawboned, sinewy six feet of muscle and brawn, as leathery as the ancient buckskins he wore. Back in the days when he was working for trapper Ashley, he had married a Crow squaw, and off and on for almost half a century had lived with the Indians. To all who knew him, he was "Old Greenwood."

He had wandered all over the West and claimed that he had been to California as early as 1826. But dates and particulars confused him. He shied from boasting very openly that he had ever before ascended the Truckee River when a group of some fifty Easterners, known as the Stevens-Murphy-Townsend Company, engaged him in 1844. Nevertheless, he led the most venturesome contingent of that party up the heights as if it were the only place where the mountains would permit the passage of a wagon.

Using guts, a frontiersman's raw common sense and an eighty-year reserve of energy, he hustled his green clientele into the hills, winding back and forth across the Truckee twenty times a day to avoid impassable obstacles; skirting pine forests too thick to let a wagon through; plowing through blankets of early snow; maneuvering up precipitous rises until he was finally stopped by a perpendicular wall.

But after a little silent scouting, even that didn't faze him.

He demanded that all the wagons be unloaded. One by one frightened, bawling oxen were pushed and prodded up a narrow fissure in the wall, and with the animals safely over the worst place, he set to work figuring out a complicated log-and-chain leverage system to take care of the wagons. Eight oxen were hitched together; one end of a length of chain was secured to the yokes, the other to a wagon; with the men heaving on log levers and oxen straining at the chains, a wagon went up the side of the cliff as lightly as a lady's phaeton. Then Caleb turned his polite clientele into pack animals and supervised them while they lugged every last item in their personal possessions, their household furnishings and barrels of provisions up the palisade. That ought to teach them to travel lightly next time, he reasoned.

"Old Greenwood" had engineered this feat. His reputation was made. He had taken the first wagon over the Sierra, delivered his party intact at Sutter's, and then insisted on going all the way back to help rescue the more reluctant members who couldn't keep up with the vanguard. His name was legend, and his services worth every dollar he demanded.

But Caleb couldn't stand too steady an association with cultivated folk, and every now and then had to escape somewhere to shake off the contamination. So he would head off into God's country for a few weeks of trapping and hunting. On one of these vacations Edwin Bryant, *alcalde* of San Francisco, accidentally encountered him on a rainy night in 1847 at Clear Lake, some sixty miles north of the Bay.

"The camp looked like a butcher's stall," commented the *alcalde* uncharitably. "The pot was filled with bear flesh and the choice pieces of tender venison were roasting. On the trees surrounding the camp were stretched the skins of various animals, and bear meat and venison enough for a winter's supply were hanging from the limbs."

The *alcalde* couldn't have cared less about the credentials of his host, but in the light of a blazing log campfire, "Old Greenwood" presented them in unsparing detail. "I am an old man," he confided, "eighty-three years—that's a long time to

live—eighty-three years last—I have seen all the Injun var-
mints of the Rocky Mountains, have faut them, lived with
them. I have many children—I don't know how many. They
are scattered, but my wife was a Crow. I can still handle a
rifle as well as the best of 'em, 'spite this infernal humor in my
eyes that I caught three years ago in bringing some emigrators
over the desart.

"I can't see jist now as well as I did fifty years ago, but I can
always bring down the game or the slinking and skulking Injun. I have jist come over the mountains with the emigrators
as pilot, living on bacon, bread, milk, and sich-like mushy stuff.
It don't agree with me; it never will agree with a man my age,
eighty-three last— I thought I would take a small hunt and
get a little exercise for my old bones, and some good fresh meat.
I came up here where I knew there was plenty. I was here
twenty years ago, before any white man ever see this
lake. . . ."

As long as there were enough guides like "Old Greenwood"
to go around, spending money on building good roads could
be postponed; but the traffic was getting heavy and the veterans were dying off. Too many amateurs tried crossing alone
and got into difficulty. March and April were the preferred
months for companies to start from Ohio, Pennsylvania, Geor-
gia or anywhere else in the East. Invariably that timing brought
the immigrants to the desert stretches in the hottest, driest
season of the year, and to the mountains late in the summer

That was when the trans-Sierran congestion was greatest.
Men and animals had passed the limit of their endurance before they approached the most formidable trials of the journey.
In the stupor from fatigue, often it was a case of the blind
leading the blind—one miserable, bewildered company making a false turn, to be followed closely by a procession of others,
until all were in a tangle of trouble. Misery always found too
much company in the Sierra. For large parties, as well as small,
a cool-headed, rough-talking pilot of the Greenwood persuasion
made all the difference between order and disaster. Fifty

men like him could at least have helped compensate for the lack of a highway.

Compared to the travel tribulations of some of the forty-niners, John Bunyan's Christian took a leisurely tramp through the Slough of Despond and the Valley of the Shadow of Death. The cross-country trip of Josiah and Sarah Royce, parents-to-be of philosopher Josiah, Jr., was a fair example.

They set out from the Mississippi border of Iowa in a prairie schooner behind three yoke of oxen and a pair of cows on April 30th, 1849, accompanied only by a couple of rheumatic farm hands and their two-year-old daughter Mary. As recent immigrants from England, they hadn't enough close acquaintances to form a company. Along the way they occasionally joined other bands, but for the most part they traveled alone, shifted for themselves, following the Mormon Trail by way of the Platte River, Council Bluffs and Fort Laramie.

Like so many others, they made the almost fatal mistake of starting too late. Misfortune seemed to accompany them the entire distance. They didn't reach Council Bluffs until June 4th. A week later they left the elder of the two farm hands in a roadside grave—stricken with Asiatic cholera. They were constantly harassed by roving bands of Pawnees, Sioux, Cheyennes and Poncas. For a few days they accepted the protection of a troop of migrating New Englanders, but paid a heavy price for it; in a wild stampede of the company's cattle one night, their wagon was overturned and the family barely missed being trampled to death.

They patched up the broken wagon and went on. Far in the rear of other immigrants, they pulled out of Salt Lake City on August 20th—two men, one woman and a two-year-old, facing the hundreds of miles of desert and wasteland by themselves. Sarah walked much of the way to save the oxen.

As they approached Carson Desert, reminders of death and catastrophe haunted the trail—abandoned wagons, skeletons of horses and cattle, rudely marked graves, discarded trunks and household furnishings, barrels of supplies; even books flung out of overloaded vehicles. The heat became so oppressive that it was necessary to travel at night. In the darkness they missed a turn in the route at Humboldt Sink and hurried on for days—in the wrong direction.

With only a few cups of water left, some scraps of food and nothing for the oxen, they had to turn back. They kept the oxen barely alive by feeding them handfuls of hay from their mattresses. After the return to Humboldt Sink, they were saved from starvation by finding a few pounds of bacon in a deserted prairie schooner. Sarah continued to walk, taking her turn at driving the lean oxen—now reduced to two span.

At last on October 12th, they came to the Truckee River at the foot of the Sierra. The snow-topped mountains loomed above. The four oxen were spent, their wagon was dilapidated and the family sick from exhaustion. They were no more capable of summoning strength to climb the mountains than scores of preceding immigrants—who all too obviously had abandoned their belongings along the river. To add to their anxiety, they suddenly detected a cloud of dust on the trail above—the kind of cloud that Indians so often stirred.

The Royces prepared for the worst, but out of the cloud, as it came nearer, appeared two white men—not Indians. To Sarah they were like a visitation of saints from heaven. They were a relief company sent across the mountains by order of the United States Government, to clear the trail of stragglers before winter set in.

But the Government men were stern and realistic. Haul the wagon over the Pass? Impossible. It had been done, of course, by summer immigrants who had plenty of time. But winter had come to the summit. It would take two weeks, perhaps a month and the help of a dozen men; the wagon would have to be completely disassembled and carried piece by piece across the canyons. The Royces had neither the time nor the men. No, the wagon would have to be left behind, and most of the goods with it.

A few packs could be lashed to the sides of the oxen. But hurry, hurry. Haste was what mattered now. Already there

were two nights of snow on the heights. Any day the trail could
be buried to a depth of six feet.

The Government men were due on another mission. They
couldn't give much further assistance, except to help with the
packing and perhaps lend a couple of animals. "The white one
there is a perfectly trained saddle mule," allowed one of the
rescuers. "My wife has rode her for miles over steep and slippery roads, and he'll be perfectly safe for the lady to ride with
her little girl in front of her. And this dark mule is just as good
for carrying packs. Yes, the two mules are yours till you get
through to the gold mines; and all Uncle Sam asks is that they
be brought safely back to headquarters in Sacramento City, as
soon as possible after you get into California." But there was
not an hour to lose.

The animals were packed, the wagon abandoned along with
the precious keepsakes that had been carried all the way from
Iowa, New York, Canada and Stratford-on-Avon in England.
There was no time to pamper sentiment or fatigue. They had to
get on. Sarah climbed astride the heaven-sent mule and
planted Mary in front of her; but the going was slow. Even
with no wagon to haul, the weary animals could barely make
their clumsy way up the steep grade, and every few minutes
Sarah was obliged to dismount and help the men shove and
prod reluctant animals over the rocks.

"On the 17th of October we reached the head of Carson
Valley," Sarah dimly remembered, "and just after noon we entered the Great Canyon. Here the road soon became so rough
and steep as to make it very difficult for me to hold Mary and
keep my seat. The men had hard work to drive the cattle and
mules over the boulders at the frequent crossings of the stream,
and in between the great masses of rock where the trail sometimes almost disappeared. As the canyon narrowed, the rocky
walls towered nearly perpendicular, hundreds of feet, and
seemed to meet over our heads. At some of the crossings it was
well nigh impossible to keep to the trail, so innumerable were
the boulders, and the scraggly bushes so hid the coming-out
places."

The Royces finally penetrated the last of the Sierra "coming-out places" and arrived at Pleasant Valley Gold Mines on October 24th—without a guide. By the narrowest of margins they had warded off death a dozen times and almost certainly would have met it in the mountains, had it not been for the charity of two Government agents. Although their possessions were gone, they were at least alive, luckier than many, and had the will to start digging to recoup their losses.

Any assemblage of overlanders could bring to light a dozen stories as melancholy as the Royces'. Men who had buried wives, children and companions along the way, and survived the last trials of the summit crossing, often arrived at the gold fields crushed, hysterical, half-demented, without the slightest lingering interest in the search for a fortune.

A company of twenty husky youngsters who had left the East for California six months before in a burst of high spirits was reduced to a single survivor. Cholera and violent death had claimed one life after another; their cattle had given out, their belongings were discarded, and when the remaining member arrived at Long Bar Mining Camp on foot, he had nothing but scorn for mining and miners.

Caustically he mocked the panners for their obsession. He had sacrificed everything for gold; his home, his health, his companions. All that had once given purpose to his existence was gone. Even while struggling up the Truckee River he had thought that he would be glad to reach the diggings. But now suddenly he saw the futility of it all. Choked for words, he tried to say that all he wanted was to find a home, some substitute for the one he had left—and knew that was too much to hope for. Spurning offers of assistance in staking a claim, he staggered on to the valley in search of something that was lost to him forever.

There was greed and groveling in the mine camps, but there was also compassion. The most callous miners couldn't accept in silence the stories of desperate predicaments that came from the mountain trails during early autumn in 1849 and 1850. Many an Argonaut dropped his pick, loaded a mule with food, medicine and supplies and set off on a mission of mercy. From grim experience they knew that a little encouragement and advice on coping with the trail could save lives.

These rescuers found appalling scenes of sick, starving companies in the last throes of despair. Like the Government men, they had to use tough talk to convince families that wagons and cherished possessions would have to be abandoned. Typically they would find parties that had reduced the weight of their loads by throwing away the last of their food in order to carry along some cumbersome, useless invention for washing gold. One group insisted on trying to get an overloaded wagon along a canyon bottom when the eighteen lacerated, dying oxen hitched to it had demonstrated beyond any doubt that it couldn't be done. Without the volunteer services of these Good Samaritans from the gold camps, scores of immigrants would have perished in the storms of early fall.

So shaken by their travel experiences were most of the overland stragglers that few could settle down at once to digging the gold they had come for. They were slow in adjusting themselves to the new environment; they wanted to make some contact with civilization first; to see the real California. Many, like the Royces, tried their hands at panning for a few days, then driften on down to the valley and Sacramento.

They were seldom heartened by what they found there. In the eight long months while the Royces and hundreds of others were crossing the continent, Sutter's farm had grown from a community of four houses to a tent city of 10,000. It was a ghastly place, yet Sacramento was the nerve center and the supply center for all the northern mining towns. With its immense commercial establishments, warehouses and wharf facilities, the city was already second in size and importance to San Francisco; but it was a valley island.

To be sure, a steady line of boats plied between the river landings and San Francisco Bay; in fact, ships cleared Atlantic ports directly for Sacramento, yet the growth had been so rapid that scattered wheel tracks were the only sign of a road between the city and the hundreds of mountain camps. Supplies had to be packed in by mule trains or on ponderous wagons. There were even daily coach services to the mines, but the stages took off for their destinations across open fields. If newcomers had been shocked by the total absence of roads on the east side of the Sierra, they found little reassurance on the west. No one appeared to have time to give productive thought to highways.

Where natural topography limited the access routes into hill settlements, beaten paths became roads through use; boulders were rolled aside and conspicuous stumps worn or chopped away, yet in the valley, pack trains and wagons veered off in so many directions that any semblance of a designated highway often disappeared. A city like Sacramento, with its teeming population, had to have streets, but they ended at the municipal limits.

When the British globe-trotting artist, J. D. Borthwick, visited the region two years later—in 1851—the only thoroughfares he could find were in Sacramento proper. He pictured a restless, booming metropolis with blocks of handsome brick buildings hemmed in by less attractive "Yankee houses"; a city unimaginatively laid out, checkerboard fashion, with alphabetized streets running east and west, numbered streets north and south.

Busy J Street marked the center. It was a mile long. On it most of the hotels had been thrown together, and the largest of them doubled as a staging house. There Borthwick, at five o'clock in the morning, forced his way through a milling mob to check in for the stage to Hangtown.

"Turned out in front of the hotel," he observed, "were about four and twenty four-horse coaches, all bound for different places in the mines. The street was completely blocked with them, and crowds of men were taking their seats, while others were fortifying themselves for the journey, at the bar. The coaches were of various kinds. Some were light spring wagons—mere oblong boxes, with four or five seats placed across them; others of the same build were covered with awnings; and there were also numbers of regular American stagecoaches; huge, high, heavy things which carry nine inside on three seats.

"The teams were all headed the same way, and these stages, four of five abreast, occupied the whole of the wide street for a distance of seventy yards. The horses were restive and pawing, and snorting and kicking; and passengers were trying to navigate to their proper stages through the labyrinth of wheels and horses. Drivers on their boxes were swearing at each other in a very shocking manner as wheels got locked and wagons were backed into the teams behind them, and also bellowing out to the crowd.

"Runners or tooters for the various stages exhausted all their persuasive eloquence in entreating the passengers to take their seats and go.—'Now then, gentlemen, all aboard for Nevada City. Who's going? Only three seats left—the last chance today for Nevada City—take you there in five hours. Who's there for Nevada City? Nevada City, sir?—This way, just in time.' —and seizing him by the arm, he drags him into the crowd of stages, and almost has him bundled in before the poor devil can make it understood that it is Coloma he wants to go to, not Nevada City. Apparently, if a hundred men wanted to go anywhere, it required a hundred more to despatch them.'"

Squeezed in among New Yorkers, Yankees, an English jack-tar and a nondescript assortment of miners gripping their carpetbags, blankets and long rifles, he was at last under way. The drivers cracked their whips and swore at their horses; grooms dashed out of the way; passengers shouted and hurrahed; and the front teams set off at a gallop, followed closely by two dozen others. But Borthwick's biggest surprise came when they reached the outskirts of Sacramento: there was no road.

"As soon as we got to the edge of town," he continued, "we spread out in all directions to every point of a semicircle, and I found myself behind four splendid horses galloping over the plains like mad. No hedges, no ditches, no houses, no road, in fact—it was all a vast open plain as smooth as a calm ocean. We might have been steering by compass. It was like going to sea; for we emerged from the city as from a landlocked harbor.

The transition to the vastness of space was instantaneous; and the other vehicles, rapidly diminishing around us and getting hull down on the horizon, might have been bound for the uttermost parts of the earth. Here we were upon an ocean of grass-covered earth, and ahead of us, as we traveled toward the mines, the wavy outline of the mountains indenting the sky—the snowy peaks of the Sierra Nevada."

Despite the suffocating clouds of dust kicked up by the horses for coach passengers to breathe and try to beat out of their clothes, this racing across the valley was comfortable travel—as comfortable as any in California. But all sense of enjoyment disappeared once the foothills were reached. The pace of the sweating horses slackened to a crawl. Able-bodied men were ordered out, to plod behind or more often to put their hands to the wheels and help work the coach over the worst obstacles.

And when it came to descending the other side of the hill and the horses were whipped into a gallop, survival rather than comfort came to mind. For an Englishman accustomed to Queen Victoria's macadamized highways it was a sobering experience. "Though the road in some places was very narrow," testified one of her subjects, "for the most part it spread out two or three times the ordinary width, was covered with stumps and large rocks, and full of deep ruts, hollows and roots of trees.

"To anyone not used to such roads or to such driving, an upset would have seemed inevitable. If there was safety in speed, however, we were safe enough, and all sense of danger was lost in admiration of the coolness and dexterity of the driver as he circumvented every obstacle—but without going one inch farther than necessary out of his way to save us from perdition.

"He went through extraordinary bodily contortions, which would have shocked an English coachman out of his propriety; but at the same time he performed such feats as no one would have dared to attempt who had never seen anything worse than an English road. With his right foot he managed a brake and, clawing at the reins with both hands, he swayed his body from side to side to preserve his equilibrium, as now on the right pair of wheels, now on the left, he cut the outside edge around a stump or a rock; and when coming to a spot where he was going to execute a difficult maneuver on a piece of road which slanted violently down to one side, he trimmed the wagon as one would a small boat in a storm, and made us all crowd up to the weather side to prevent capsize."

The fifty miles from Sacramento were covered at a respectable average of six or seven miles an hour. Before midafternoon the coach careened into Hangtown—a place twice as dismal as Sacramento, for here men were actually digging for gold in all the mud and filth of the main street.

But the hill trail into Hangtown was only a teaser for what lay beyond toward Strawberry and other mountain towns, particularly in spring before the last of the snows melted and mule teams were working overtime to replenish exhausted supplies in upland trading posts. It was an unnerving junket even for a toughened, travel-seasoned journalist like J. Ross Browne, who ventured it one April, and in restrained understatement admitted it would be a violation of conscience to recommend the route to anyone.

"The melting of accumulated snows of the past winter had partially washed away the trail," he noted, "and what remained was deeply furrowed by the innumerable streams that sought an outlet in the ravines. In many places it seemed absolutely impracticable for wheeled vehicles; but it is an article of faith with California teamsters that wherever a horse can go, a wagon can follow.

"There are some exceptions to this rule, however, for the road was literally lined with broken-down stages, wagons and carts, presenting every variety of aspect from the general smash-up to the ordinary capsize. Wheels had taken rectangular cuts to the bottom; broken tongues projected from the mud; loads of dry goods and whisky barrels lay wallowing in the general wreck of matter; stout beams cut from the roadside were scattered here and there, having served in vain efforts to extricate the wagons from the oozy mire.

"Occasionally these patches of bad road extended for miles, and here the scenes were stirring in the highest degree. Whole teams of pack mules struggled frantically to make the transit from one dry point to another; burros, heavily laden, were frequently buried up to the neck and had to be hauled out by main force. Now and then an enterprising mule would emerge from the mud, and by attempting to keep to the edge of the road, lose his foothold and go rolling to the bottom of the canyon, pack and all.

"Amid the confusion worse confounded, the cries and maledictions of the *vaqueros* were perfectly overwhelming; but when the mules stuck fast in the mud, and it became necessary to unpack them, then it was that the *vaqueros* shone out most luminously. They shouted, swore, beat the mules, kicked them, pulled them, pushed them, swore again; and when all these resources failed, tore their hair, and resorted to prayer and meditation."

Come what would, the mules claimed the right of way on any California road, and they monopolized the mountain trails. Saddle trains had served as dependable freight transports anywhere and everywhere since the earliest days of the Spanish padres. Mules had been used to break the first paths into the mountains, and as if by right of prior conquest or eminent domain, they stolidly held to them long after wheels had stretched the paths to wagon width.

Mining camps far back in the hills were entirely dependent on mule packs, and in many cases these settlements sprang into existence, boomed into populous towns and died before a road ever reached them. By mule pack went all the lumber, liquor, pork and pianos that gave them life.

With some forty mules to a train, each animal loaded with three or four hundred pounds, and countless strings of them reaching out from cities like Stockton, Sacramento and Marysville, they were an impediment to all competing traffic in the valleys; in the mountains they were a menace, for the nudge of a mule trotting down a steep grade carrying ballast of close to a quarter of a ton, could unbalance a horse and rider or a stagecoach and send them over a cliff to kingdom come. At the first sound of the tinkling bell from a lead mule or the clatter of hoofs, the only recourse for anyone in the path was to dash hellbent for the nearest turn-out, whether up or down the mountain. When the trail was clogged with snow, the threat was diabolic.

"Now, boys, hang together. Your lives depend on it," was the warning from the captain of a group of twelve horsemen, setting out from Strawberry. It was spring, and the worst season of the year for mules. Ahead of them was the notorious "Grade," a steep narrow stretch cut into the sheer eastern slope of the Sierra. "Watch out for the pack trains, and when you see them coming, hang on to a wide place! Don't come in contact with the mule packs, or you'll go over the grade for certain."

The horsemen safely evaded train after train by taking refuge in the wide places in the road and waiting until the rear guard had passed. It was precarious going, for the trail was a mass of slush after a late snowfall, the threat of avalanches from above was constant and fresh tracks of animals that had been sent over the cliff were a grim reminder of the danger.

The riders were at last caught just short of a turn-out, as a lead mule with its jangling bell suddenly appeared around a sharp bend, followed by thirty-nine others; all loaded with whisky, gin and brandy—barrels, half barrels and kegs, three to an animal. Moreover, at that point the trail was scarcely more than a foot wide, banked on the left by packed drifts of last winter's snow, and bounded on the right by nothing but space and a spectacular view.

"Dismount all! Wheel! Cut back for your lives!" yelled the captain. But his order came too late.

"The mules were on us before we could turn," reported the spokesman for the group. "Some of us were overturned, horses and all, in the banks of snow. Others sprang from their horses and let them struggle on their own account. All had to break a way out of the trail. The mules stampeded, and kicked, brayed and rolled in turns. The *vaqueros* were in a frenzy of rage and terror combined—shrieking *'Maladetto!' 'Carambo!'* and

'*Caraja!*' till it seemed as if the reverberation must break loose the snow from above, and send an avalanche down on top of us all.

"Bridles got foul of stray legs and jerked the owners on their backs; riatas were twisted and wound around horses, mules and whisky barrels; packs went rolling hither and thither; men and animals kicked for their bare lives; heads, legs and bodies were covered up in snowdrifts; and nobody knew what everybody else was doing, or what he was doing himself. The scene would have been amusing, had it not been intensified by the imminent risk of slipping over the precipice. It was at least a thousand feet down into Lake Valley. But upon picking up our scattered regiment, with all arms and equipments used in the melee, we found as follows: dead, none; wounded, six; mortally frightened, the whole party; lost, a keg of whisky, which some say went down to Lake Valley; but I have my suspicions where that keg went, and how it was secreted."

That melee above Lake Valley was perhaps one of the last to occur on a major trail over the mountains. The day when riders, teamsters and coachmen could claim the right of way over the barking *vaqueros* and their jackass trains was long overdue. The columns of stubborn mules were about to be crowded off the road.

When Californians—who had so recently been Midwesterners, Yankees and Southerners—made up their minds to do something, there was no stopping them. Immediacy was their motto. All at once construction of highways became the obsession of the hour. Phalanxes of Chinese, Mexicans and miscellaneous laborers from many nations armed with picks, shovels and dynamite, and backed by mobile units of horse-drawn scoops, scrapers and dumpcarts, swarmed over the worn trials and began converting them into roads.

The campaigners worked with a fury that seemed to assert that the job must be done overnight, and remarkable achievements were made in record time. Suddenly the highways were there, like ribbons dropped in some sleight-of-hand hocus-pocus. They appeared with the same abruptness that characterized the birth of mining towns or valley cities. A teamster who laboriously urged his horses up a jagged, furrowed incline one season would unexpectedly find a hard-packed road there the next. Immigrants who risked life and limb crossing from Carson City to Sacramento in 1855 returned to ride over something that could easily be mistaken for a road in 1856.

The new thoroughfares weren't much to brag about, and even newspaper editors realized it. By all rules of news evaluation, the completion of a first highway over the Sierra would stand out in the West as a monumental, history-making event, worthy of the boldest headlines and the shrillest cries of paper venders. But San Francisco's leading chronicle, *Alta California*, buried the report in a column of miscellany, and in a prosaic announcement informed its readers on August 25th, 1856, that the Immigrant Road from Murphy's to Carson Valley was complete—"The workmen came in several days ago, and all who have passed over the road speak of it in the highest terms of praise. A day or two ago a buggy containing two gentlemen started for Carson Valley by this route, but as yet has not returned. Now that the road is completed, travelers from Sacramento to Carson can accomplish the journey easily in two days, and without wearying unnecessarily either horses or riders."

Despite the indifference of editors, the new trans-Sierran road was a godsend to immigrants, as well as to the constantly shifting population of miners, to the draymen, to coach drivers and their animals. It was a highway primarily for wheels, not pack trains. Two years later a more direct wagon route from Placerville to Carson City, by way of Lake Tahoe, was on the map. Private investors were shortly pushing a highway along the headwaters of the American River to Dutch Flat, heading over Donner Pass to Truckee; and still another road was being built over Sonora Pass farther to the south.

State funds and federal funds went into the new traffic lanes, but for the most part the backing was in private capital. Men with big money had a notion that someday a railroad might zigzag up the cliffs, and they knew that a supply road would have to come first. Less farsighted capitalists who had cleaned up in the gold fields saw investments in toll roads as a way of multiplying their resources. Then the discovery of the rich Comstock Silver Lode in Nevada made construction of a highway to the bonanzas on the east side of the Sierra an urgent necessity.

Within little more than half a decade, the heights that had long been the terror of travelers were cut by smooth thoroughfares as fine as any in the Adirondacks or Appalachians of the East—and to add a touch of incredible luxury to the Placerville-Carson route, horse-drawn water wagons moved up and down the mountain in the dry season sprinkling the surface to keep down the dust and pack the bed, while in winter endless relays of drag chains and scrapers cleared the snow.

The opening of the Placerville Road changed everything along its 160-mile route almost overnight. The pack trains moved over to make way for giant freight wagons and smart coaches. In the foothills pleasant frame houses took the place of the tent cities. Orchards, sheep and cattle ranches appeared on former wastelands. The rip-roaring shanty colonies where *vaqueros*, peddlers, red-shirted miners, teamsters and traders had put up for the night in a bedlam of drinking, cursing, gambling and brawling, turned into respectable inns and taverns. And spaced every few miles along the route were orderly stage stations, each complete with hotel, bar, stables and blacksmith shop.

Day and night the traffic rumbled by, the almost endless procession of freight wagons hogging the road. At the foot of a slow incline, they would sometimes back up for miles. Drawn by sixteen or twenty mules, or as many horses, and burdened with ten or fifteen tons of freight, the vans got larger and larger. Behind the leading freighter was hitched a second wagon, and behind that a tender. Annual freight hauls during the boom years ran to 70,000 tons, and at the rate of ten cents a pound for the entire distance, the teamsters struck it richer than the miners. Their income for the one year, 1863, totaled $12,000,000.

The Placerville, of course, was a toll road, and its builders, if anything, had far underestimated the potential income. They had gambled the fantastic sum of almost $500,000 on the road, yet in a single season over $600,000 was collected.

But the most remarkable change among all the transformations brought by the Placerville Road was in the people traveling on it and the vehicles they rode. Now de luxe Concord coaches, imported all the way from New Hampshire, made daily runs over the Sierra, and they were drawn by six slickly groomed horses. The depot in Sacramento had all the bustle and most of the sophistication of an eastern terminal— "Stages backed up in a long row; prancing horses in front; swearing and sweating porters, baggagemasters, drivers and passengers all about and behind; anxious ladies, prolific in crinoline and gorgeous silks and satins, fretting and scolding over crushed bandboxes; and stern-looking men of an official cast shouting fiercely, 'This way, gents! 'Ere's the place for your baggage! Bring it along if you want it weighted; if you don't it won't go —that's all!

" 'Thirty pounds allowed; all extra baggage twenty-five cents per pound. Fifteen dollars for you, sir. Twenty-five for you. Forty-six for you, madam. Seventy-five for you, Miss—heavy trunk that, miss. Quick, if you please, ladies and gents! Stage's behind time—won't get to Placerville before dark. Your names, gents. Pile in. Get down from the front seat, you, sir—place engaged. All aboard!' "

And the men that drove those coaches were the best in the trade. It took more talent to pilot a coach down the Sierra than to serve as a Congressman, admitted the Honorable Schuyler Colfax, Speaker of the United States House of Representatives, after a trip over the mountains; and Colfax was not deprecating the qualifications of a politician. What with the narrow roads, lacking so much as a log buffer to keep the stage from plunging over a thousand-foot precipice, the heavy counter-traffic in wagon trains, the washouts and fallen trees that had to be reckoned with, and an average speed of ten or twelve miles an hour to be maintained night and day, driving a coach in the Sierra required artistry, supreme self-confidence and considerable sleight of hand.

The coachman handled his vehicle as a skipper would a yawl. His passengers were his crew, and he counted on their services in making his hairbreadth maneuvers, shouting at the top of his lungs as he rolled down the mountain: "Forward!" "Hard to right!" "Back!" "Everyone, now, sit up to windward!" And on they plunged behind six racing horses, never slacking speed for the craziest of turns. The most exciting man-made spectacle ever to visit the Sierra was the coach-and-six thundering down the grade.

J. Ross Browne took a second trip one moonlit night in 1863, and lived to tell of it exuberantly: "For a distance of five or six miles the road winds around the sides of the mountains, crossing ravines and doubling up occasionally in turns so rapid that the stage seems to run one way and the horses another. Some of these whirling turns reminded me of the flight of an Australian boomerang.

"As we strike the straight road again, the driver gives rein to our spirited animals; crack goes the whip, and down we plunge over narrow bridges, along the edges of terrific precipices a thousand feet deep, through dark forests of pine and along frowning banks of granite, hewn from the solid bed of the mountain.

"Despite the ridiculous stories we had heard of accidents and alarms, every passenger with a nervous disposition clung tenaciously to the stage fixtures, as if determined to follow the stage wherever it might go, and there were moments when we even held our breaths to keep up a balance. I flatter myself I saved the lives of the whole party several times by hoisting at the lee rail and holding my breath hard, while I leaned over on the weather side. It is not comfortable to look down when you are flying along at the rate of ten miles an hour and see no bottom short of fifteen hundred feet.

"Yet there is a charm in this dashing, reckless journey by moonlight. The danger is just sufficient to give it relish. The excitement keeps the blood warm; the fresh mountain air invigorates and inspires every faculty; the spirit rises with the rapidity of motion, and before you get halfway to the valley, you find yourself in a condition to sing, shout or dance."

But this conquest of the Sierra by stagecoach wasn't enough. Visionaries now were talking seriously about crossing it with a more powerful vehicle. "Men of the East! Men of Washington!" cried Samuel Bowles, editor of the Springfield, Massachusetts, *Republican,* just after Appomattox in 1865, "You have given the toil and even the blood of a million of your brothers and fellows for four years, and spent three thousand million dollars to rescue one section of the Republic from barbarism and from anarchy. Lend now a few thousand men and a hundred millions of money to marry to the Nation of the Atlantic an equal if not greater Nation of the Pacific. Here is the completion of a Republic that is continental; but you must come and take it with the Locomotive!"

V

BUT MORE PARTICULARLY
THE WIDOWS

There were Pennsylvanians who claimed that *E Clampus
Vitus* originated back in the Keystone State. Loyal Missourians
would swear on a stack of dictionaries that the charter chap-
ter was organized in St. Louis. Vermonters contended that
Ethan Allen and his Green Mountain Boys were the first
Clampers, and if the Yankees were interested in provoking a

brawl, all they had to do was uphold their bogus premise in the presence of a few Southerners who firmly believed that the vital impetus for *Vitus* came from Alabama.

Then while representatives from a dozen states were maintaining their priority claims, brethren from West Virginia would step in and attempt to demolish them all. They were the original founders. In fact, they could name the prime author and creator of the fraternity—Squire Ephraim Bee, blacksmith and tavern keeper of Meat Horse Fork on Middle Island Creek, Dodridge County, West Virginia.

But once *E Clampus Vitus* took root in the gold towns of the Sierra, all these apocryphal claims lost focus. There the true universality of the Order came to light. No narrow bounds either of time or place restricted the sweep of the brotherhood. It could be traced back through G. Washington, William the Conqueror, Nero, King Solomon, to Babylon and the Garden of Eden. Adam was the original Clampatriarch, St. Vitus the adopted Clampatron. The glorious company of progenitors included Aristotle, Socrates, the Caesars, Napoleon, Will Shakespeare, Patrick Henry and any other illustrious figure a plenipotentiary cared to pluck out of history.

In *E Clampus Vitus* was found a common catechism that resolved all the differing ideologies brought to California by men from every quarter of the nation and the globe. Sharp, boisterous humor cemented human relations as no parson, judge or do-gooder ever could. It was that element that knit the miners and their contemporaries into an indigenous society—the devotion to spoofing, rambunctious horseplay and straight-faced humbuggery; the absorption in practical jokes, so complicated and contrived that their inventors often forgot the point in the process of execution; the love of corny hoaxes carried under such beguiling camouflage that even the press, fellow pranksters and the public were taken in.

Of their own free volition, no men ever undertook harder, more backbreaking labor than working the diggings. After wielding a sledge hammer or wheeling wet gravel to the sluices for a ten-hour day, they craved companionship and some form of amusement. They found it at the saloons and gambling hang-outs, but the whisky and the cards didn't entirely fill the bill. There had to be an outlet for the inventive spirit and the excess animal energy. Usually it was exhausted at the expense of some gullible greenhorn. Pool the reserve of buncombe and buffoonery that was trapped in a saloon, along with the smoke and liquor fumes, and something had to explode. The fuse to set off the explosion was supplied by the Ancient and Honorable Order of *E Clampus Vitus*, a burlesque on fraternal orders, monstrous enough to end forever all such caricatures.

Between Honey Lake and Kern River there wasn't a respectable mountain town without its clique—like Tuolumne Chapter No. 28, Gobbler's Lodge No. 107,368 at Columbia, Balaam Lodge No. 107,402 at Sonora, or Mokelumne Hill Lodge No. 100, titular See of the Grand Consectory.

Ostensibly *E Clampus Vitus* was a service club and benevolent fraternity combined, a mysterious supersecret organization formed for "the relief and protection of widows and orphans—but more particularly the widows." Since one was hard put in the 1850's to find a legitimate orphan nearer than Missouri, and since widows were scarcer than unclaimed maidens, the fraternity was free to direct its endeavors into less specific channels.

The Clampers ran the diggings. They ran highfalutin' impostors out of town, routed grafting politicians and made short work of any other individual with whom they chose to cross swords. The organization was dedicated to the putting of every man in his place. Anyone who took himself too seriously was fair game. As one Clamper expressed it, "We made fools out of men and men out of fools." Actually they did good deeds too—every now and then. For families in distress they took up collections unobtrusively, sympathetically, efficiently. And nobody could complain that he was shortchanged for entertainment in the Fourth of July parades, oratorical shindigs and masquerades gotten up by a chapter for the public benefit —even though the proceeds were all for the liquid assets of the members.

But the real purpose of *E Clampus Vitus* was to *take in* new members and convert initiation fees quickly into good wholesome hard liquor. All other *raison d'être* was admittedly dispensable. It was virtually a labor union—closed shop—with membership compulsory to those with the ready capital. Nor was it limited to miners and their minions. Every male bartender, innkeeper, lawyer, doctor, merchant, minister, visitor and vagrant had to belong to avoid social ostracism.

No grocer could hold his customers for a week without taking the oaths. No political aspirant dared consider running for office until he had joined. A drummer could tote up an order for $2,000 worth of merchandise, only to have it canceled when his client discovered that he wasn't one of them. The only means by which a court defendant could avoid certain conviction was to flash the *E.C.V.* signal as the jury filed out. Barnstorming theatrical companies were boycotted until the manager paid his dues.

Men of distinguished birth, wealth and high position were no less eligible for membership than the rudest tramps. The claws of *Clampus* welcomed all gullible humanity. Even nobility was given the business. When Lord John Shalto Douglas, eighth Marquess of Queensberry and celebrated originator of modern boxing rules, was billed for an appearance at Marysville, miners were ready to sacrifice their shirts to see him, but not until he joined the club. He faced an empty house the first night—except for a few hecklers. Then someone tipped him off; he was hastily initiated, and the next night STANDING ROOM ONLY signs had to be posted an hour before the performance.

Serious students of the Order noted that its entire creed was fabricated around certain lunar conceptions, with particular emphasis on moonshine. Even the calendar of the organization followed the lunar month. All regular assemblies of a Lodge were scheduled before the full of the moon, or after the full of the moon—just how long before or after was immaterial, as long as there were enough meetings to observe properly all interim phases of the moon. Between these regular meetings, irregular ones could be called at any hour of any day or night.

Monotonous blasts from the "Hewgag," an eight-foot tin trumpet, summoned the clan to meetings of either type. Normally the sound of the Hewgag meant that another prospect had been pledged and all brothers were being rounded up for a business meeting in the back room of their favorite saloon. No urging was required to assemble a quorum. The men came on the run.

During the first rounds of drinks at the bar, the new candidate was introduced. He was always impressed with the spirit of hospitality, the liberal flow of alcohol and the apparent generosity of the house—until the saloon proprietor later presented him with a well-padded bill for the total consumption. Soon the honored candidate was solemnly ushered to the back room where he made his first acquaintance with the mysteries of the Order.

The Shining Sword of Justice Tempered with Mercy was unsheathed—all seven feet of it; the Blunderbusket, a ten-foot fowling piece with a two-inch bore, was reverently brought out of hiding. The Royal Grand Musician demonstrated the use of the Hewgag. A billy goat, with elaborately gilded nether extremities, went on parade. And to the stirring rendition of the Clamper anthem, "We'll Take a Drink with Thee, Dear Brother," the emblem of the society was slowly raised—a hoop skirt inscribed with the motto: "This is the flag we fight under."

With these preliminaries over, the formalities of the formal initiation began. The neophyte was blindfolded and invited to seat himself in the symbolic Expungent's Chair, on which he would be conveyed in state over the royal highway to the spiritual stronghold of Clampalia. The chair proved to be a wheelbarrow cushioned with a large wet sponge, and the royal road a ladder laid on the floor.

Unless he insisted on having nothing further to do with *E Clampus Vitus* after that ordeal, he presented himself for the Inquisition. This was a brief inquiry into his religious convictions, terminating always with the test question regarding his belief in the Elevation of Man. As soon as the affirmative answer was given, the candidate found himself astride a taut, narrow saddle being elevated by block and tackle.

Such humiliation could go on for hours, depending on the constitution of the customer and the sobriety of his torturers. If he passed safely through the Cave of Silence, endured the Obliterating of Obfuscation and recited the solemn oaths of secrecy with proper aplomb, he was at last ready to receive the Staff of Relief and be admitted to all the privileges and immunities appertaining to the Order.

The only immunity was freedom from ever being taken in again. There was an assortment of privileges: thereafter a member was eligible to partake of the entertainment and liquid assets of the chapter; he was entitled to claim fraternal compensation if ever injured while drunk (sober brethren were expected to look after themselves); and he would receive old-age compensation of eighty dollars a month, payments to start eleven years after burial, provided he would appear in person to collect. His name went on the roster of the local chapter and a jumbo-sized certificate placed in his custody was to be carried in his hip pocket at all times as evidence of his affiliation. The passport was good anywhere in the Sierra— High or Low.

The democratic principles of *E Clampus Vitus* were made evident to the initiate from the start. Every man held an office of equal rank and dignity. All were chairmen of the Most Important Committee; all were given titles of equal elegance, such as: Clamps Petrix, Clamps Matrix, Royal Platrix, Great Mountageon, High and Mighty Hangman, Grand Iscutis, Noble Grand Chiseler. Only the presiding officer, the Noble Grand Humbug, and perhaps the Guardian of the Hewgag, held responsibilities that placed them a peg above their fellows.

With painfully vigorous backslapping and handgripping, the new member was once more led back to the bar where the anthem, "We Take a Drink to Thee, Dear Brother," was sung repetitiously in more or less close harmony into the small hours of the morning, each rendition representing another round of drinks for which the honored initiate would receive the bill.

That bill constituted the initiation fee. It could amount to half a year's wages.

The efficiency with which the Clampers worked in remedying sticky local problems of civic interest was well exemplified at Sonora. At this booming mining city the bull ring was the major entertainment attraction. But certain clergymen and their converts looked askance at the brutality of this Sunday exhibition. They wanted to do away, not only with the bullfights but also with the bull-and-bear fights, and were making quite a to-do about it, claiming that they were a distraction to churchgoers, that the bull ring was an eyesore and the hideous racket of cheering that rose from the amphitheatre on a Sunday afternoon was a desecration. The pulpiteers were even making an ethical issue out of the fights. Sonora's morals, they insisted, needed to be reconstituted.

The beneficent guardians of widows and orphans weren't quite ready to concede that such drastic action was necessary. By unanimous vote they enthusiastically endorsed all kinds of bullfights, and with the same unanimity appointed their own Morals Committee. To prove that they never acted under pressure from the home office, they seceded from the Ancient and Honorable Order and, in a superfluous bit of buffoonery, went local under the name of Royal Order of George's Sons Mighty and Terrible, though the change did not mean that they were straying very far from either the Clamper's objectives or its canon law.

A bold advertisement shortly appeared in the Sonora *Herald* announcing the most spectacular bull-and-bear fight that had ever been held in the amphitheatre. And the bill wouldn't be limited to that. It would be followed by a dog-and-bear fight and then a man-and-bear fight; a professional bear hunter would battle to the death, if necessary, the fiercest grizzly ever brought into captivity.

As soon as the *Herald* reached the streets, the rumpus started. Clearly more than bulls, bears, dogs, bear hunters and morals were involved. This was open defiance, a challenge to the forces of righteousness, a contest for supremacy between

church and an insolent fraternity. Church rallies followed cau-
cuses of the deacons. There were revival meetings and indignation meetings. The spirit of the Christian martyrs of Rome
was rekindled. George's Sons lay low.

For once, the church denominations presented a united
front. They had a surprise for the bear fighters; a courageous
and daring plan. On the day of the great contest the clergymen led their flocks through the streets, singing hymns as they
marched. Their destination was the ring of the amphitheatre,
where they intended to assemble and remain through the
bloodshed. Let the bulls, bears and dogs be brought in; they
would die for the cause of better Sonora morals.

The thin line of hymn singers stormed boldly into the ring at
the hour announced for the fight. They were ready to make the
supreme sacrifice. But as they marched through the heavy
doors, the chorus dropped a pitch. The line faltered. Embarrassed clergymen turned to scan the wilting faces of their following. The amphitheatre was empty.

Suddenly the crusaders caught on to the fact that the whole
affair was a magnificent hoax, carefully plotted for their benefit.
There weren't going to be any fights; none had been planned.
Sheepishly they made their retreat. George's Sons Mighty and
Terrible had won the first round in the struggle for control of
Sonora's morals.

The Clampers set a standard for California hoax and humor,
but by no means did they hold a monopoly on the field. Practical jesting belonged to the period rather than to any one
group. The biggest, most costly hoax of the gold rush had nothing to do with the Clampers. It grew like Topsy, fed from half
a dozen different sources, but primarily by none other than
Old Caleb Greenwood, who was far too independent a customer to stoop to social regimentation imposed by anything
like the Ancient and Honorable Order. That classic hoax of
hoaxes was known to everyone west of the Rockies as "Gold
Lake."

According to the most reliable hearsay of the early 1850's,
Gold Lake was located in the northern Sierra between the

Feather and Yuba Rivers, or near their headwaters. That meant that it might lie anywhere within an unmapped, unexplored wilderness of some five thousand square miles. Reportedly it nestled at the foot of three sharply peaked mountains, and its shores were inhabited by a tribe of tricky, hostile Indians. However, any risks were worth taking to establish a claim there. Its broad sloping beaches were pebbled with globs of gold—yellow nuggets as copious as cobblestones in a gravel dump; such an inexhaustible wealth of gold that the native Indians had long since ceased to attach any value to it. They preferred harder, less malleable minerals.

When the first rumors of Gold Lake began to circulate, "Old Greenwood" was at once consulted. Though he was getting on toward his dotage, he was never to be outtalked by a competing frontiersman. He readily acknowledged that he knew all about the lake; he had been there and could vouch for the fact that the beaches were strewn with the yellow stuff; he hadn't given it much thought because that kind of hardware didn't interest him.

Yes, one would have to be wary of the Indians thereabout. They were ornery but could be brought to terms. As for locating the lake, it was easy enough to find with those three buttes to mark it. No one could go wrong. He'd be glad to take a party there, but he was too busy just then; he'd lend his half-Indian son John, instead.

Following the directions mapped by his father, John set out for Gold Lake, trailed by a heterogeneous group of Tenderfeet. In the course of a week they combed a lot of territory, found innumerable bodies of water that roughly answered the description, but found no gold-rimmed lake and returned in disgust.

That failure only whetted the appetites of other gold seekers. News of the lake spread through the diggings like wind-blown fire over a parched hayfield. By early June of 1850 the discovery of Gold Lake had become an established fact in the public mind. From Oregon to the Mexican border the stampede was on, everyone intending to get there ahead of someone else.

Mining camp after mining camp was deserted as men took off en masse. Marysville became virtually an abandoned city. Shopkeepers closed and boarded up their stores—except vendors of prospecting gear, who were doing a wholesale business at retail prices. Verification of the existence of the lake by Indian chiefs east of the Sierra and west of the Sierra spurred on the search. Thousands upon thousands of Argonauts were wandering aimlessly over the mountains north of Donner Pass, where there were no less than fifty lakes that would pass for the one "Old Greenwood" had described.

Old-timers like Peter Lassen, the Danish blacksmith who had come overland in 1839 to establish an immigrant route north of the Sierra, postponed his plans for building a Utopian city at Deer Creek and went off looking for Gold Lake. Goldsborough Bruff, ex-West Pointer, experienced topographical engineer and president of the Washington City Gold Company, joined the search, as did dozens of other men of respectable standing.

Every few days reports of incredibly rich strikes were judiciously circulated. A party of Kanakas was reported to have gathered chunks of gold worth $75,000 in a few hours. Guides at Marysville and Nevada City advertised their services with a money-back guarantee if they failed to locate the lake. Armies of treasure hunters in the hinterland firmly believed the story that mule trains were daily freighting gold into Marysville by the ton.

But always there was a certain vagueness about the location and circumstances of a find. Secret maps that led parties to the lake were too often accidentally destroyed. Repeatedly, men who presumably reached the golden shores had time only to snatch up a few hunks before being attacked and driven off by Indians. The size of the lake seemed to vary from five acres to five square miles and the size of the gold nuggets from marbles to bowling balls.

In the background were editors and well-informed people who apparently knew that the whole thing was a hoax of majestic proportions. For a time they did their best to dissuade earnest prospectors from joining the goose chase. The effort was futile. They suffered public rebukes for expressing their skepticism. They tried a different tack—exaggerating the glitter of Gold Lake to put its absurdity in proper perspective. That failed too. People were more inclined to accept the exaggerations as the latest intelligence from the front.

On June 19th, 1850, the Sacramento *Transcript* joined the jokesters with a reckless plug. "We are informed by a gentleman just in from Marysville," read the tongue-in-cheek account, "that it is currently reported there that the Indians upon this lake use gold for the commonest purposes—that they have a rude way of knocking out square blocks which they use for seats and couches upon which to place their beds, which are simply bundles of wild oats which grow so profusely in these sections of our State.

"According to reports also, they use for fishhooks crooked pieces of gold, and kill their game with arrows made of the same material. They are reported to be thunderstruck at the movements of the whites and at their eagerness to collect and hoard the materials of the very ground upon which they tread. A story is now current that a man at Gold Lake saw a large slab of gold floating on the lake, which he succeeded in getting to shore. So clear are the waters that another man saw a rock of gold on the bottom. After many efforts, he succeeded in lassoing the rock. Three days afterward, he was seen standing, holding on to his rope, pale and emaciated."

Readers even missed the point of this all too simple satire, and enlarged their vision to include quarrying gold, rather than bothering with mere nuggets.

Few among the thousands of searchers for Gold Lake during the 1850's were ever convinced that it did not exist. Their not finding it was just a turn of bad luck. In the process of looking for the dazzling shores, they uncovered superb deposits in the Yuba and Feather River country, established dozens of camps like Whisky Diggings, Hepsydam, Poverty Hill and Poker Flat; but the tens of millions in treasure that came from these diggings never quite compensated for the elusive gold of phantom Gold Lake. A good hoax died hard.

Occasionally the spoofery in the mining towns brought re-percussions that reached far beyond the domain of the diggers, beyond the Sierra, beyond California and the West. The un-known perpetrator of a bizarre little prank at Cherokee Flat certainly didn't intend to upset the entire scientific world—but he very nearly succeeded.

Undoubtedly that incident started with a spat over the harsh handling of a molar while the prankster was seated in Dr. Kelly's dental chair at Angels Camp; the patient had to get even with the dentist. On the way out of the office, he spotted the skull which Kelly kept on display as his badge of trade. A perfect souvenir. He light-fingered it under the jacket carried over his arm and disappeared. At least that is the way it could have happened.

In all the clutter of his office, Dr. Kelly didn't miss the skull for a long time, and by then it was too late to pin the theft on any single suspect. He first missed it in February, 1866, when gossip reached him that a skull had been found in a gravel bed at the bottom of a mine shaft, 130 feet under Bald Hill. The thief had probably tossed it there to get rid of it, and to startle some nervous wielder of a pick and shovel. The doctor wanted it back, but, alas, he was now at a loss to prove that it was his. It had been pickling so long in the wet gravel and volcanic ash that the bone had turned black and the familiar facial expres-sion had changed.

The finding of this amusing prop created quite a sensation among the miners. Something very special had to be done with it. Why not pass it off as the "bony fide remains of an aboriginal Homo Californianus?"

As usual, one thing led to another. The most unpopular char-acter to make recurrent visits to the mines was Dr. J. D. Whit-ney, State Geologist, who was forever throwing monkey wrenches into machinery contrived by local financiers for sell-ing wildcat stocks. The State Geologist might care to look over the specimen and express an opinion regarding authenticity of its age. A long chance, but one well worth taking.

The Clampers were canny enough not to ship their brain box directly to headquarters. Miner Jim Matson, who took credit for unearthing it, naturally turned it over to the local dealer in flesh and bones—his grocer. The grocer passed it on to his family physician Dr. Jones, with a few appropriately naïve remarks, and here at last the prize came up for its first serious scientific appraisal.

The unsuspecting Jones was swept off his feet. He knew enough about geology to realize that no human remains had ever before been found at such depth beneath ancient lava flows. It could predate the formation of the Sierra, predate the Piltdown Man and the Pekin Lady, and incidentally stir up a fuss among scientists and anti-evolutionists that would be heard around the world.

"This knocks hell out of Moses," Jones is alleged to have remarked, as he rushed it off to Whitney in San Francisco.

The scheming of the Clampers and the process of passing the fossil from hand to hand had taken time. It was unearthed on February 25th; Whitney didn't receive it until July. Its arrival in San Francisco turned the Geological Survey rooms into pandemonium. The disinterment of the head was an event more momentous than Jim Marshall's discovery of gold at Sutter's in '48. Whitney had been maintaining all along that man made a much earlier appearance in California than anthropologists were willing to concede. Here was the evidence to prove his theory. After the county in which it was found, it was at once christened the "Calaveras Skull."

The State Geologist dropped everything and dashed up to Cherokee Flat to make a thorough investigation. The miners were waiting for him. Among them there wasn't a single disagreement on the details of the discovery. All stuck to pecisely the same story and avoided any mention of Dr. Kelly. Whitney wanted to climb down the mine shaft. They had even anticipated that, and broke the news that unfortunately it was flooded.

The doctor who had predicted that the skull would "knock hell out of Moses" underestimated the forthcoming furor. With a zealous assist from Whitney, the Calaveras Skull was going to knock hell out of college professors, museum curators, science writers and sermon writers, as well as Genesis. Every life-science textbook in the world would have to be revised to make room for the man of Calaveras.

Within a few weeks the storm had passed from the daily press and the pulpit to popular magazines and the science journals, and the famous profile was being calipered at Harvard.

"This relic of human antiquity," the *American Journal of Science* learnedly expounded, "is easily seen to be an object of the greatest interest to the ethnologist as well as the geologist. The previous investigations of the Geological Survey have clearly demonstrated the fact that man was contemporaneous with the mastodon and elephant. . . . But in the case of the skull now laid before the academy, the geological position to which it must be assigned is apparently still lower than that of the mastodon. . . .

"There is every reason to believe that these great proboscidians lived at a very recent date (geologically speaking) and posterior to the epoch of the existence of glaciers in the Sierra Nevada, and also after the close of the period of activity of the now extinct volcanoes of that great chain. In fact, they belong to the present period. The bed, on the other hand, in which this skull was found must have been deposited at the time when the volcanoes of the Sierra were still in vigorous action, and, as seems to us highly probable . . . previous to the glacial epoch of the Sierra, and also previous to the erosion of the canyons of the present rivers. . . . On the subject of the ethnological relations of this skull, I should suppose that it belonged to the type of Indians now inhabiting the foothills of the Sierra. It is certain that the facial angle is not one indicating a low order of intellect. The skull, however, seems to have been very thick and solid."

Before the controversy was over, there were scientists who began to question the thickness and solidity of Dr. Whitney's skull. They failed to come up with conclusions that matched those of the State Geologist, after careful analyses of the Calaveras Man.

For a few turbulent seasons, paleontologists were divided into two contentious camps—anti-Calaveras and pro-Calaveras. Yet Whitney stood by his guns to the last. Thirteen years after the great find, he made a final report in which he reiterated his steadfast conviction regarding the authenticity of the skull: it was definitely Pliocene. But by that time it had become a discarded issue.

The textbooks weren't revised, after all, to accommodate the Clampers. Instead, Bret Harte, who may have been in on the secret from the start, memorialized the hoax in a few unsparing stanzas addressed "To the Pliocene Skull." Perhaps some of the scientists overheard, too, the rolls of laughter coming from the Cherokee Flat saloons and even the plaintive murmur of dentist Kelly who still wanted his showpiece back.

The mine-town flux of practical jests seemed to be inexhaustible, but few of them received the fanfare of the Calaveras and Gold Lake hoaxes. For the most part the miners were content to keep their fellow-ribbing localized. They found hilarious entertainment in challenging two louse-ridden prospectors to race a duet of lice from their respective persons across a soup plate—with stakes set at a thousand dollars. They got equal pleasure out of wagering an un-Christlike crackpot that he couldn't walk on water, as he claimed he could, but cheerfully paid off their bets when he fooled them and did it on pontoon shoes he had invented. And they went into spasms of merriment watching their favorite fire company repeatedly beat a competing team, through the simple expedient of doping the competitor's tank with soapsuds. The idea was for each company to put the hose nozzle of their hand pumper into the tank of the other and pump like mad until the loser's tank overflowed. The froth from a few pails of soapsuds, surreptitiously turned into the tank before the race, always brought an early victory—and profitable returns on the odds.

Sometimes the practical jokes miscarried or backfired in a

bad way. To sell a claim that had proved worthless, a gang of bamboozlers thought up the bright idea of peppering the prospect hole with gold dust fired from a borrowed cannon. The scheme would undoubtedly have worked, but the cannon exploded and there weren't enough survivors to repeat the experiment.

Into Mokelumne Hill drifted a Negro, Joshua, with a lazy shuffle and a soft southern drawl; he inquired of street-corner gossips—known everywhere as the "Grand Jury"—what they did for a living and where he might pick up a few days of work.

"Here we figure on doin' narthin' but dig holes in the ground and lift out nuggets," Joshua was told. He wanted to know where he could start digging. So with the usual mock-serious drollery, he was sent to the nearest hilltop where the sod had already been turned over unsuccessfully so many times that it looked like a hard-won battlefield.

Joshua outfitted himself with a pick and shovel, and two days later returned to the same street corner carrying a poke of gold dust, his pockets bulging with shiny lumps. He merely wanted to thank his beneficiaries. The Grand Jury quickly recovered from its shock and ran for the hill to stake out claims of its own. "Nigger Hill," it was called thereafter—one of the richest discoveries in the region.

And during an uncommonly bitter winter when it was too cold for treasure hunting in the mountains, hibernating miners improved their time by circulating the whopper that Emerald Bay in Lake Tahoe, which never gets a coating of ice, had frozen solid all the way to the bottom; prospectors had moved their rigs to the lake, were driving shafts through the ice, and mining trout.

The fish story worked its way down to San Francisco Bay, where it was accepted as gospel truth and whipped into a news story without the trace of a smile. "In the general freeze which has converted the lake into a sea of ice, Emerald Bay has been frozen solid," asserted *Alta California* on its front page. "It is one vast ledge of ice from the surface of its transparent water to the bottom. For some reason best known to themselves, the fish, especially the trout, have fairly swarmed here. When the great and sudden freezing came, it imprisoned them by hundreds of tons all over the bay. There they are fixed, like a bee in a drop of amber.

"The fishermen are reaping a rich and novel harvest. The present abundance in the Carson market is due to this remarkable occurrence. The bay presents a wonderful appearance. Some associates have actually sunk a winch in the ice between the boat landing and Captain Dick's Island, and by dint of tunneling and stopping in the solid ice, they are mining out the imprisoned trout by the cartload.

"This class of phenomena occurs only at very rare intervals. In 1845, Black Cove, an arm of Casco Bay, Maine, was a scene of such a freezing as this. All sorts of salt-water fish, such as frequent the more shallow bays and estuaries—smelt, tomcod, eels, flounders—were frozen in and captured by the million. The tomcod, when thus frozen, may be thawed out in cool water and restored to life. For this reason, this small member of the finny tribe is known as the 'frost fish.'"

It was evident that a spellbinder from Down East had engineered that one.

Mark Twain, of course, was the champion of all this mountaineer humor, its recorder and promulgator par excellence—though he was adept at sifting some of the corn out of it. From his hut on Jackass Hill, "The Jumping Frog of Calaveras" hopped to world renown. It was there that he helped to institute the chimerical "Hospital for the Insane on Jackass Hill," for which he successively assumed roles as director, resident physician, attendant and inmate. There he drilled and tongue-lashed his "Jackass Squad of Invisible Swordsmen."

The humor and hoax spilled over the mountains to Virginia City and Gold Hill where Twain's celebrated holdup occurred late one night in the fall of 1866. Highway robbery was on his mind as he started walking back to Virginia City after a lecture at Gold Hill, accompanied by his agent Denis (Mike) McCarthy. Only two weeks before, stagecoaches had twice been held up on that road, and the stretch over which he tramped in the black darkness was a noted hang-out for hoodlums and highjackers.

As Mark Twain himself described it with a touch of exaggerated realism, "The divide was high, unoccupied ground between the towns; the scene of twenty midnight murders and a hundred robberies. As we climbed up and stepped out on the eminence, the Gold Hill lights dropped out of sight at our backs and the night closed down gloomy and dismal. A sharp wind swept the place, too, and chilled our perspiring bodies through."

" 'I tell you I don't like this place at night,' said Mike the agent.

" 'Well, don't speak so loud,' I said. 'You needn't remind anybody that we are here.'

"Just then a dim figure approached me from the direction of Virginia—a man, evidently. He came straight at me, and I stepped aside to let him pass; he stepped in the way and confronted me again. Then I saw that he had a mask on and was holding something in my face. I heard a *click-click* and recognized a revolver in dim outline. I pushed the barrel aside with my hand and said: 'Don't!'

"He ejaculated sharply: 'Your watch! Your money!'

" 'You can have them with pleasure—but take the pistol away from my face, please. It makes me shiver.'

" 'No remarks! Hand out your money!'

" 'Certainly—I—'

" 'Put up your hands! Don't you go for a weapon! Put 'em up! Higher!'

"I held them above my head.

"A pause. Then: 'Are you going to hand out your money or not?'

"I dropped my hands to my pockets and said: 'Certainly! I—'

" 'Put up your hands! Do you want your head blown off? Higher!'

"I put them above my head again.

"Another pause.

" '*Are* you going to hand out your money or *not?* Ah-ah—again? Put up your hands! By George, you want the head shot off you awful bad!'

" 'Well, friend, I'm doing my best to please you. You tell me to give up my money, and when I reach for it you tell me to put up my hands. If you would only— Oh, now—don't! All six of you at me! That other man will get away while— Now please take some of those revolvers out of my face! . . . If I had four hands—so that I could hold up two and—'

" 'Throttle him! Gag him! Kill him!'

" 'Gentlemen, *don't!* Nobody's watching the other fellow. Why don't some of you— *Ouch.* Take it away, please! Gentlemen, you see that I've got to hold up my hands; and so I can't take out my money—but if you'll be so kind as to take it out for me, I will do as much for you some—'

" 'Search him, Beauregard—and stop his jaw with a bullet, quick, if he wags it again.' "

The robbers made off with Twain's watch, keys, wallet and the fat carpetbag of currency his agent had just gathered up at the Gold Hill box office. Mark and Denis were commanded to keep their hands held high for ten minutes and remain where they were. Except for their shivering, they didn't budge for the allotted period of grace.

An hour later the two showed up at one of the more civilized saloons in Virginia City, "as unruffled as a mountain lake," according to one observer. Mark calmly announced to his friends that he had been robbed. He wanted to borrow some money. Demonstrating more excitement than either Mark or Denis, a sympathetic crony quickly counted out a hundred dollars and handed it to him.

The company adjourned animatedly to the office of the Virginia City *Enterprise*, where accounts of the robbery were immediately dispatched to other newspapers. Mark set to work composing an award advertisement for apprehension of the thieves. Someone suggested that now he would have to give another lecture at Virginia City to recoup his losses; the robbery would make a wonderful subject for it. It would be the biggest entertainment event ever to hit the place. People would pay five dollars apiece for seats. Entering into the spirit of the thing, and beginning to recover from the shock of the encounter, he laughingly agreed.

But the robbers had made one mistake. In their resolve to give Mark a taste of the medicine he spooned out so liberally to others, in their eagerness to provide him with the subject for another hilarious lecture, the hoaxers had let one too many of their friends in on the fake holdup. They had told Sandy Baldwin, and Sandy, thinking that the joke would be funnier for everyone if he confided to Mark what was going on behind his back, let the cat out of the bag. He explained that the grim characters who staged the robbery were Mark's best friends, identified them one by one, and informed him that even the hundred dollars he had been loaned was his own money.

Mark Twain canceled his lecture, rode out of town next day in a huff, threatened the robbers with prosecution to the full extent of the law, and in dead seriousness swore that if ever he saw the perpetrators of the holdup mounting the scaffold and it were within his power to save them, he wouldn't so much as turn his hand.

The very best of the practical jesters couldn't take it when the jests were turned the wrong way.

VI

THROW DOWN THAT
TREASURE BOX, SIR

For horse thieves, murderers and highway robbers, the mountain towns had a code of justice all their own. Returning from a hanging party, a vigilante stopped at the late home of a victim to break the news to the widow. "We just hanged Jim for horse-thieving," he announced cheerfully. "But come to find out, 'twant him who done it, so I guess the joke's on us."

Or there was the case of the oafish judge who listened in mounting confusion half an afternoon to the haranguing of two opposing attorneys, and finally interrupted: "Can't make head or tail out of it, men. Guess you'll have to settle it between yourselves."

The gold rush lured the prize desperadoes of six continents to California. Seldom in history had so many convened in one region. The creditable congress of North American crooks and shysters was augmented by past masters in crime from the Orient, Europe, the Mediterranean countries, Latin America and even a batch of "Sydney Ducks" from New South Wales. Assembled in San Francisco, the ruffians soon grew too competitive for the accomplishment of their own purposes, so they drifted off to the Sierra.

No legal agency could possibly keep track of the offenses among such strays. According to one estimate, 4,200 murders were committed in California during the five years between 1849 and 1854; in San Francisco alone the count ran to 1,200 —with only one conviction; and as an indication of what went on in the hill country, seventeen murders reputedly were committed in seventeen consecutive weekends at Mokelumne Hill.

Within a year and a half after the first gold strike, the situation was completely out of hand. Neither sheriffs nor courts could cope with the chaos. Moreover, officials duly elected to enforce law and order were commonly the nominees of hoodlums. Criminals had better protection than the innocent. Uncommitted justices weren't going to risk their necks and political futures by treating malefactors too severely. And juries ready to take similar risks were nowhere to be found. Murder was more likely to go unpunished than ordinary thievery—and that could be a capital offense.

It was at this point that lynch law and the vigilantes took over. Time-tried legislation on the books was abandoned. Around the yellow light of a kerosene lamp in a hill-town saloon, a new set of lawmakers sat down to find answers to the problem of lawlessness, as they saw it. They began from scratch, waving aside the Code of Hammurabi, Mosaic and

Common Law, the Constitution of the United States. All that mattered to them could be reduced to four or five sentences—sentences with some bite in them.

After heavy philosophizing and the downing of an inordinate number of whiskies, they would unanimously decide, for example, that anybody who shot, slugged or otherwise killed a man, woman or child on purpose should be hung; that anybody who deliberately struck or otherwise injured anybody else would have to face up to a jury and take the punishment voted by it; that whoever was guilty of robbing or thieving should be punished with stripes or banishment, whichever the jury figured was best; and anyone guilty of threatening or attacking with a gun would be treated the same.

With those four decisions made, they had something to go by. As a self-appointed Vigilance Committee, they might sometimes have to double as a jury and even supply the judge, if a regular one wasn't handy. Fine points, of course, would arise, but they could be handled as they came up; the machinery and the details weren't too important. And out of fairness to everyone, circumstances and public opinion should always be taken into account.

Strangely enough, the system worked. Under constitutional law, a murderer, caught red-handed, might be jailed—if there happened to be a jail—until an outraged public calmed down, until some sly lawyer was summoned to twist the facts or until the culprit was forcibly freed by confederates. Under lynch law, there was no waiting. A quorum of Vigilance Committee members could be rounded up on short notice, and if the circumstances warranted it, the case disposed of on the spot. A rope thrown over a high limb on the nearest oak ordinarily settled the matter.

Disturbed by the reaction of Easterners to this California justice, editor Enos Christman of the Sonora *Herald*, who had seen both systems in operation, went to bat for the vigilantes in a strong letter written for the edification of the home folks in Pennsylvania. "I see by late intelligence from home," he chided, "that the Atlantic papers have taken grounds against

the Vigilance Committees in California and denounce them as
'mobs' and 'lynchers.' They do not understand the causes
which have driven the people to take upon themselves the
speedy and prompt trial and punishment of criminals. In the
old states where society is properly organized and law and order prevail, such a course might properly be denounced as
'mob-law' and 'lynch-law.' But criminals and adventurers from
every part of the globe have flocked to California in great numbers for the past three years. If a criminal was brought up before Court, charged with some heinous offense, a confederate
was always ready to step up and prove an alibi, and of course
the prisoner had to be released.

"The murderer, the assassin and the incendiary lurked
around in open day. The people were compelled for their own
protection to take upon themselves the responsibilities they
did. And what has been the result? Law and order and justice
again prevail, security is given to life and property, and a number of vile marauders have met the fate they so richly merited.
Not a single one of all the wretches executed by the Vigilance
Committee, but confessed enough of crime to deserve the hal-
ter.

"In this city these wretches were all tried before a jury of
Sonora citizens and that jury's verdict fixed their punishment.
The vexations, delays and technicalities of the law through
which so many criminals escape punishment were laid aside,
and justice quickly and promptly vindicated."

Even a British visitor, who otherwise was inclined to look
askance at barbaric American ways, agreed implicitly with the
Sonora editor. "When lynch law prevails here," he argued, "it
strikes terror to the heart of the evildoer. He has no hazy and
undefined view of his ultimate fate in the distant future, but a
vivid picture is before him of the sure and speedy consequence
of crime. The formalities and delays of the law, instituted for
the protection of the people, are for the same reason abolished.
Californians are eminently practical and earnest; what they
mean to do, they do right off with all their might, and as they
really mean to do it; and lynch law is administered with char-

acteristic promptness and decision. Sufficient time, however, or at least what is considered sufficient time, is always granted the criminal to prepare for death. Very frequently he is not hanged till the day after his trial."

There was good reason for prompt action. In twenty-four hours the witnesses, bereaved companions, incensed townsmen, even the vigilantes might be on their way somewhere else, responding to the latest buzz on a gold discovery a hundred miles away. The outrage of one day could be forgotten the next, as the population shifted its interests. Miners seemed to spend half their time on the move, and outlaws had merely to drop out of sight in the anonymity of a migrating crowd to get beyond the reach of retribution.

Lynch law was devised to hamper such escape. It had more to do with masses of people in transit than with a settled population. Essentially it was legislation for highways—such as they were. The vigilante reign undoubtedly played a large part in suppressing violence at the diggings and on the trails between them. Utter anarchy might have come to California, had it not been for the lynch lawyers. But it was a pretty haphazard effort. For every desperado that was strung up or rusticated, there were nine others who managed to escape.

"Our roads are swarming with highwaymen, and scarcely a day passes but we hear or read of some instance of robbery," complained an editor of the Placerville *Press* on August 16th, 1856. He was not exaggerating, for he could cite chapter and verse for a dozen cases of outrageous armed robbery that had occurred within the week.

On Saturday last a softhearted teamster had taken pity on a hitchhiker limping along the road outside of Placerville; he helped him onto his wagon and bedded him down in the rear, only to have the patient suddenly shake off his infirmity, come to life with a gun and relieve the driver of every cent he possessed—$32. Then still at gun point, the teamster was forced to unharness one of his horses and let the scamp gallop off on it.

Sunday afternoon at Whisky Creek a scared-looking young

fellow named John Barry rushed into the home of a vigilante with a breathless tale of being robbed a half mile down the road. The vigilante ran for his horse and took off after the villain. But the moment he was out of sight, John turned robber himself, pulled a gun on the vigilante's wife and walked off with $43.

On Monday morning at Clear Creek a masked bandit had robbed a peddler of $170. Monday afternoon at Tehama a trio of highjackers had collected $280 from one of Major Bidwell's drivers. And later the same day at Rabbit Creek, a shoddy character had stepped out from behind a tree to demand Hal Gibson's purse; Hal reached for it in such haste that the challenger figured he was going for a gun and pulled the trigger. Luckily it didn't go off.

On Wednesday, after a victim had been relieved of $20 near the Calaveras Bridge, he took flight on his horse before his highjacker gave the word, and was rewarded with two pistol shots, one of which lifted his hat off his head.

Thursday, near Oroville, a freight driver had forfeited $14 to two highwaymen, and would have lost a lot more, but from experience he had learned to distribute ready cash in packets hidden among the freight.

Late Friday afternoon between Drytown and Volcano, "Dutch John" was driving peacefully along with a big cargo of lager beer, when he was halted by a group of cheerful liars who said they were taking up a collection for charity. They didn't make it clear just whom the charity was for, so "Dutch" declined to come across. Thereupon the collectors lost patience and demanded his money. "Dutch" counted out $30.25, explaining quite honestly that it was every cent he had. Graciously the two bits were returned to him with the suggestion that he'd need it for a drink.

And around ten o'clock Friday night Fred Schroeder, en route from Mound Springs to Mud Springs, encountered a thug who politely requested him to shell out. Fred sized him up and responded by knocking him over the head and beating it. Almost immediately, however, he was overtaken by a half dozen of the thug's teammates, and surrounded. In the scuffle that followed, Schroeder's shirt was ripped off and his pockets emptied. He was released a little the worse for wear. But the joke was on the thugs, for foxy Schroeder had $220 hidden in a scarf tightly wound around his middle. They missed that. As soon as Fred reached Mud Springs to report his assault, the usual party of vigilantes dashed off in pursuit of the robbers, and toward morning, as happened all too frequently, they returned empty-handed.

These pickings were all pretty small—the work of amateurs, a public nuisance. But there were plenty of artists in the game. For their elementary lessons the amateur knights of the road were indebted to a semifictitious character, Joaquin Murrieta. He was the exemplar. The only difference between their operations and his was a matter of refinement. For real competence in the art of highway robbery it was necessary to have a calling, a conviction, a chunk-sized chip on the shoulder. One needed to believe steadfastly that he was merely recovering his rightful heritage, serving humanity by evening a score or redistributing the common wealth. Joaquin had such a credo; most of his imitators dabbled in the art for kicks and small change.

Murrieta may have been real; he may have been a myth; possibly he was the composite of half a dozen Joaquins. But his story was too good not to be true. Only sticklers for verified fact ever doubted the tales that embroidered his biography.

Murrieta could undoubtedly claim a lot of justification for carrying a chip on his shoulder. Before the Americans came he was doing all right for himself in the Calaveras-Tuolumne country; a smart, mild-mannered, hard-working *ranchero,* studying on the side to be a priest. Like any other sharp Mexican, he took off for the diggings as soon as gold was discovered, staked out some substantial claims and was working them peaceably when the new law taxing foreign prospectors twenty dollars a month went into effect. This had been Mexican land for a long time and he wasn't going to accept any such imposition. He refused to pay the tax and was driven off his property by belligerent gringos.

Even that setback he took in stride, moved on to Murphy's where he got a good job at a sporting house as a three-card monte dealer, married a sparkling little Mexican girl named Rosita and settled down in a cabin outside of town. While on duty at the sporting house one night, a gang of drunken Americans broke into his cabin, assaulted Rosita and left her dying.

With his younger brother, he set out for more congenial surroundings, only to be overtaken by a posse of whites rounding up horse thieves. As Mexicans, they were guilty until they could prove themselves innocent. Joaquin's brother lost his temper. He roasted his accusers and declared his innocence in such unequivocal fulmination that he was hung on the spot. Out of consideration for Joaquin's more moderate attitude, he was merely tied to a tree and ruthlessly flogged forty stripes.

This was the last straw for the youngster who had wanted to become a priest. In the hands of the Americans he had been robbed of his rightful land; he had lost his wife and his brother. He swore revenge; he would get every last one of his attackers and any gringos that stood in the way.

Joaquin went about it systematically. The country was crowded with Mexicans who had suffered almost as much humiliation as had the Murrietas. Within a month he had recruited the bloodiest gang of cutthroats to be found north of the border, and they went to work. Volunteer spies and informers were planted in every region he planned to harry. There was always a refuge, a disguise and an alibi waiting for him or his men. Numbered among his ardent followers were experienced desperadoes like Tiburcio Vasquez of Monterey and Three-fingered Jack, who went after Chinese as impartially as Americans, and established a reputation for stringing up Orientals by their queues or wrenching heads back with a deft twist of the queue, to slit the throat.

Joaquin's campaign started in 1851, and during the next two years he took revenge aplenty. One by one every last Yankee who had done him dirt was put out of the way, along with a great many suspects and their associates. Nobody had any clear idea of how high Murrieta's score ran. Beside the killings, miners were robbed, saloons shot up, stores looted, travelers waylaid. Joaquin Murrieta was the terror of the Sierra, popularly known as "Robin Hood of El Dorado." The State of California, so ran the tale, posted an award of $2,000 for his capture; it was raised to $5,000. Somebody else offered the weight of Joaquin's decapitated head in gold.

Intermittently a posse of three hundred men combed Calaveras County for him. During the heat of the hunt any hombre could pass for the notorious bandit and innumerable Joaquins were shot down in cold blood or hung. But the real Robin Hood always lived to strike again. He was here, there and everywhere.

Between card deals in Zumwalt's Saloon at Mokelumne Hill one night, the conversation shifted inevitably to Murrieta and his exploits. Flushed with whisky and simulated courage, a cardshark abruptly interrupted the badinage by plunking a sack of gold on the table. "Here's five hundred dollars that I'll get Murrieta," he shrilled in a brave boast, "if I'm ever lucky enough to come face to face with the bastard."

The game stopped, and there was a shuffling of chairs. Onto the table leaped the braggart's card partner, holding out a scarred hand. "I call you on it," he shouted. "Here's your chance. Meet Joaquin Murrieta—face to face. I'm your man."

In a stunning silence Robin Hood leisurely stepped down from the table, bid his adieu and strolled out of the saloon. No one made a move as he rode away.

Into the center of busy Stockton rode a nonchalant Mexican. He dismounted, elbowed his way to the stage station where his eye was caught by a bold broadside advertising $5,000 for the capture of Joaquin Murrieta. He paused to read it. A smile turned into a careless laugh. As others looked on, he scrawled across the bottom in black crayon: "I raise it to $10,000—Joaquin." Then, unmolested, he galloped off through the crowd.

In the safety of city parlors, gossiping women freely admitted their infatuation with the daring adventurer. Kids loved him and fought battles among themselves in his name. He became a popular hero. But in the course of his rampages he had made enemies, too—Mexican as well as American. Clues on his whereabouts came into headquarters more frequently. He was obliged to flee from the Sierra and seek refuge in the arroyos of the Coast Range.

There—appropriately enough—in Priest Valley, the would-be priest and his gang were tracked down and surprised by a posse of twenty State Rangers in July, 1853. Three-fingered Jack was one of the first to fall, shot squarely between the eyes. Joaquin almost made good his attempt to escape, but in the pursuit his horse was shot from under him. One pistol shot brought him to his knees; a second felled him.

Whether or not this was the real Joaquin, the victim was beheaded, and in a demonstration of the crude sadism that belonged to the era, the head was pickled in a glass jar, along with the right hand of Three-fingered Jack, and shipped up and down California for years, so that the curious and the unconvinced could see for themselves—at a dollar a look—that Robin Hood of El Dorado was no figment. He had lived, and was no more.

One doubting old *señora* paid an extra dollar to have the head lifted from the jar. She claimed to have known Joaquin when he was a young boy in Sonora, Mexico, before he came to California. He had a great scar under the chin then. Until she saw the scar she wouldn't believe the wizened face was his. The scar was there. She was convinced.

The high standard of brigandage set by Murrieta was hard to beat. His lieutenant, Tiburcio Vasquez, who survived the Priest Valley purge, carried on from where the master left off, but he never succeeded in making the name for himself that Joaquin had. Scores of other trainees robbed, pillaged and raised hell in general, yet they didn't have the artistry, the all-consuming passion, the solid chip on the shoulder. With them it was mostly a question of evening some petty score or picking up extra cash—nothing wholehearted like revenge against mankind.

The Mexicans left it to the Americans to think up a new wrinkle in crime. In all the Murrieta sorties, not once was a coach robbed. To be sure, not too many of them were plying through his territory at the time, but he knew as well as the drivers that what few stages there were carried express boxes containing thousands of dollars in gold. Joaquin played square. He couldn't stoop to the level of coach robbing. The stage was inviolable. He let the Yankees undertake the first holdup.

The news came with stunning impact on August 13th, 1856: BOLD ATTEMPT AT HIGHWAY ROBBERY—BRAVE RESISTANCE—WOMAN KILLED—SEVERAL MEN WOUNDED. And the details were appalling: "Yesterday afternoon at four o'clock as the Camptonville stage was coming to Marysville, and when it was near Dry Creek, it was stopped by six mounted highwaymen, who were after the treasure amounting to $100,000.

"They commanded the driver of the stage, John Gear, to stop and threatened to kill the first man who should oppose them in their designs. Mr. Dobson, Langton's Express messenger, immediately drew on them and commenced firing. His first fire took effect on the spokesman of the crowd and unhorsed him. Indiscriminate firing commenced between the robbers and the passengers. As many as forty shots were fired on both sides. The robbers, finding themselves stoutly opposed, retreated, leaving the passengers masters of the field and treasure."

The driver had been shot through the arm above the elbow. The wife of a Marysville barber was killed by a stray bullet that ricocheted into her right eye. Another passenger was badly wounded in both legs, and a third narrowly escaped death when hot lead shaved off an eyebrow.

The coach carried a full load—seventeen passengers. As the shooting exchange started, four men leaped from their seats and dashed for cover. The driver didn't wait for them; at the first break in the firing, he whipped his horses into a gallop, only to be attacked again by a mounted Mexican and two Yankees sheltered in a thicket. Dobson shot the horse out from under the Mexican, and Gear, in spite of his injured arm, drove on. The stage arrived at Marysville a half-hour later splashed with blood and riddled with bullet holes.

"This is the boldest robbery ever chronicled," ventured a San Francisco newspaper. "But for the bravery of the driver, the express agent and passengers, it would have resulted in the loss of the treasure and more lives."

From descriptions given by the survivors, it didn't take the press and the police more than two hours to pin the outrage on one Tom Bell. He was an escapee from the San Francisco jail, a gangster heading a syndicate of thirty or forty hooligans who had been terrorizing the mining country in groups of twos, threes and sixes all summer. They were responsible for innumerable robberies, bludgeonings and daring shakedowns.

By the press, Bell was pictured as a strapping giant who carried six loaded revolvers and a dozen bowie knives, and wore a breastplate of thin boiler iron; he was a cattle rustler, killer and fiend who shot on sight and showed no mercy.

As posses scoured the countryside, Tom Bells began to appear on every sweep of landscape. Less than forty-eight hours after the battle of Dry Creek, three masked villains stormed into the store at Grizzly just before midnight, demanding food and threatening proprietor Argrave and three members of the household with immediate death if they resisted. The leader of the trio brazenly introduced himself as "Tom Bell, the Highwayman." Even though there was no resistance, Argrave was clobbered over the head with a pistol and left unconscious while the bandits scooped up seventy dollars in cash and their pick of supplies from the counter.

"This Tom Bell seems likely to become as notorious as the ubiquitous Joaquin," chorused the newspapers. "He is probably about as much a myth as many a petty scoundrel, as well as a desperate villain—assuming his name from mere bravado— as was done in the case of his Mexican prototype, until the very name of the bold robber became a terror wherever he was heard. We would not be surprised if this Tom Bell should turn out to be a sort of general appellation used by the cutpurse gentry in common."

That wasn't a bad guess. A few days later three horsemen crossed the toll bridge near the mouth of the South Yuba. Toll Collector Woods stepped out of his shanty and held out his hand for the fee. "As a general habit we pay only in lead," snarled one of the men waving a pistol. "Ever heard of Tom Bell? Nobody in Bell's company gets charged for crossing bridges."

The three rode on, but before they were out of sight, Woods took a pot shot at them. Then he saddled his horse and pursued them courageously all the way to French Corral, where he managed to recruit a few vigilantes. All day and into the night the toll dodgers were pressed closely—as far as Cherokee. But all they got for their pains was an abandoned horse which proved next day to have been stolen from a man in Grass Valley.

Yet among the stories about Tom Bell, there was one very inconsistent characteristic that didn't tie in with his reputed ferocity. On recounting earlier affrays, people kept referring to a kindly, genial soul with a broken nose and a rounded sandy mustache—the unmistakable marks of Tom Bell—who appeared to be shocked at the sight of injured victims or a bludgeoned head, and took the time and trouble to bind up wounds with an almost professional interest. The persistence of the report baffled sheriffs and newspaper readers alike.

Four days passed and Tom Bell was in Sacramento. Under the heading, MOST WANTED, a local daily noted breezily: "We understand that the notorious highwayman, Tom Bell, was in town yesterday. He was seen and recognized by several persons who knew him before he took to the road à la Turbin, near the corner of Seventh and J Streets about 10 A.M. playing with a dog. He is a large man with a broken nose; had on dark pants and a white shirt; without either coat or vest. The police got wind of the distinguished arrival and sought anxiously for the visitor, in order to extend the hospitalities of the city to him, but Tom was not to be caught napping."

Indeed Tom was not napping. He was on the run. The biggest manhunt in California history was under way. Sheriffs, deputies, constables and vigilantes from all the counties touching the Western Sierra were out for him. They were joined by a special delegation of Marysville police, headed by Captain William King; and two of the most relentless detectives in the West were assigned to the case by Sacramento, with explicit instructions to capture or destroy Bell's gang.

The northern mining country which Bell had favored for all his depredations of the summer was getting too hot. A friend had a secluded ranch near Knight's Ferry on the Stanislaus River; that would be the perfect hide-out until the excitement died down; nobody would recognize him that far south. On long night hitches he headed for Knight's Ferry, but en route he took time out to send an insolent letter to Captain King: "Don't think for a moment that your vigilance causes me any uneasiness, or that I seek for an armistice. No, far from it, for I have unfurled my banner to the breeze and my motto is 'Catch me if you can!'"

Tom moved into the secluded ranch and lay low, but he had reason to be more uneasy than he admitted. Communications with his partners in crime had broken down and he was out of touch with the world. He didn't know that one group after another had been picked up while he was sneaking away to his hide-out, and he didn't know that they had talked.

On October 4th, not quite two months after the big holdup, Judge Belt of Knight's Ferry led a quiet posse into the yard of the ranch and caught the fugitive off guard.

"I believe you are the man we are looking for?" queried the Judge.

"Very probably," replied Bell.

"Tie him up," ordered the Judge.

Late that afternoon, before anyone could raise bothersome points of law about proper legal charges, defense or trial by jury, Tom Bell was put beyond the reach of such amenities.

In a quiet little ceremony he was strung up on the limb of a convenient sycamore.

Gradually the truth was pieced together that Tom Bell was none other than Dr. Thomas J. Hodges, a young physician from Rome, Tennessee, who had distinguished himself in the War with Mexico as a medical attaché in the regiment of Tennessee Volunteers—as timid and inoffensive a character as ever crossed the line into the State of California.

In all likelihood he had never knowingly injured a man; the shooting had all been done by his disciples. Caught in the coils of pennilessness and frustration, he had adopted the name of a genuine Tom Bell, killer and cattle rustler of Northern California, and to confuse the public had instructed all the different groups of his gang to identify themselves as Tom Bells or Tom Bell's men. He didn't want to be a bandit. He loathed guns and gunning.

For him one venture into crime just seemed to lead to another. The outlaws had looked to him as their field marshall, and he had played along until he had become so enmeshed he couldn't extricate himself. He'd hated every hour of it. But he had had to make a living somehow. Doctoring hadn't paid; prospecting a claim near Rough and Ready hadn't paid; and just before the noose was tightened around his neck he confided that robbery hadn't paid very well either.

Though Dr. Hodges' get-rich-quick scheme proved unprofitable to him, he nevertheless had established a precedent, knocked the stuffings out of an old notion that robbing stagecoaches just shouldn't be done. Waylaying of stages shortly became the latest fad among the knights of the road and "Throw down that treasure box!" their war cry.

Generally they were choosy about the coaches that were stopped. The preference was for vehicles well-loaded with passengers, for as long as people were aboard, the driver and express agent hesitated to open fire. Resistance always set off a shooting match in which innocent men and women stopped the bullets, and the publicity about injuries was bad for the stage business.

In proportion to the number of coaches traveling the highways by the late 1850's, the number of holdups was hardly worth mentioning, but a half dozen robberies could easily be multiplied in the public mind to apply to most of the vehicles on the Sierra run.

Then the undemonstrative newspaper accounts, written in the slightly bored style of a third-rate reporter who had been relegated to covering holdups, made them sound routine. The story of May 4th, 1858, date-lined Nevada City, was typical: "The stage on its way to this city from Sacramento was stopped one mile from here this morning by six robbers armed with guns and pistols. One of them seized the lead horses, while the others presented their arms and demanded the treasure box. The Alta express box was handed them, but they refused it saying, 'You can't fool us; give us the Wells, Fargo box.' This box, containing $21,000 was turned over to the highwaymen, and the stage was allowed to pass on. No resistance was offered. Wells, Fargo and Company has offered a reward of $3,000 for the apprehension of the robbers."

The hasty extermination of the Murrieta and Tom Bell gangs didn't stop stage robbing, but it did bring on a reshuffling in gangster organization. Highwaymen seemed to be convinced that cumbersome clubs were a disadvantage in the long run. The swag had to be split too many ways; gang feuds couldn't be avoided; a single squealer could jeopardize the whole outfit. Much more satisfactory to work in small fly-by-night groups, they reasoned. The fewer the better.

That was the way "Dutch Kate" of Marysville figured it—the first woman to horn into the masculine ranks of highway knighthood. Kate could drink, swear, smoke, gamble and hold her own among the most accomplished ruffians of the mining country. And she had a hankering to try her hand at the latest fad of playing the coaches.

Her immediate incentive was the loss of $2,000 at monte. She needed that money back. In men's clothing and with two men to lend moral support, she nervously flagged down the Camptonville coach just four months after the Nevada City incident. To her utter astonishment she discovered there was nothing to be nervous about. The passengers and driver were more scared than she was. At her command the express box was dropped, and ten passengers seemed all too ready to contribute their valuables. Manfully she waved aside the private hand-outs; all she wanted was the box, thank you. It was dropped at her feet. The coachman was ordered to get up and get. He drove on, and that was all there was to it.

With the assistance of her male associates, Kate wrenched open the box. It was empty. And to add to her chagrin, she read in the newspapers next day that one of the passengers carried a plump purse of $15,000. The experience was such a shattering blow to her pride that "Dutch Kate" stuck to her bottle, cigars and cards after that and let the men do the stage robbing.

The empty box was a common ruse. A spare was often carried to fool the amateurs. One coachman went further and filled it with gilded lead. All sorts of devices for foiling highwaymen were tried. Locked iron safes were substituted for wooden containers, and some of them were bolted to the floor under the seats for the passengers to guard. Rattlesnakes were even mixed in with the gold.

The outbreak of the Civil War introduced a brand-new novelty to stagecoach rifling. It happened on the old Placerville route, one July day when traffic was so heavy that a second coach had to be ordered out at Carson City to cover the run. Fenton Blair took the driver's seat in No. 1; Charley Watson drove No. 2. One closely followed the other over the mountains, and aboard No. 2 coach was a widely traveled woman tourist who could boast of encounters with brigands in the Campagna of Italy, in the Abruzzi and the Pyrenees. With this perspective, she was well equipped to appreciate the trials of travel in the Sierra and to narrate an account at least as lucid as that of the average California journalist.

"We were about twenty-eight travelers in all," she recounted. "We were bound over the Placerville route, and nothing occurred beyond the usual incidents of travel until we reached a point about fourteen miles from Placerville. About ten P.M.

just as we turned the bend in the road, we found that Blair's stage was standing in our front, and someone called out, 'Hold on,' or he would fire.

"Thinking that some accident had occurred to the forward coach, Watson reined up. As the stage stopped I, being an inside passenger, looked out the window and heard someone say: 'We won't detain you but a moment; all we want is Wells, Fargo and Company's treasure'; at the same time assuring the passengers that no harm was intended them if they would remain quiet.

"Here was a dramatic situation—robbers in our front, and for all we knew, on all our surroundings. Prudence dictated silence—and I can assure you it was with some difficulty that prudence prevailed. The robbers took possession of the treasure in the forward boot—three sacks of bullion in all; and then ordered the driver to proceed. The gang surrounding the stage was seven in number, armed with revolvers—I think two pistols each; and I assure you, pistols never before appeared so formidable to me as well as to the others, for in the dark the bores seemed at least as large as six-pounders. One of the crowd had a rifle or gun.

"They came up to our stage, some of them remarking that they ought to shoot us all, but our driver coolly remarked that no shot had been fired at them and consequently no harm ought to reach his passengers. Watson had requested the passengers not to fire, as we were on the grade and if the animals were startled we would go over the side and all be dashed to pieces.

"The gang surrounded us, presenting its weapons, and I noticed that one man had a tin cup and bowie knife slung to him, in addition to a revolver in each hand, leveled at the driver. At this time one of the robbers advanced, claiming to be the captain, who informed us as follows: 'Gentlemen, I will tell you who we are. We are not robbers, but a company of Confederate Soldiers. Don't act foolish. We don't want anything of the passengers. All we want is Wells, Fargo treasure to assist us to recruit for the Confederate Army.'"

As if he were any too willing to promote the Confederate Cause, Watson threw down two sacks of gold. But his political leanings became clearer when the mistrusting men of Jeff Davis's uncovered another sack of bullion and two extra treasure boxes. Altogether it made a tremendous haul.

While all this was going on, a sly little flirt in the back had caught the ear of a gun-toting guard, and on her own was doing some frivolous teasing and effective sleuthing. She was curious to find out whether this really was a Confederate invasion. Brushing pistols away from her face, she allowed that she had a five-cent postage stamp in her pocketbook. Would that help the Southern Cause? How could they possibly carry away all those sacks and boxes? Did they really need all that money? Would they mind showing their flag? When it was proposed that a collection might be taken from the passengers to assist the Confederacy, she lightly countered that they had nothing but greenbacks. Would they have any use for Union money?

The guard took up the spirit of the banter. He wasn't going to be outwitted by a young girl, and improvised a quick comeback for all her quips. He talked too much. The passengers were convinced that they were dealing with no Southern gentlemen.

Watson was politely given an official receipt for the lucre, signed by "Henry H. Ingraham, Captain Commanding, Confederate States of America," and told that he could drive on.

Shortly after midnight the coaches thundered into Placerville with the latest news, and long before dawn posses were fanning out over the countryside. The testimony of one coolheaded young girl had persuaded the authorities that the seven Confederates were seven Yankee impostors. Wells, Fargo promptly offered an award of $1,000 for recovery of the treasure and $300 apiece for each robber—a stingy amount, thought some, considering the total at stake. But early next morning the first two culprits were arrested, and the execution of the leader followed soon after.

Such quick settlement of Wells, Fargo accounts didn't happen often. In fact, various editions of one of the company's posters fluttered on bulletin boards for seven years before they were taken down. BLACK BART—WANTED DEAD OR ALIVE, read a late version. "The criminal is always armed with a double-barreled shotgun, which he unbreaches and rolls in his blankets as soon as he is safe from immediate pursuit; always brings an old ax to the scene of the robbery, which he uses to open the box, and leaves in the vicinity of the robbery. In opening the mail sacks, he cuts them with a sharp knife, making a 'T' on top of the sack near the lock. He has never manifested any viciousness and there is reason to believe that he is adverse to taking human life. He is polite to all passengers, and especially so to ladies. He comes and goes from the scene of the robbery on foot, seems to be a thorough mountaineer and a good walker, as he sometimes covers long distances in a day—getting food from houses in out-of-the-way places—but has never been known to remain overnight in a house that is occupied; never allows himself to be seen in the vicinity of the robbery, and never shows up for food until twelve or fifteen miles away. His only baggage when traveling is a roll of blankets generally tied with bale rope at the ends, although at one time he had a long valise. Four times he has attacked two lines of stages terminating at the same point, with but a day or two interval."

The statistics and data on the flier had to be modified all too frequently. Before the efficient detectives of Wells, Fargo nabbed Black Bart, he had built himself up as the most portentous desperado in the annals of California gangland, and had twenty-seven stage holdups to his credit. Yet he turned out to be a more docile little fellow than Tom Bell. Stripped of his aliases, his shotgun, the flour sack and long linen duster he wore while on duty, Black Bart was Charles Boles, Civil War veteran, schoolteacher; a religious man who never went anywhere without carrying along a Bible lovingly inscribed on the flyleaf by his wife.

Back at his home town in Illinois, he was highly regarded as an intelligent, well-educated citizen. In San Francisco, where he resided intermittently at 37 Second Street, he was

known as a prosperous businessman with large mining interests—a dapper, immaculate gentleman of expensive tastes who
always carried a swaggish cane, wore a handsome derby and
beautifully tailored pepper-and-salt suits, sported a gorgeous
diamond on his little finger and a conspicuous gold watch
chain across his waistcoat. He dined regularly at one of the
better restaurants of the city—the New York Bakery—frequently in the company of prominent public servants like Captain Lee, head of the police detective force.

His friends were charmed by his cultured conversation and
his courteous, almost gallant manners. The long, slender hands,
the piercing eyes—startlingly blue—a high forehead, gray
hair and carefully groomed mustache, the delicate cheek
bones, all marked him as a man of genuine distinction and
singularly artistic leanings. One minor disfigurement, however, spoiled the total effect of his appearance: there were
just enough arrogance and superiority about him to keep his
closest friends from inquiring why in hell he didn't get those
three missing front teeth fixed.

Like thousands of others, Mr. Boles came to the Sierra foothills for gold. He worked claim after claim in five different
counties and every one of them was a failure. Hard pressed
for cash, he took a temporary job as clerk in a stage-express office. The work was a bore, but it was there that he got his first
inspiration on a quick remedy for his embarrassing state of
destitution. He was packing millions in gold into those express
boxes, and he could see for himself how totally inadequate
were the provisions for protecting them. Waylaying a coach
should be the simplest thing in the world.

But he was wise enough to refrain from taking immediate
advantage of his inspiration. He switched from one clerking
job to another, making a careful study of shipments, schedules
and drivers. He postponed a change in occupation for months
until he became thoroughly familiar with the business. And
during those long weeks of boredom he managed to develop a
stock of resentment against wealthy capitalist firms like Wells,

Fargo, until he could carry a chip on his shoulder as large as Joaquin Murrieta's.

At last he was ready to strike, on August 3rd, 1877. To avoid association with his regular beat as clerk, he journeyed as far afield as he could from the Sierra—clear over to the coast. The Point Arena-Duncan's Mills stage that swung along the Russian River was his first objective.

At a turn in the highway, he stepped out from behind a tree into the middle of the road, signaled to the driver to stop, grabbed the lead horse, and in a hollow voice, as casual as a man asking for a match, addressed the coachman: "Would you please throw down your treasure box, sir?"

The box landed in the gutter with a metallic ring.

"Thank you, sir. Drive on."

The thing went off more easily than Boles had dared imagine. He ripped open the box and was disappointed to find only $605.52. But it was worth a laugh. He pocketed the money, and on the back of a waybill borrowed from an express office, he scrawled a message, slipped it into the box and left the container exactly where the driver had dropped it.

When investigators arrived on the scene the next day, they were more baffled than amused by the message:

> I've labored long and hard for bread,
> For honor and for riches,
> But on my corns too long you've tread,
> You fine-haired sons-of-bitches.
> —Black Bart

The first posters with the award inducement went out from Wells, Fargo, but there was nothing to go on—no description except the hollow voice, a self-confident manner, the shotgun, a figure of medium height disguised under a flour sack and linen duster—and, of course, the unprintable stanza. Nothing like this had ever been known to students of California crime.

The next holdup was the Quincy-Oroville stage, a hundred and twenty-five miles from the Russian River. Unquestionably it was the same gangster. The hollow, polite voice was unmistakable: "Don't be alarmed, ladies. You will not be hurt or robbed. I want only the treasure box and the mailbag." The tone was almost apologetic.

That time Boles did better. He took in $5,000, plus miscellaneous small sums from the contents of the mailbag. But Uncle Sam was now involved. The Federal Government added $500 to the paltry $300 offered by Wells, Fargo. But still they had nothing to go on, except the usual costume, an awful-looking shotgun with an outsized bore, and another jingle signed B.B. and what was supposedly a touch of hieroglyphic humor, Po8, for "poet":

> Now I lay me down to sleep
>   To wait the coming morrow,
> Perhaps success, perhaps defeat
>   And everlasting sorrow.

> Yet come what will—I'll try it on;
>   My condition can't be worse;
> And if there's money in that box,
>   'Tis money in my purse.

Other brigands who dared try their luck more than once had been caught in days, weeks or at most, months. But Black Bart carried on for seven years. All the northern gold-mine regions were his bailiwick. It was the Sonora-Milton stage one time, La Porte-Oroville the next; then on to the Covello-Ukiah route or the Weaverville-Shasta—always skipping from one locality to another.

Little by little a better description was pieced together. His roll of blankets had been spotted, the pattern of his robberies defined, the fact that he always traveled on foot pointed out. A woman up Eel River way described a "gentleman tourist" for whom she had prepared a meal. He had piercing, brilliantly blue eyes, slender, genteel hands; looked like a preacher; engaged in intellectual conversation; and, oh, yes, had three front teeth missing—two uppers and a lower. This portrait was discounted; there were lots of "gentleman tourists" and roving preachers now. Even Detective Lee in San Francisco wouldn't have thought of connecting the description with the fine old gentleman who sat opposite him at the New York Bakery.

The twenty-seventh robbery came on November 3rd, 1883, three miles east of Copperopolis, just after stage driver Reason E. McConnell had let off a young hitchhiker to whom he had given a lift to go rabbit hunting. There were no passengers, but $4,700 was in the treasure till, and that box was bolted firmly to the floor of the passenger compartment.

The holdup was carried off as easily as twenty-six others, except for a slight delay in prying the box off the floor and breaking it open. In that delay the rabbit hunter, assuming that the stagecoach had broken down, appeared on the scene with his rifle, unobserved by the bandit. McConnell commandeered the rifle, and as Black Bart was escaping into a thicket, he opened fire.

Bart got away, but his left hand was hit. This time no poetry was left in the abandoned box. Instead there were bloodstained papers. Next morning Wells, Fargo's competent sleuth, James B. Hume, picked up not only the abandoned box, but also a stained cuff, a handkerchief and an old hat. On the handkerchief was a laundry mark FX07—the first tangible clue he had managed to lay his hands on in seven years of the chase. It was just a guess that the mark belonged to a San Francisco laundry.

Including all the Chinese establishments, there were ninety-one places that took in washing in the Bay City. Methodically Hume started going the rounds of them all. He found the information he wanted on Bush Street, between Kearny and Montgomery.

"Oh, my gracious," exclaimed a dumbfounded landlady at 37 Second Street, where Hume took her into his confidence. "That man a stage robber! Lan' sakes! Who would have thought it? Why, he told me he was a mining man, and he has been living here for something like five years."

Ten days after the crime Charles Boles was in the clutches of the law and newspapers were peddling the news as if it were the end of a war: "Black Bart, the famous lone highwayman, the hero of twenty-seven stage robberies, a person whose poetical effusions have been copied by the press all over the country and who has led innumerable sheriffs and county constables a wild chase for seven years, was captured in this city at seven o'clock last Monday evening.

"In the incarceration of this audacious highwayman, the express company and the Postal Department of the United States have rid themselves of one who has been a terror to stage drivers and passengers, and a most expensive hamper to the safe delivery of valuables and treasures consigned to Wells, Fargo and Company. The suddenness with which he appeared, like an evil spirit, upon the lonely desolate road, and his calm demeanor—tempered and suggested, so to speak, by his trusty gun—commanded the respect and obedience of all who beheld him."

Charles Boles, alias Black Bart, alias Po8, was now San Quentin prisoner No. 11046.

In rummaging through his belongings, police were puzzled by the absence of artillery to go with the ugly shotgun wrapped unbreached in a roll of blankets—the gun that had horrified hundreds of passengers and twenty-seven stage drivers.

"Oh," laughed Boles in answer to their queries, "I never did have any ammunition for it. Wouldn't know how to fire it. It never was loaded."

Black Bart was the last notable hero in a long generation of highway knights. His employment was out of date. The genuine artists, by the 1880's, had long since given up highways for railways.

VII

THE B'AR ALWAYS STANDS
HIS GROUND

The interlopers could just as readily have picked an antelope
or a lynx, a bighorn or a beaver, an elk or a rattlesnake to sym-
bolize the new Republic. If the Indians had been given a say,
their demigod, the coyote, would have been chosen. A seaman
would have held out for the California elephant seal. If John
Muir had been present, he certainly would have insisted on

139

that "bolt of life," the Douglas squirrel, "fiery, pungent, full of brag and show and fight, the most influential of the Sierra animals, the squirrel of squirrels."

Any one of them would have been a good choice, for in 1846, California was still teeming with such representatives of the animal kingdom. But the choice had to be made in a hurry. Sonoma, the northern outpost of Mexican California, had just been conquered by a band of three dozen villainous-looking Yankee trappers and settlers. They were proclaiming California an independent republic, and to create the right impression on the vanquished Mexicans, a new flag had to be raised without delay. But first they had to think up something to put on it—something different, distinctive, striking.

For materials they had a yard of homespun, a pot of brown paint and a four-inch hem of red flannel salvaged from an old petticoat. All right, they could stitch the red flannel across the bottom; a proper flag, though, ought to have some stars on it. How many? Let's not overdo it. The supply of paint was limited. A single one would answer the purpose. Sure, one star, kind of reminiscent of the Texas Lone Star. But that left a lot of blank space. For real distinction, they ought to put in an animal—a typical California animal. Mule? Elk? Mountain lion? Wolf? Seal? Bear?

"Reckon we ought to fix on a grizzly, then," advised trapper Benjamin Dewell, one of the prime movers of the revolution, "'cause the b'ar always stands his ground."

There wasn't a dissenting voice. No question about it, the bear was the logical choice, king of the California menagerie. Cute idea, too, to pick the grizzly—a left-handed tribute to the Mexicans, in a way. Warn't Sonoma set up in the first place to beat off the Russian bear?

A trapper, less awkward with needle and shears than some of his fellow rebels, went to work with the materials. Will Todd, nephew of Abe Lincoln's Mary, painted the star into the corner, and adjacent to it, an animal faintly resembling a grizzly. To the hurrahs of thirty-six roisterous conquistadors, the bear flag of California was raised over Sonoma late in the afternoon of June 14th, 1846. Biased Sonomans, when told what the symbol fluttering over their heads was supposed to represent, laughed their heads off. It looked like a pig, they claimed. But regardless of the awkwardness in portraiture, the bear that day became California's permanent totem.

It was well chosen. No other animal could ever have properly taken its place. From the initial invasion of the Far West by Americans, the bear—grizzly or black—was chairman of the reception committee. Frequently Sierra bear rump was the first fresh meat overlanders had tasted since leaving the buffalo country. The providential appearance of these prowlers saved the lives of scores of starving pioneers, and scared the daylights out of many more. They were prized and despised, eagerly sought and cautiously avoided, depicted as the most ferocious tenants of the mountains and as the most innocuous.

Immigrants also encountered impressive herds of deer and antelope, elk and wild horses, but the bears were remembered most vividly. All could recount some amusing or exciting experience with them. And long after miners and settlers had chased surviving grizzlies farther back into the bush, they continued to be a perennial source of entertainment and alarm— as well as sustenance. Every red-blooded Californian had to catch a bear, and if he weren't successful, he could at least concoct a thriller about the monster that almost caught him.

Barroom broodings and fireside gab fests never lasted long enough for a rehearsal of all the trumped-up tales. The grizzlies got larger and the escapades more hair-raising as the evening wore on. After ten o'clock and the third bottle, no one ever mentioned a bear smaller than 1,500 pounds. In some of the accounts there was even an element of truth and, to prove it, many a narrator had the immodest habit of stripping off his flannels to display the crusts of hideous scars.

Those ranking themselves as "profess'nals" had the best repertoire. One who entertained J. D. Borthwick for an evening in 1854, at a public ranch appropriately called the "Grizzly-Bear House," had exactly the right make-up—"a dry, stringy-looking man with light hair, keen gray eyes and rather handsome features, but so dried up and tanned from exposure and the hard life he led that his face conveyed no idea of flesh. One would rather have expected on cutting into him to find him composed of gutta-percha or something of that sort, and only colored on the outside."

Characteristically, he too pointed out the various scars on "his gutta-percha person" received from the paws of grizzlies, and launched into a yarn to go with a set of them. It seemed that on one occasion he had twice fired at a bear without effect, and the bear, "infuriated by the balls planted in his carcass, was rushing upon him. He took to flight and, loading as he ran, turned to put a ball into the bear's left eye. The bear winked a good deal, but didn't seem to mind it much—he only increased his pace. So the hunter loaded again, turned around and put a ball into the right eye; whereupon the bear, now winking considerably with both eyes, put his nose to the ground and began to run him down by scent."

The story savored too much of phantasy to be swallowed whole by one of Borthwick's companions, and at that critical point in the story he had the indiscretion to burst out laughing.

"What are you a-laafin' at?" bristled the hunter. "D'ye mean to say I lie?"

"Oh," answered his detractor, "if you say it was so, I suppose it's all right; you ought to know. But I wasn't laughing at you. I was laughing at the bear."

Grizzlies were a source of extravagant humor, but when a raconteur overreached the bounds of plausibility, rather than confronting him with an honest charge of fact-stretching, doubting Thomases were more likely to assume a dead pan and deflate him by bringing out of hock a reliable old chestnut like the one about Jenkins:

"Yar, it was down at the camp in Grizzly Creek. Jenkins wa'n't huntin' that day. Left his gun ta' home. He was eatin' berries, stuffin' 'em into his maw by the hatful. Wonderful patch of berries. And he'd just squshed another fist of 'em in when he heard a rustlin' on t'other side of the patch. He knew right off, of course, it was a b'ar. He could tell. You know the way b'ars take to berries.

"Wal, if he didn't swaller that mouthful without ref'rence to further munchin' and masticatin'. Mind yer, though, he didn't run. Jenkins just stood there courageous and stone cold, hearin' the b'ar threshin' into the bushes, comin' nearer all the time. He dasn't run, fer fear of 'tractin' the b'ar and gettin' chased.

"He waited, fingerin' his knife and plannin' how he'd stab the brute just afore the big hug. Them bushes was so thick, he couldn't get a good look through no matter how much strainin' he did on his neck. From the sound he knew it was a monstrous critter. Then of a sudden it came to him that 'twan't one b'ar but three, maybe four, all large b'ars, an' he got an uncontrollable hankerin' to git to a spot where he could squint at 'em and size 'em up. So Jenkins backed away, quiet-like, and stepped across the Creek to a point about a half-mile downstream, but when he turned to look, he'd lost so much time that the b'ars had got away."

No matter how many times variations of the Jenkins story were repeated, it was good for a laugh as long as it was at someone's expense.

Many of the close calls with California bruins were self-provoked, and the string of sight-seers and naturalists who began flocking West on the first transcontinental stage lines were among the most indiscreet. "Don't injure a bear; stay away from she-bears with cubs," they were told, "and you'll find them utterly harmless."

Even John Muir took the counsel too literally, and came close to having his career curtailed during his first season in the Sierra. It was on a tramp to the crest of the Dome above Yosemite Valley. He was on the lookout for bears; for weeks he had wanted to get a good close-range view of the animal in his wilderness setting, and at last he was to be rewarded.

His dog Carlo gave the warning. Muir quieted the pooch, posted himself on the leeside of a great fir and peered out from behind it expectantly. There was bruin within a stone's throw, sniffing for trouble, aware that he was not alone—"a broad rusty bundle of ungovernable wildness, probably five hundred pounds in weight"—his front feet on a fallen log, head raised high, as if he were posing for a photograph.

Muir studied the animal for a long time, watching the gestures; noting the sharp nozzle, the broad chest, the stiff, erect ears; scrutinizing every aspect with a trained eye. "He made a telling picture standing alert in the sunny forest garden, harmonizing in bulk and color and shaggy hair with the trunks of trees and the lush vegetation; as natural a feature as any in the landscape."

The spectator wasn't satisfied. He wanted to inspect the congenial creature in motion, to see the running gait and the play of muscle. There was nothing to be timid about; no cubs were around and he had no intention of inflicting injury. Turning himself into a veritable windmill, he charged out from behind the tree, rushing toward the animal, shouting, wildly swinging his arms and hat.

But this specimen didn't follow the rules. To Muir's embarrassment, the bear, far from showing any inclination to accommodate his human ally by exhibiting his locomotion, held his position; ready to defend the forest domain, ready to fight. He lowered his head, thrust it forward savagely. Staring back at the intruder with fierce, burning eyes he rose up to full height flexing mighty forearms, eager to crush and kill.

Muir was willing to call a truce and back away. He considered high-tailing it himself if the bear refused to co-operate, but his legs wouldn't move. He was too awed by the spectacle of ferocity to run. Hypnotized, he stood less than a dozen yards from the arrogant beast, wanly gaping back.

"How long this strenuous interview lasted," mused Muir, "I don't know. But at length in the slow fullness of time, he pulled his huge paws down off the log and with magnificent deliberation turned and walked leisurely up the meadow, stopping frequently to look back over his shoulder to see whether I was pursuing him, then moving on again, evidently neither fearing me very much nor trusting me."

The contest was counted a draw, but the roving naturalist had a more respectful attitude toward the king of the Sierra after the experience.

It was still on his mind some weeks later when he was threading his way at dusk over Bloody Pass, one of the more tortuous routes across the Sierra to Mono Lake—a lonely trail known only to the Indians, until 1858. Muir had just entered the "gate" of the pass. Sheer, gaunt rocks closed in on every side. It was some of the wildest country into which he had yet ventured alone.

Suddenly in the half-darkness ahead, he made out a staggered line of hairy creatures advancing toward him with the unmistakable wallowing movement of bears. There was no escape up the sides of the mountain, and an attempt to retreat would be futile. The creatures shambled and shuffled toward him while his fears rose. But unhesitatingly he faced them —only to discover as they drew nearer that they were a file of unsociable Mono Indians decked out in ceremonial attire made of sage rabbitskins; make-believe bears so filthy that the accumulation of dirt on their faces was "old enough and thick enough to have geological significance." Muir felt let down by the scare; he would as soon have met a family of grizzlies.

Despite his predilection for the society of bears and his eagerness to make sure that they had at least an even chance in battle, John-of-the-Mountains did acquire a great affection for the memory of the greatest bear killer of the Sierra, an all-time champion, David Brown of Brown's Flat. But beside his aptitude for slaughtering grizzlies, David also had in him a streak of the naturalist that appealed to Muir.

An early arrival in the mountains, he had staked out a vast estate for himself on a scenic plateau between the North Fork of the Merced and Bull Creek. That placed him on the edge of what was to become Yosemite National Park, west of Big Grizzly and Little Grizzly, and slightly north of Bear Creek.

Brown divided his time between admiring mountains, gold hunting and bear hunting—with emphasis on the bears. "Where could a lonely hunter find better solitude?" reflected

Muir. "Game in the woods, gold in the rocks, health and exhil-aration in the air; while the colors and cloud furniture of the sky are ever inspiring through all sorts of weather."

Neither clock nor calendar were allowed to dictate Brown's habits. Whether in search of gold or bear, there was always time for a detour to the summit of a commanding ridge to soak up scenery—a man after Muir's heart. His dog Sandy tagged him everywhere, and no man ever had a closer partner. In deer hunting the mongrel trotted behind him so silently that the master rarely caught the sound of a rustling leaf or the snap of a twig. But in bear hunting his role was more aggressive. Sandy was the tracker. He led the way. No matter how rocky the terrain, the dog kept the scent. Once Dave Brown and Sandy set out to corner their quarry, neither gave up until the victim was downed.

The search could take them over a circuitous route of fifty miles; it could take hours, days, weeks; but they wouldn't think of returning to the home flat without a token of conquest. A pocketful of ammunition and a sack of flapjack flour were enough to keep the two on the go indefinitely.

The hunter knew all the bear habits there were. He cat-alogued them by season. In spring and early summer bruin was most likely to be found along a stream bank or in a swamp feeding on clover and lupines, or in an open meadow feasting on strawberries. Toward the end of summer he could be lo-cated on dry ridges guzzling manzanita berries, squatting on his haunches pulling the branches down and pressing them together into clusters for a luscious mouthful. In Indian sum-mer he would be under the pines teasing the squirrels and hogging the cones the squirrels dropped. In late autumn his feeding grounds were in the oak thickets of the canyon flats.

Brown's uncanny sense for locating bear never failed. As soon as Sandy indicated that he was closing in on a hot scent, a long halt was called. They knew how dangerous a grizzly was when cornered, and didn't take chances. Topography and vegeta-tion were closely studied and the attack leisurely planned. Regardless of how much circumvention was required, Brown and dog kept to leeward. Dave would stalk to within a hundred yards of his prey, then establish a base at the foot of a tree too small for the bear to climb, but large enough to hold him if necessary.

At that point he always shed his shoes, for toes could be very useful in a quick ascent. He waited patiently until the bear exposed one side for a clear target, then squeezed the trigger. Knowing that a bear had poor eyesight and would be attracted only by movement, Brown avoided making a perceptible motion, though he did have to worry about the smoke from his discharge. Frequently he could get in a second shot before the bear detected the smoke.

If the victim started to wander off into the brush, Brown let him go a good safe distance before he followed. Sandy did the scouting and the worrying. He usually found a dead bear, but a bark was the signal to come up with caution. When the animal still showed fight, Sandy dashed in for a distracting nip while Dave chose a secure stand for a final shot.

"Bear hunting is safe enough," confided Dave. "If an old hungry mother with cubs met a man on her own ground she would, in my opinion, try to catch and eat him. This would only be fair play anyway, for we eat them. But nobody hereabout has ever been used for bear grub that I know of."

Dave was too modest to venture even a guess as to how many bears he had felled in his quiet, cautious way—so different from the methods of a more impetuous school of hunting. It was a prodigiously large number. There were a lot of bears around Brown's Flat when he first took up residence there, but by persistent effort he did himself out of his profession. Close calls? Oh, yes, he and Sandy had experienced a few; nothing to brag about. The truth was, their operations had been so calculated that Dave didn't leave behind him even a legend of a wrestling match or an eye-to-eye encounter.

Brown's reassurance notwithstanding, there were plenty of authentic accounts of less prudent hunters who had met their ends in the claws and clutches of aroused bears—including the story of Peter Lebeque who crept up too soon after planting a lethal shot in a grizzly's chest. Peter's remains were buried under the very tree he had used as cover in the battle, and his companions memorialized the tragedy by carving the brief facts on the trunk:

PETER LEBECK

KILLED

BY

A X BEAR

OCT^R 7, 1837

On an expedition a few years earlier, Captain Joseph Reddeford Walker kept coming across the bodies of Indians that had been mauled by grizzlies; and later he lost one of his own men who tried to chase a grizzly from a thicket ambush. The daredevil had followed a bear into the brush where it turned on him in close quarters. The enraged animal caught a leg as the man was escaping up a tree. He lost the leg and bled to death.

Disfigured men who had tried their luck once too often in these tussles were not an uncommon sight in the mountain country; casualties hobbling about on limbs that would never heal; strapping fellows with an arm and shoulder gone; hunters blinded in one eye or with a mask of hideous scar over half the face.

Around San José in the 1850's was a young Negro without the wherewithal to sit down. While strolling in the hills, unarmed, he had surprised a grizzly with cubs, but the family had just finished a meal, had no appetite for the intruder and was in a playful mood. A haymaker felled the Negro. More scared than hurt, he lay on the hillside for an hour or longer, playing dead man, while the bears frolicked nearby. Hoping that they had lost interest in him, he at last eased up from his cramped position expecting to take to his heels. But no sooner was he on his feet than he was given another bruiser that stretched him out a second time.

Toward dusk the bears ambled off and the Negro took advantage of their absence to make one more attempt at escape. He hadn't gone twenty feet when the animal overtook him

again from a different quarter. This time she did him great
damage, with both claws and jaws. She knocked him senseless,
gashed his back and gouged his haunches, then, scratching a
few leaves over him, she called it a day. By accident, he was
shortly found and nursed back to life, but he never again had
much use for a chair.

"A wounded bear is a worse enemy to encounter than a
tiger," claimed Frank Marryat, British-bred sportsman, actor
and adventurer. He could speak from experience, for in September, 1854, he had participated in a memorable bear-hunt-
ing expedition in the Sierra, accompanied by several veterans,
including two old hands named Sheldon and March.

"It was not until the afternoon that we struck upon fresh
bear sign," he wrote. "The sign led into thick underwood—the
worst of all places for a kill. March disposed us in couples; we
then spread and entered the thicket. Almost immediately I
heard a crash and an angry roar, and then a shot was fired to
the left. The bear was in view. I was astonished at his size,
standing on his hind legs with his mouth open like a thirsty
dog. Working himself up and down, he indicated that he felt
the inconvenience of the pellet that March had intended for
his heart but lodged in his alimentary canal.

"At that instant, as if by sudden impulse, he again assumed
the position of a quadruped and bounded toward March and
Sheldon, clearing as much ground at each stride—for he was
as big as an ox—as would have done credit to the winner of
the Liverpool steeplechase.

"A shot from the right altered his course again in that direction, for the grizzly bear will turn to the last assailant, and this
enforces the necessity of bear hunters supporting each other.
A momentary uncertainty on his part gave me opportunity of
troubling him with one of my one-and-a-half-ounce balls; but
this only elicited a grunt and a rush in my direction.

"I confess that as soon as my rifle was discharged, I felt great
inclination to disregard March's directions not to use my revolver, but to reload my rifle under all circumstances. While
I was in a curious state of uncertainty on this point, though

loading, the bear swerved suddenly on one side in chase of the little high-couraged dog that belonged to Sheldon.

"The dog had been in other bear hunts and I fancy he must have got hurt or lost his pluck, for he now rushed straight to his master, and the bear followed. Sheldon fired as the grizzly approached, but without effect; and the next moment poor Sheldon was down, bathed in blood. One blow had carried away the flesh entirely from one side of his face, fracturing his jawbone in the most frightful manner.

"The bear disappeared, probably to die, while we carried Sheldon home, with what feelings of grief I need not say. He afterward recovered, though dreadfully disfigured, and with the loss of an eye. It was, perhaps, on account of this accident that we made up no more parties for the express purpose of bear hunting."

For beasts so prone to rough up their human combatants no treatment seemed to be too barbarous. The danger and difficulty in killing a grizzly came from his relative invulnerability to the light arms and ammunition generally used. The keenest marksman rarely felled a bear with a single shot. He had a choice of three vital spots to aim for—the back of the ear, the spine and the heart. An ounce ball would glance off the stoutly framed head; bullets pumped at random into the tough hide only enraged the animal; and many an old-timer would testify that even when a shot had gone clean through a bear's heart, he would live long enough to do serious mischief.

A cornered grizzly kept in constant motion, and the sudden rushes of fifteen hundred pounds of muscle, claw and open mouth did something to the nerves of the most intrepid hunter. Yet one contingent of steelhearted backwoodsmen maintained that the only way to bring down a savage bruin was to *let* him attack; to stand firm and composed until the beast was within six feet, then discharge the muzzle directly into the yawning mouth. It took courage, they admitted, but the procedure guaranteed the safety of the sportsman and was calculated to produce "a very bad cough" in the animal.

That was the kind of courage possessed by Peter the Hunter,

half-breed son of a Sioux squaw and a French-Canadian trapper, a tall, gaunt, lank character with sunken cheeks and restless black eyes, known throughout the West more fondly even
than "Old Greenwood" or men like Dave Brown. He was more
a man of the world, at home anywhere between the Rockies
and the Coast, but since the Sierra was in between, he
regarded that range more or less as his home base.

In his lifetime he had been much farther afield. While trading a batch of hides at Montreal in his boyhood, he had been
spotted as a likely candidate for the British army; was impressed into service, shipped across the Atlantic and toted a
gun in the Battle of Waterloo. To hear him tell of it, Peter the
Hunter deserved a good share of the credit for the overthrow
of Napoleon Bonaparte.

After seven years in the British ranks, he was discharged in
Oregon, where he married a faithful Catholic squaw and settled down long enough to have three daughters. Between
trapping jaunts deep into the continent, he took off time
enough to teach his girls to use lasso, rifle and hunting knife
as skillfully as any of the local lads, and to build up a small
ranch. Then his wife suddenly died and he was left as sole
guardian of three comely daughters.

To assuage his grief and his lust for wandering, he tried alcohol, but it didn't work, so he packed up and took to the road
with the teen-age girls in tow—as devoted a father as ever
roamed the West. Protecting his daughters became an obsession. Whether he was trapping, bear hunting or prospecting,
he never let them out of his sight. Together father and daughters teamed up as bear killers for the sheer delight of the sport.

But in the mining country of California the eligible girls became a real problem. They could ride like devils, match any
Mexican at tossing a lasso, bring down grizzlies, swear like
troopers and recite good Catholic prayers like Holy Sisters.
Wherever they went they attracted attention.

Time and again one of them caught the lusty eye of some
gold panner or ranch hand, and Peter was hard put to fend off
the advances. Not that he was against their marrying. He was

perfectly willing to see a daughter happily tied to an honest man—provided the prospective husband would agree to take in the rest of the family too, so that he could keep an eye on them all. Marrying, however, wasn't what the men seemed to have in mind; they were all interested in a more temporary arrangement. Getting hitched to a wild half-breed, under the auspices of a preacher, was much too permanent, and as for accepting the other terms, well, Peter could keep his daughters. So the Hunter was never successful in striking a matrimonial bargain.

Armed to the teeth, the four set out on their horses one morning in the spring of 1850, on another bear hunt. But they weren't blessed with their usual good luck. High in the broken mountain country, Peter finally dismounted and pushed his way through the chaparral toward a shelf on a sharp cliff where he could better survey his surroundings. Both hands were needed to hoist himself up the last six feet, so he leaned his rifle securely against a rock and scrambled up unarmed.

To his horror he saw that the shelf was already occupied. A huge grizzly towered above him not three paces away. For the first time in his life the Hunter confronted his prey without a gun. As the monster sprang, Peter instinctively drew his knife and plunged it into the animal's side. In a fury the grizzly struck back. Peter's scalp was torn half off his head; vicious jaws rent his shoulder; and he was enveloped in the bear's mighty hug. Then, thrown off balance, both rolled over the side of the cliff.

By all ordinary laws of chance, Peter should have been killed, or at least knocked senseless in the fall, but he was safely cushioned in the bear's belly and the animal took the shock. Even as they rolled, Peter, still gripping his knife, was jabbing it again and again into the leathery chest. For a few seconds the stunned bear released the viselike arms. The Hunter sprang away. More infuriated than ever, the grizzly pounced again. But he shuddered and dropped halfway to the man.

True to her training, one of the daughters had trailed her

father, witnessed the whole bloody scene and yelled to her sisters to hurry with their rifles. While bear and man were doing their tumbling act over the edge of the shelf, she was sliding down the rocks close behind. The barrel of her rifle was trained on the bear, and in the brief moment the two antagonists were separated, she fired. But the shot was only enough to halt the bear. He was now ready to take on a second foe— a third and a fourth, for the other two sisters had joined the fray. As the frenzied grizzly started to lunge for his latest tormentor, the girl grabbed her sister's rifle, thrust the gun at the animal's ear and pressed the trigger. The bear crumpled at her feet.

Desperately wounded, Peter was carried back to camp by his daughters, and under their care he miraculously recovered. After that he was less solicitous of his daughters' welfare. He was getting on in years, and concluded that if he'd reached the stage where he had to depend on them for protection from grizzlies, they were quite capable of contending with the advances of Mexicans and miners.

Like many other professional hunters, Peter in his old age turned to the more lucrative employment of trapping grizzlies for bull-and-bear fights in the mining-town arenas. During the 1850's and 60's these fights burgeoned into the greatest entertainment spectacle in the State, and fierce live bears were very much in demand for them. At a Sacramento meat market a fresh carcass might be worth $100, but a live specimen, weighing half a ton or more, easily brought $1,500 from the fight promoters in towns like Downieville, Sonora or Mokelumne Hill.

WAR! WAR!! WAR!!! screamed a typical placard advertising one of these contests. "The celebrated Bull-Killing Bear, General Scott, will fight a Bull on Sunday, the 15th inst. at 2 P.M. at Mokelumne Hill. The Bear will be chained with a twenty-foot chain in the middle of the arena. The Bull, perfectly wild, young, of the Spanish breed, and the best that can be found in the country, will be freed in the arena and not hampered in any way whatsoever. . . ."

It took a gang of six or eight to lasso a monster like General Scott, tether his feet, cage and haul him to town. Or another favorite method of capture was to construct an enormous log trap with an open bottom, hoist it six feet off the ground from the limb of a tree, and bait it with a leg of lamb in such a way that a tug on the meat tripped the hoist and let the cage come crashing down to ensnare the brute. Capturing live grizzlies became a favorite occupation for aged frontiersmen, and a highly remunerative one.

Bullfights, of course, had been imported to California by the Spanish, but the Mexican addition of bull-and-bear contests proved much more popular with the American clientele. In fact, they were such an attraction that private shows were often staged for the entertainment of visiting celebrities.

The Reverend Walter Colton, first *alcalde* of Monterey, was so honored. He helped to capture both bull and bear and enthusiastically participated in the outdoor banqueting and other preliminaries. But he wasn't particularly thrilled with the big event, when the horsemen finally drew back to form a large circle around the two enemies.

"Neither turned from the other his blazing eyes," he wrote, "while menace and defiance began to lower the looks of each. Gathering their full strength, the terrific rush was made. The bull missed. The bear with one enormous bound dashed his teeth into his back to break the spine. The bull fell, but whirled his huge horn deep into the side of the antagonist. There they lay, grappled and gored, in their convulsive struggles and death throes. We spurred up and with our rifles and pistols closed the tragedy. And it was time; this last scene was too full of blind rage and madness even for the wild sports of California."

The spectacle had acquired a few refinements by the time captive bulls and bears were let loose in the mining-town arenas. The more gruesome parts were omitted and the animals were usually dispatched before they reached the stage of death convulsions. But it was a colorful, rowdy show, complete with band, bar, souvenir hawkers and red-shirted miners

—all confined in a crudely built amphitheatre of rough lumber, tiered seats sloping down to a tiny arena not more than forty feet in diameter.

"The bull was a beautiful animal," recalled one spectator. "His horns were regular and sharp and his coat as smooth and glossy as a racer's. He stood taking a survey of the bear, the ring and the crowds of people. After looking at the bear for a few minutes, as if taking aim at him, he put down his head and charged furiously across the arena. The bear received him crouching down as low as he could, and though one could hear the bump of the bull's head and horns upon his ribs, he was quick enough to seize the bull by the nose before he could retreat. This spirited commencement of the battle was hailed with uproarious applause.

"The bear, lying on his back, held the bull's nose firmly between his teeth and embraced him around the neck with his hind feet, shaking him savagely by the nose. A promiscuous scuffle ensued, until the bear threw his antagonist to the ground. For this feat the bear was cheered immensely. But the bull soon regained his feet and, disengaging himself, retired to the other side of the ring.

"Neither of them seemed to be very much the worse for the encounter, excepting that the bull's nose had rather a ragged and bloody appearance; and after standing a few minutes steadily eying the bear, he made another rush. Again poor bruin's ribs resounded, but again he took the bull's nose into chancery, seizing him just as before. The bull, however, quickly disengaged himself and was making off when the bear, unwilling to part with him so soon, seized his hind foot between his teeth, and holding on with his paws as well, was thus dragged around the ring before he quitted his grip. The round terminated with shouts of delight from the excited spectators."

For round after round the gory conflict went on. When it became clear that the bull was going to be the loser, a second was let in, and together they tackled the bear. But after an hour or more of excitement, the grizzly came off an easy victor—"the finest fight ever fit in the country."

Between the toll in grizzlies for the fights and their slaughter for sport and steaks, the species didn't last long in California. In a few years the grizzly was completely exterminated and the black bear took over as the ursine king of the Sierra forests. But there are enough Grizzly Peaks, Grizzly Gulches, Grizzly Boulevards, Grizzly Creeks and Valleys to remind the public of the prowess the brute once knew. And from high places his vestige still flutters nostalgically on the state emblem—a much more sophisticated representation than the pig Will Todd daubed on the homespun, back in 1846.

VIII

RAILROAD ACROSS
THE MOUNTAINS!
ARE YOU CRAZY?

The panting Central Pacific locomotive labored up the
slopes of the Sierra foothills, its flaring stack belching clouds
of pungent wood smoke. Bathed in the smudge, a tender and
seven passenger cars snaked behind. The bantam engine

seemed hardly capable of hauling itself up the mountain without anything in tow, but as if Central Pacific officials were intent on demonstrating the capacity of its rolling stock, the cars were crammed to the aisles and platforms with four hundred excursionists—stockholders of the company, their guests and noisy children, all on a Saturday-afternoon jaunt to review the latest wonders wrought by the builders of the western leg of the transcontinental line.

The night before—June 3rd, 1864—another mile of the line had been completed. The rails now ran all the way to Newcastle, thirty-one miles from Sacramento. Almost a thousand feet of the seven-thousand-foot elevation to the summit had been conquered. The construction had taken a year and a half, so perhaps it wasn't too much to brag about, but reaching Newcastle was something of a milestone; the event couldn't be allowed to pass unobserved.

There had been speeches and celebrations for the groundbreaking at Sacramento on January 8th, 1863, more speeches and celebration when the first locomotive was rolled onto the tracks in November, and still more when eighteen miles were laid to Roseville. The public was getting fed up on oratory and fireworks. Company officials were accused of being long on talk and short on action. So it was decided that the Newcastle rites would be a quiet affair just for the stockholders and their friends, an outing without any formal program. At least it would give investors an opportunity to see for themselves the kind of action their money had bought.

Huffing and puffing, the locomotive eased along an open ridge beyond the Rocklin granite quarries, high above a deep ravine. For passengers fortunate enough to have window seats on the left, there was a breath-taking view, and for a moment their exclamations almost drowned out the racket of driving pistons and grinding wheels. Someone shouted and waved to a group of miners far below.

The train chugged into the twilight of a dense sugar-pine grove, picked up speed on the level and came roaring out of it into glaring sunshine on the height of a spectacular wooden trestle so narrow that for all the cringing passengers could see, they were being drawn through mid-air. Then began the last, slow climb up the hills to Newcastle. The train jolted along unevenly here. This was track that had been laid only the day before and gangs of workmen were still busy with picks, bars and wheelbarrows on the embankment. The engineer tooted a salute to the laborers; they waved back, and youngsters in the car windows added their hurrahs.

Newcastle was around the bend. The train crept past a ramshackle construction camp of tents, shacks, rough-lumber shelters and open kitchens. Beyond was the supply dump; an acre or more cluttered with piles of rails, ties, lumber, tools, lines of horse carts, wheelbarrows and nondescript machinery.

"Newcastle. Newcastle," sang the conductor half facetiously. "End-o'-track!"

The train thundered past the sidings, a turntable and the freight depot bulging with crates and more equipment, and ground to a jerking halt in front of the brand-new passenger depot, from which the carpenter's scaffolding had not yet been removed. Two long triumphant screeches from the locomotive whistle were taken as the signal for the boys in the aisles to make a rush for the doors. The thirty-one-mile trip from Sacramento had taken exactly an hour and forty-five minutes.

Waiting statuesquely on the station platform and looking as though he were about to dim the occasion by making a speech after all, was sedate Leland Stanford, President of the Central Pacific and host for the day. But as people streamed off the train, he waved them on, jovially urging them to look over the town, take a tramp in the hills, walk the tracks if they wished; and be sure not to miss the wonderful view of Sacramento Valley. "Return train leaves at five," he cautioned.

For the most part, the host's counsel was ignored. The youngsters made a collective dash for the locomotive, swarmed into the cab, fought for footing on the cowcatcher, took over the tender and lionized the engineer. Their parents headed for the nearest bar.

Newcastle was a dismal place, with two saloons for every

shop. Like the nearby mining villages that had mushroomed into existence ten years before, this break in the wilderness was suddenly booming into a populous railroad center before Main Street could be cleared of stumps and boulders, or decent shelters built for the invasion of laborers. It was another shackville and tent town.

For the afternoon excursionists, the views of the valley were magnificent, the walks to lookouts mildly refreshing, the bar service prompt and expensive; but the one thing that made the greatest impression was "Newcastle Gap"—a yawning gulch sixty-feet deep and nearly a quarter of a mile wide. The track stopped at the lip of this gulch. It had to be spanned before the railroad could proceed farther toward the summit. Certainly the thirty-second mile of rail line was going to be the hardest yet. There was something foreboding about that great chasm.

Late in the afternoon parents rounded up their children; the whole crowd gathered around the largest saloon Newcastle boasted; glasses were raised to the future of the Central Pacific; three sonorous cheers were given that grand old man of Coloma and Sacramento, General John Augustus Sutter, and three more to Governor Stanford. Then everyone was ready to board the cars for the biggest excitement of the occasion—the roller-coaster plunge down the mountain.

In a prosaic memoir a cub reporter from the Sacramento *Union,* who went along for the ride, filled in the details: "The engine blew the whistle. Cars were quickly filled, and in good season the stockholders and their families were safely returned to the city. No observant traveler can pass over the road without appreciating the substantial character of its construction. The last four miles ascend at the rate of 105 feet to the mile, the maximum grade of the entire road. Notwithstanding the opposition from rival roads and various antagonistic interests, the managers have steadily pressed forward their work, and their efforts have been crowned with the fullest measure of success. They now have material enough, purchased and available, to complete thirty more miles. Strong assurance is felt of its speedy construction to the eastern boundary. . . . All will realize the importance to the city, the State and nation of so gigantic an enterprise."

Local readers hardly needed to be reminded again of the significance of a transcontinental line funneling a nation's commerce through Sacramento. For a decade California editors and orators had been reciting the facts, and for much longer than that, eastern visionaries had been spouting eloquence on what it would mean to America and the world. But now that a small start was actually being made to translate the dream into reality, Western capitalists were catching on to the machinations of the Sacramento promoters and were balking vigorously.

Jealous San Franciscans couldn't bear to see the little capital city stealing the commercial show. Affluent Wells, Fargo was up in arms; the railroad would ruin its vested interests. All the stage companies—the Pioneer, the California and particularly the Overland with its superb line running between Missouri and the Coast—were violently opposed. The Pacific Mail Steamship Company, commanding commerce between Panama and the Bay, objected to a rail line cutting in on shipping business from the East. The California Steam Navigation Company, operating between the Bay and Sacramento, foresaw an end to its monopoly. The Overland Telegraph Company, between Salt Lake City and Placerville, realized that it would have to compete with a Central Pacific system.

Freight-wagon contractors, with some 10,000 employees and millions of dollars invested in horses and wagons, would be doomed. Even the Sitka Ice Company, which imported Alaska ice to retail for five cents a pound, predicted that it would be put out of business by quicker transportation from the Sierra snow belt. Everywhere forces antagonistic to a ruinous railroad were gathering.

If the public was invited to express an opinion, undoubtedly the railroad builders would get an overwhelming vote of confidence, but outside of Sacramento, the capitalists had the press pretty tightly sewed up; the vocal minority wielded a powerful influence. Keenest of all was the resentment against four business upstarts in Sacramento who thought they had the savvy to organize, build and run a great railroad.

The sophisticated critics couldn't be censured too severely. They had something on their side. They looked upon the contrivers of the Central Pacific as the most pompous small-town operators in transportation history—a wholesale grocer, a dry-goods dealer and two partner-proprietors of a hardware store; all unknowns outside their limited business and political circles.

The grocer was Stanford; the dry-goods dealer, Charles Crocker; the partners in hardware, Mark Hopkins and Collis P. Huntington. For their fervent interest in a railroad across the Sierra, they were indebted to a young engineer, Theodore Judah, who before his untimely death had convinced himself and a great many others that the only logical place to cut a transcontinental rail line into California was over the route the Donner Party had traveled in 1846.

With all four, the first vague preoccupation had quickly developed into a mania, and while their capitalist adversaries were arguing about whether the quartet was really insane or inspired, they had rushed ahead with impetuous haste, ignoring the indignation of powerful business and transportation bigwigs of the West, and gone straight to the top. Within three years they had received the endorsement of the United States Congress, President Lincoln and even the State Legislature. Meantime, Stanford had somehow managed to get himself elected Governor of California.

Events had ticked off with magic precision. The Company was incorporated in June, 1861. A year later Congress was persuaded to pass the Pacific Railroad Act, authorizing construction of the line and granting fat subsidies. Hundreds of individuals, the State, adjacent counties and towns had supported the cause with the purchase of stocks and bonds. The Big Four were not wealthy, but each had put up a few thousand dollars so that ground could be broken and actual grading started early in January, 1863.

An undertaking originally colored by Sacramento pride and prejudice was redecorated by "Stanford and Company" to look like a proposition of momentous national and international importance. The transcontinental railroad, they argued, was to be the principal thoroughfare for traffic between the Orient and the Occident—a pathway for all nations. They even turned to good account the rivalry between North and South over the location of the route, by convincing Northern legislators that the Civil War now made the road a military necessity.

Without their railroad, California might be lost to the Confederacy, the State might declare itself an independent nation, or become subject to foreign invasion and exploitation. They worried Senators and Congressmen into believing that rails were the only tie that could permanently marry the Pacific states to the East.

Specious as many of the arguments were, they had their effect. Congress and the President responded magnanimously. In successive acts the Central Pacific was granted subsidies of $16,000 per mile for construction over level terrain, $48,000 for construction in the mountains, and a land grant of 12,800 acres to go with every mile of road. But as a guarantee of its capability and good intentions, the Company would have to complete forty miles before any government beneficence would become effective.

Then, with a frugal eye on the larger bonus, a fine point was raised as to just where the Sierra began. The California Supreme Court settled on a line thirty-one miles east of Sacramento—the Newcastle region. Big-hearted Abraham Lincoln, far from the scene, was shown some old topographic maps and persuaded that the western bounds of the mountains were only seven miles from Sacramento. With a stroke of the Presidential pen, the Sierra was moved twenty-four miles off base, giving the promoters an unexpected additional subsidy of almost three-quarters of a million. They were sitting pretty.

But the Big Four weren't to get all the gravy, said Congress. They could start building from the west, while another company, the Union Pacific, would start building from the east. The two corporations could set their own construction pace, compete for mileage until they met, and each claim profits and right of way for the distance they covered. The race was on.

It wasn't exactly a fair match; the line-up gave Central Pacific more than its share of handicaps. Every length of rail, every spike, dump wagon, flatcar and locomotive had to be ordered a year in advance at factories and foundries in the East and shipped 18,000 miles around Cape Horn—unless the company chose to pay three times the freight rate for transshipment across the Isthmus of Panama.

A locomotive, for instance, after traveling from inland factory to eastern port, had to be disassembled for ship transportation around South America; laboriously deposited on a lighter when it arrived six months later at San Francisco; hoisted to the deck of a river boat for shipment to Sacramento; transferred there to flatcars on the levee and hauled to shops for reassembly. If it went by way of the Isthmus, the cost for additional flatcar and lighter reloadings had to be added. By the time a $12,000 locomotive reached Sacramento it could have a freight bill of $8,000 tagged to it.

As the Civil War progressed, freight rates of $15 a ton rose to $45. With Southern privateersmen on the loose, marine insurance rose from 2½ per cent to 17 per cent. Railroad iron jumped from $115 a ton in New York or Boston to $267.50. Nor was the equipment always available. Time and again priority orders ready for shipment were grabbed by the military for urgent use on the war front.

The Union Pacific could draw on the pools of Irish labor in the Atlantic states, while workmen were difficult to get in California, at any price. The Sierra gold mines were playing out, but the silver bonanzas in Nevada beckoned any man willing to swing a pick. In daily rounds of labor markets at San Francisco and other cities, agents could usually assemble a few roustabouts, yet chances were that half of them would accept the free ride to a construction camp, only to wander off next day to the nearest mine.

But the greatest handicap in the race across the continent was the Sierra. Until the rails were laid over the mountains, the Central Pacific could hardly consider itself in the running for the easy, lucrative miles across Nevada and Utah. That barrier came at the start. Threading a line over the hundred and thirty miles of upland was the greatest problem ever faced by railroad builders anywhere. Here lay the same formidable impediment that had frustrated pioneers, overlanders, trail hounds and highway engineers for a generation. Now the Big Four were tackling it.

One of the first decisions was to build a toll road, adjacent to the rail right of way at the outset. It was needed for transporting supplies; would serve as a source of income while the rail line was under construction; would swing the Placerville trade to Sacramento grocers, dry-goods and hardware dealers; turn every depot, as fast as a new one was erected, into a feeder for the railroad. And if, by some misfortune, the Central Pacific never got all the way over the mountains, rail and road in any case would be a profitable combination.

"Stanford and Company" made allowance for almost every exigency, but it didn't make allowance for the blast of controversy that the toll road set off. Long before it was opened in July, 1864, the public jumped to the conclusion that the Big Four had no intention of extending the rails to the Nevada line; they would stop at Dutch Flat and let the project go at that, after cornering the freight traffic. No amount of reassurance could dispel the idea, so for two years the popular name for the Central Pacific had been the "Dutch Flat Swindle."

Carping citizens became more and more certain that no feat of engineering could possibly push a railroad over the mountains. Trains weren't constructed to climb precipices, and if they got to the foothills, the titanic snowdrifts on the summit would halt them there for seven months of the year. Rank and file were all for giving the venture a try, but newsmen, under pressure from capitalistic interests, were viciously hostile. In repetitious tirades editors warned the public of the enormous fraud that was being put over on them.

Stanford's closest friends tried to bring him to reason with arguments that all the fortunes of the company would be buried in the snow of the Sierra. "The road will end high in the air and nowhere else," they told him. Others worked on Huntington, on Hopkins and Crocker with the same talk. "Why, Crocker, are you crazy?" ridiculed a respected colleague with whom he had been doing business for years. "You think of building a railroad across the mountains? Why, you have a good business, what more do you want?"

Crocker wanted to build a railroad. Nothing, nobody would stop him. He sold out his "good business," sunk his money in the crazy venture and formed a construction company to do the building. While his three partners worked in the background, he moved to the front line.

Crocker never shortchanged people, never exaggerated. He unhesitatingly told them how competent he was and lived up to his self-appraisal. He wasn't burdened with any sense of false modesty, with any feeling of timidity or any abstruse engineering theories. Admittedly he knew nothing about engineering, civil or mechanical. At the age of twelve he had given up all schooling as a bad job. He could read, write, spell, do simple arithmetic and find places on the map, but book learning wasn't for him. "I had a wonderful schooling in experience," he alleged.

If the public and press had fully realized what rank amateurs at railroading the Big Four actually were, and if they had been given an inkling regarding their shaky financial status in 1864, the quartet might well have been ridden out of the State. "We none of us knew anything about railroad building," boasted Crocker unblushingly long after the job was done, "but at the same time we were enterprising men, anxious to have a road built and have it come to Sacramento where our interests and property were. . . . We had no idea how we were going to build the road. We all said to each other that if anyone could do it, we could. . . . We actually spent our own money building that road to Newcastle and it left every one of us in debt."

Fortunately no such careless statement was aired while the appeals for financial backing were in circulation. Despite the debt and the inexperience, come hell or high water, they were going on from Newcastle to Dutch Flat, to the Summit, to the Truckee River, Nevada and Salt Lake City.

At one time or another, each member of the strong-willed Big Four allowed that he was entitled to the major portion of glory for completion of the Central Pacific, but Crocker was more inclined to put things into perspective and distribute credit where it was due—after making ample deductions for the credit due himself.

"My faculty for leadership developed more and more as I grew older," he confided. "We all came together and were anxious to succeed—all ambitious—and each one dropped into his place and filled it. My department was construction. I had charge of the construction from first to last. . . . When it came to judging of men and the working with men and execution of work on the road, I was the man. . . . I had very great success in judging men. . . . I did not care about being president, nor taking any position, but I was always on the watch that a dollar came as near buying a dollar and five cents worth of material as possible.

"Mr. Stanford was the president and attended to the finances here in California. . . . Mr. Huntington was in New York and attended to financial matters there . . . to dealings with the government, to the purchase of material and locomotives and all such matters. He was supreme in the east. I was supreme on the road. Mr. Stanford was supreme in financial matters here and Mark Hopkins was a general advisor to all of us. . . . He was senior in years, and always disliked to execute or direct. He was the treasurer of the company, but the finances were generally managed outside the treasurer's office. He was never very active outside. He was a long-headed man without much executive ability, but was a wonderfully good man for an executive officer to counsel with. . . . The work of building the road was mine."

Charley Crocker didn't intend to have his analysis of who did what disputed. Within a few days after the jovial stockholders' party at Newcastle he had an opportunity to begin to put his superior schooling in experience and his faculty for leadership to the test.

The first thirty-one miles of the road had been relatively easy going. According to the judgment of the California Supreme Court, the ascent of the Sierra was just beginning. Somehow the line had to be snaked up the mountains another 6,000 feet, and it was a long 100 miles over the top to the other side. Moreover, the pressure was on. In a grand ceremony, ground for the Union Pacific had been broken at Omaha more than six months before, on December 2nd, 1863, and although the speeches hadn't yet spurred anyone on to start the grading or track laying, it could start any day. Every mile that Union built would be one less mile on which the Central eventually collected revenue.

According to Judah's survey charts, the nine miles east of Newcastle were one of the ruggedest stretches on the whole route. They called for a succession of sweeping detours and prolonged grades, trestles, fills and cuts. The string of twenty locomotives which had just arrived from the East were put to work hauling flatcars loaded with rails and freight to Newcastle, but the equipment poured in faster than it could be used. Five hundred men were all that Crocker could round up— and sometimes they were 500 too many as payday approached. Funds were running low. The promoters managed to keep to themselves the fact that for an anxious period of seventeen days there was not a dollar in the treasury.

As the summer wore on, discouragement seemed to be in the air. County and State bonds were being held up; lawsuits were pending; worst of all was the news from the war front. General Grant had just lost 7,000 men in the horrible slaughter of Cold Harbor, and 60,000 in his ill-fated Wilderness Campaign. But despite the common depression and all the physical difficulties,

Crocker kept pushing ahead. If worst came to worst, he seemed capable of building a road without money. Those nine miles had to be finished as soon as possible; for until they were done the company could not claim a dollar of the federal subsidies.

It was slow, slow work, but the weather at least was with them. The winter of 1864-65 proved to be one of the mildest on record. Hardly a day was lost because of storms, yet it wasn't until May 10th that the tracks reached Auburn, a modest five miles from Newcastle. Cutting and grading, however, had been completed far ahead, so that by June they were at Clipper Gap, forty-three miles from Sacramento. The last great financial hurdle had been cleared. Government aid was now assured, and after Appomattox on April 9th, the future for the Central Pacific hadn't looked so bright since the day Abraham Lincoln moved the Sierra those seventeen miles into the valley.

Already the railroad was bringing in substantial earnings. The gross for May was $740 a day; for June $1,080. Passenger rates were ten cents a mile; freight fifteen cents a ton, per mile —all gold. To four old hands used to working behind counters, this was a kind of business that made the returns from merchandising look like small pickings.

If less than fifty miles of rail could bring in income like this, what would 500 yield? But it was no time to gloat; according to the latest intelligence from Omaha, Union Pacific was now hard at work, building more miles of railroad across the rolling hills of Nebraska in a month than the Central was building in a year.

By August, Crocker had licked another eleven miles. Illinoistown was the new end-of-track, and the supply base was moved there. Toward the middle of the month the garrulous Speaker of the House, the Honorable Schuyler Colfax, on a political junket through the West, blew into Illinoistown to look over construction activities and pronounce a few stentorian words of encouragement. As one of the most outspoken Congressional advocates of "transcontinental bonds of iron," he was greeted with wild acclaim.

"I believe the Pacific Railroad to be a national and political and military necessity," he ranted, as he had at Virginia City and other mining towns. "I believe that there should be a railroad binding this great continent together with its iron bands. It is riveted and banded together now by mountain and river and plain, upon which are written, 'What God hath joined together, let no man put asunder.' . . . When we have a Pacific Railroad opening to this vast interior region . . . it will pay back to our national treasury far more than the bonus which may be given to aid in the construction; it will add to our national wealth, beside being a bond of union firm as the eternal hills."

So impressed were his listeners that they promptly voted to scratch Illinoistown from the map and rename the town "Colfax." Endorsement from a national figure like the Honorable Speaker added real spirit among laborers handling the drills, shovels and pickaxes. Crocker took advantage of it. He went up and down the road, as he asserted, "like a mad bull, stopping along wherever there was anything going amiss and raising Old Nick with the boys that were not up to time. It put everybody on the alert and kept them right up to their work; and it did good, because everybody was afraid, and when I came along they were all hard at work, I can tell you."

But Charley had his troubles too. Leland and Mark were now providing him with ample funds and Huntington was keeping up a steady flow of equipment from the East. Labor was his nightmare. Regardless of the number of times California and Nevada towns were scoured, the agents couldn't produce enough men. He was desperate. Transporting husky Irishmen and Italians all the way around the Horn was out of the question; the expense would be prohibitive. Employing gangs of Mexicans was proposed. Impatiently he discarded that; he was all too familiar with their indolent habits.

The State was flooded with cheap Chinese labor, handy men engaged in light housework, gardening, cooking, laundering. He had an extravagant idea that they might be fitted in somewhere. His partners, foremen, supervisors, straw bosses—everyone he queried—either scoffed or laughed. "You're not thinking of it seriously, are you?" they asked. He was. They wanted nothing to do with Orientals—men totally lacking the natural physique and stamina needed for mountain work. Even when he pointed out that their ancestors had built some rather famous walls, they were unimpressed.

Nevertheless, Charley had his way. He brought in fifty coolies, on trial, and in less than a week supervisors were begging for more like them. Another gang of fifty was hired. Then they came by hundreds and thousands. They were the most efficient, adaptable, tireless workers he had, and available in unlimited numbers; willing to work for a dollar a day and provide their own food and quarters.

When San Francisco and the valley towns began to run out of Chinese, agents were dispatched to Canton for more. By the fall of 1865, Crocker had 7,000 of them on his payroll, and before he was through a total of almost 12,000. Everyone from Stanford down to the lowest American apprentice was delighted, for chances were that the apprentice got an advancement under the new order and became foreman of a gang of coolies at twice his previous wage.

In the weirdest assortment of hovels ever attached to a big construction job, the Orientals made themselves at home. They lived in individual dugouts and caves along the tracks, in kennel-sized hutches made of rocks or shakes, in tiny huts and shanties thrown together from discarded lumber and packing boxes; and they were the healthiest, happiest toilers on the line. Each compound had its cook and makeshift kitchen to provide a diet of rice, fish and tea. Pots, kegs and barrels of well-brewed tea accompanied the little men wherever they worked.

Decked out in basket hats, blue blouses and flapping pantaloons, "Crocker's pets" swarmed along the Central Pacific right of way. At handling horses or teams they were useless, but with baskets and wheelbarrows, picks and spades they were capable of completing an assignment in less time than it took white men to do the same with horsepower and mechanical equipment. Crocker never could have put his line over the mountains without them.

End-of-track remained at Colfax that fall, while Crocker's 7,000 pets, 2,500 whites and 600 teams worked ahead, grading, trestling, bridging, tunneling. Across one great gorge slowly rose a curving trestle 1,100 feet long. Beyond were the awesome slopes of Cape Horn, a precipice so sheer that there was not a toe hold on it. The road had to be built into that cliff. Squads of laborers, yellow and white, were suspended by ropes, to chisel, hack and blast a shelf into the solid granite, while swaying in the wind 2,500 feet above the roaring American River.

Steadily gaining height, the trail edged past old mining camps like Gold Run, Red Dog, You Bet and Little York. In May 1866 the first train steamed across the giant trestle and wound precariously along the shelf blasted into Cape Horn. The eve of Fourth of July was celebrated in Dutch Flat, and Americans took the next day off for a grand flatcar excursion to Sacramento, but while they were watching the bands parade down J Street, industrious Chinese were blasting the heading out of a 508-foot tunnel under Grizzly Hill, ten miles beyond Dutch Flat. That, suggested Crocker, ought to squelch the talk of Stanford's "Swindle."

The Flat immediately became the new supply terminal, with its mountainous piles of iron and acres of timber and ties. Alongside it, went up another labor camp including a thousand new oddities in huts and shanties. Three freight and passenger trains from Sacramento made daily runs to connect with the stagecoaches for Nevada and points east. Dutch Flat was end-of-track for regular transportation service, but the real end-of-track seldom remained the same for two consecutive days.

The heavy construction train set the pace, shuttling constantly between the supply base and the foremost point on the line. One load carried blasting powder, timber for a trestle, tools and concrete to be hauled by teams miles ahead. The next was heaped with rails and fastenings to be transferred to the low track cars which gangs of coolies pushed forward by hand, as soon as a new length of rail was secured to the ties.

Everything had to be planned far into the future. Bridges had to be ready for track at the right time, trestles built, grading and ballasting done, fills prepared, trees cut, stumps blasted, ground grubbed. Each step depended on another. An error in the schedule, a delay in delivery, could hold up a thousand men for hours or days.

And as the railroad was pushed eastward, stations had to be constructed, water towers erected, sidings installed, telegraph lines strung, and sawmills for ties and timber set up. Crocker had a host of bosses, field superintendents and department supervisors to tend to the details, but ultimately the responsibility was his, and he wasn't one to overlook any of the details.

It took the rest of the summer and fall to reach Cisco, fifteen miles from Dutch Flat and close to 6,000 feet in altitude. Snow was already deep on the ground when the last track was spiked on November 24th, 1866. Crocker would have been the last person to conjecture that this point, fourteen miles from the summit, would stand as the terminus of the road for nine months. He knew that there was some tedious, troublesome work ahead, was fully aware of the fifteen tunnels shown on the engineer's maps—including one at the summit, almost a third of a mile long. He had anticipated that weather might create some tough complications as they approached the crest, but the most chronic pessimist would have failed to anticipate such a winter as suddenly gripped the High Sierra.

When it started snowing early in October, no one was particularly troubled. Get winter over with before Christmas, was Crocker's ambition; let it snow and let it melt. It didn't melt. The snow kept coming. By December the slopes east of Cisco were buried under fifteen feet.

Even with that formidable blanket to contend with, Crocker refused to give up. Bundled in furs from ears to ankles, he continued to patrol the line, though half his army of nine thousand were employed in nothing but shoveling snow. By working in shifts around the clock, they managed for a few weeks to keep enough short stretches open so that the work could go on, after a fashion. Then plows couldn't combat the monstrous drifts that formed on the road below Cisco, and hundreds of men had to be taken off construction to help dig out the trains and plows.

Finally, in January, Charley was compelled to yield. It was impossible to keep the paths open between the camps and the line. Where nothing else could defeat him, snow had succeeded. He divided his men into three groups, sent one half-frozen contingent down to Sacramento to thaw out, another over the mountains to start grading along the Truckee River, and assigned the third to tunnel work deep underground. But reaching the granite faces of the cliffs was a considerable undertaking in itself. Under forty-foot drifts, tunnels had to be cut for distances of a hundred feet or more. All winter and into the spring, 3,000 men lived like moles, tramping from work to living quarters in their burrows deep under the snow.

With the first wet storm, the horrors of avalanche were added to the miserable existence. The only warning was the dull crunch, followed in an instant by the engulfing tidal wave of white. A work squad that had ventured into the open was swept away; a bunkhouse was enveloped; an entire camp was sent catapulting down the mountain beyond any hope of rescue. Frozen victims, still clutching shovels and picks, were uncovered in the spring.

The thunderous detonations of blasts in the tunnels were in part responsible for the slides. So great was the threat of complete annihilation at Donner Peak tunnel that the work had to be stopped, but elsewhere the dangers were taken in stride. To speed up excavation on the 1,659-foot length of Summit tunnel, a shaft was sunk at the halfway point. Working on twelve-hour shifts, coolies drilled and blasted both ways from the middle, as well as at the ends; yet the rock was so hard that the advance on the four fronts was seldom more than eight or nine inches a day.

An incredible nine feet of snow fell in a single storm, and even in the face of that disaster the road to Cisco was kept open. Two engines behind the snowplows couldn't buck the drifts; four were tried; six; finally twelve. Week after week through the winter the procession of plows thrust up and down the tracks. Regardless of expense, the line had to be kept running. Closing down could spell the end of the Central Pacific. Adversaries had been waiting for this kind of catastrophe. Halting trains for a day would be interpreted as acknowledgment of defeat.

While the Chinese were advancing by inches on Summit tunnel, word kept coming through from Nebraska that the Irish on Union Pacific were doing a mile a day. It was too much for Charley to stand. His 3,000 men slaving away in the Truckee River canyons needed equipment, and the only way to supply it was by sled—a distance of twenty-four miles.

He rounded up hundreds of ox teams and had scores of runners shaped from split logs. Onto the runners were loaded rails, ties, fastenings, forty freight cars, three locomotives; and in one of the most fantastic transportation feats in history, these tons of massive bulk were hauled to the summit from Cisco, across the mountains in snow eighteen-feet deep on the level, forty to sixty feet in drifts, and down the east slopes to the open country around Donner Lake, where they were transferred to mud skids and logrollers and dragged four more miles to Truckee. Properly equipped and unhampered by snow, the forces on the Nevada side could at last make some progress to brag about.

With the first break of spring, the gangs dismissed for the winter were recalled. For weeks their principal occupation was shoveling snow. Sixty-foot drifts had to be cleared to get down to cuts and gradings, and much of that accumulation had to be pitched from pile to pile a half dozen times before it could be heaved over a cliff. The drifts were so solid that the sun of June, July and August failed to thaw them. Off and on, men were shoveling snow during the whole summer of 1867.

Though end-of-track remained at Cisco many months, cutting, grading and filling were completed miles beyond, and when the last heading of Summit tunnel was pierced in August, track laying proceeded at a frantic pace. By late summer the first locomotive crossed the divide, fourteen miles from Cisco, saluted Nevada on the horizon, and eased two miles down the eastern slope. In the Truckee region below, a twenty-four-mile stretch already reached across the State line. The gap between the two ends-of-track was only seven miles.

A lone tramper who ventured over the mountain during the peak of activity that year was astonished at the sight. "Twelve miles of delving men!" he exclaimed. "Massive stone culverts hanging on the steep slopes of granite mountains, a constant succession of blasts with their grand reverberations, a granite roadway through tunnel and cut, and over fill; an immense serpent whose convolutions rest on mountain spines and bridge deep ravines!

"Coming from perpetual summer, the first objects to attract the attention of a climatologist were patches of snow. Snow! The idea was quickly brought home by the sight of hard-working Mongolians in thick coats with mittens and tippets, of buckets fringed with ice, cuts gemmed with icicles. . . . Here and there among the moss-covered trees bordering the cuts were thousands of hewn tamarack ties ready to take their places on the road. I walked along a granite cut where Chinamen were as thick as bees—where a score and a half of carts and two hundred and fifty men were working crowded together in a space of two hundred fifty feet. From its lower side one could look down a thousand feet—a wall of rock on one side and empty space on the other.

"The loud, sharp blasts, as of large-rifled guns seem to crack the very mountains. . . . An immense broadside cleared a little of the shell from the mountainside, transforming a goat's path to a way for the iron steed. In one blast, three thousand tons of granite were torn away. I observed one rock measuring seventy tons, a third of a mile away, while another weighing two hundred and forty pounds was thrown a distance of two-thirds of a mile.

"A thousand feet beneath me I saw the 'mountain schooners'

each drawn by twelve mules, their bells tolling the knell and their wheels creaking the dirge of their last year's labor on this route."

Crocker's "pets" were indeed hurrying along the day of doom for the toll-road caravans. The need for haste was urgent: the Union Pacific was already in the Black Hills of Wyoming. Along the Upper Truckee the tracks were building both ways. Another winter almost as severe as the one of 1866-67 had to be faced, and it was now clear that thirty-seven of the forty miles of rail across the heights would have to be roofed with sheds and galleries, at a cost of from $10,000 to $30,000 a mile. But these were minor undertakings. The end was in sight.

Already the *Overland Monthly*, in San Francisco, was crowing that the railroad was "the greatest work of the age. Even the Suez Canal, which will change the front of Europe and divert the course of the commerce of half the world, is not to be compared with it." And for San Francisco, the city that was so reluctant to back the Central Pacific, the *Overland* summed up the extent of her inevitable benefits and asked rhetorically: "Is it too much to say that this city of ours must become the first city on the continent, and is it too much to say that the first city of the continent must ultimately be the first city of the world?"

On June 15th, 1868, when the last mountain gap was bridged, the significance of the event was all but overlooked, for the tracks then ran beyond Reno, and Crocker was out in the Nevada desert racing eastward, far more interested in where the wedding of Central Pacific and Union Pacific would take place than in his sensational triumph over the Sierra.

The marriage came off at Promontory, Utah, on May 10th, 1869. By then the snowsheds were nearly completed, trains were running on schedule over the mountains, the Big Four of little Sacramento were well on their way toward becoming multimillionaires, and the country was whistling Henry Clay Work's new tune, "Crossing the Grand Sierras":

" 'Neath timbered roofs unending, from winter snows defending,
  Through canyons wild descending, to the city of the plain,

We leave the scenes terrific; we pass the field prolific
And view the broad Pacific, the Golden-gated Main!

    We sing a wondrous story, no nation sang before!
    A continental chorus that echoes either shore!
    We sang it on the summit! We sing it on the plain!
    We've climbed the Grand Sierras
    With the Lightning Palace Train—
    With the Lightning! The Lightning! The Lightning Palace Train."

IX

THEY THOUGHT THE TREES
WOULD LAST FOREVER

Uncle Sam was very generous in granting fringe benefits to
the Central Pacific. Along with a broad right of way and the
acreage in public lands went authority to take earth, stone,
timber or any other material useful in building a railroad and
telegraph line. The timber was most important. Great had been

the greed for lumber; trees were cut unsparingly and ruthlessly —millions of them.

For the stretch between Sacramento and the summit, redwood from the Coast Range was requisitioned, but from the crest on—all the way to Utah—the Sierra supplied the lumber. The demand was insatiable. Some 2,500 ties were required for every mile. Telegraph poles were cut by tens of thousands. Inordinate quantities of lumber were needed for trestles and bridges. Secret Town trestle, for example, was nearly a quarter of a mile long and ninety feet high, a veritable fabric of four-by-sixes, and there were scores of other viaducts built with the same lavish use of lumber.

Miles of tunnels had to be lined, not with ordinary boards, but with planks five inches thick and twelve wide, supported by beams of much heavier stuff. Into the $2,000,000 complex of snowsheds, resembling a hay barn 37 miles long, carpenters fitted 65,000,000 board feet of lumber—so much lumber that it took 900 tons of nails, spikes and bolts just to hold it together.

Then coincidental with all this railroad construction was the building of towns and cities on the eastern edge of the mountains, to accommodate the Nevada silver strikes. The hills there were barren; the Sierra was the nearest source of timber supply. Millionaire miners wanted vast quantities of lumber for their palatial residences, their gambling halls and opera houses. More than that, miles of underground shafts and tunnels had to be lined with wood sturdier than even that of the rail subways.

When William H. Brewer of the State Geological Survey took a field trip into the Gould and Curry Mine at Virginia City, he was more astonished at the lumber hidden in the depths than at the silver. "It requires great skill to keep the sides from caving in," he noted. "The timbering is unlike anything I have ever seen. Stout timbers, a foot square, in short pieces five- to seven-feet long, placed in a peculiar manner, run entirely across the mine in every direction, further strengthened by braces where the pressure is greatest. Yet at times these timbers are crushed as if they were but straws."

Between railroad and mining interests, the competition for products of the Sierra forests was keen. While Charley Crocker was constructing his line, 600,000,000 board feet were being buried underground in Nevada—enough to build a city of six-room houses for 150,000 people. Both had to depend on cordwood from the mountains, too, for locomotive fuel, household fuel and steam-engine fuel. The Central Pacific boilers were stoked all the way to Ogden on Sierra pine, and in a few years the hoisting works and mills of the Comstock mines accounted for consumption of 2,000,000 cords.

Before the gold rush and the railroad, there hadn't been much call for lumber in the West. California wasn't lumber-minded. The Spaniards and Mexicans preferred adobe architecture. In fact, the supply of sawed wood was so short that the first frame houses in Monterey were built of eucalyptus boards shipped from Australia, and a few San Franciscans boasted of living in homes made of pine transported 9,000 miles around South America from Penobscot Bay, Maine.

In those years Marin County, the peninsula north of the Golden Gate, was one great gorgeous expanse of redwood forest, and there on Bodega Bay, California's first sawmill went into operation in the 1820's. It was another *first* for the Russians: when the seal hunting, for which they had invaded the Bay region, played out, they turned to lumbering. But the operation was short-lived. They sold out to John Sutter. Yet when the General was digging his famed gold-bearing mill-race at Coloma in 1848, the mill for which the water was intended was only the third since the American occupation. For three or four years after the tidal wave of immigration began, the supply of lumber was so limited that more people were living in canvas tents and temporary shelters than in frame houses.

By 1855, however, Yankees had as many as eighty mills buzzing around the State, and within five more years that number was quadrupled—practically all of them in the redwood country or on the western Sierra foothills. Not until Crocker and the Comstock Lode got into the headlines were the forests of the

High Sierra invaded rapaciously. Then, as if the devil himself had ordered annihílation of the woodlands, lumbermen went after the tall timber.

Where there had been sylvan silence since the beginning of time, "the woods of the Sierra suddenly rang with the strokes of axmen," observed a poet-realist. "The streams were bordered with camps of lumbermen and choked with floating logs. At one place on the Truckee River twenty-five sawmills went into operation. The forest solitudes of the Sierra thundered to the roar of falling trees."

Fifteen thousand railroad laborers raised unholy havoc with mountain scenery, but it was a mere surface scratching compared to the devastation of the loggers. In a few short years the lumbermen created an industry more overwhelming than all the gold business of California and the silver business of Nevada combined.

The assault of the Sierra timberlands was only a flank engagement in a portentous nationwide campaign against the great forests. The lumber barons were the *generalissimos*—speculators who bought up gigantic tracts of virgin woods, furnished capital for the conquest and did the necessary political wangling far from the front; their field commanders and lieutenants were the lumbermen who set up the mills, recruited loggers and took most of the rap from citizens who objected to the spoilation; the sergeants and companions-at-arms were rugged French Canadians and Yankees from Maine—veterans of the New England wars of the woods.

While the overlanders and forty-niners were trudging West, the loggers were advancing, too, over a slightly different route. Having let light into the forests Down East and along the headwaters of the Connecticut River, they moved on across New York and Pennsylvania into the lake country of Michigan, Minnesota and Wisconsin. Streams of them headed for the big stands of the Northwest and California. A few were caught up in the surge leading to the gold fields, but, for the most part, the arrival of the loggers on the Coast at the right moment was historic accident.

Into the lumber camps of the Sierra the men from Maine and French Canada transplanted the rudiments of their trade, as they had known it back East. They did have to make adjustments to a different climate, to longer logs and steeper terrain. They doffed their mackinaws and woolens and substituted waterproof cottons—"tin pants." In the East, winter had been their big season; in the Sierra, where the deep snows stalled everything, it was a long layoff.

And somehow in the transition from Maine to California, the lingo of lumbering had suffered a number of disrespectful alterations. For instance, where trees were chopped and sawed in Maine, they were "felled" and "bucked" in the West; collective bunks in the lumber camps were "muzzle-loaders," greenhorns were "hoosiers," cookhouse assistants, "flunkies," and oxen, "bulls." But aside from such superficial changes, the job was pretty much the same.

Distance had inspired no improvement in living quarters or camp fare. The bunkhouse for a hundred or more was one long cavernous room with a huge stove in the center, a continuous two-tiered "muzzle-loader," mattressed with hay or spruce boughs running the length of the room on two sides, and a board bench, known everywhere as the "deacon seat," extending from one side to the other. Into this bunkhouse were compressed more indelicate noises, odors and ribaldry than could possibly be forced into even the crew's quarters of a tramp steamer.

The cookhouse was a structure on the same order, incorporating a central range, rough pine tables, covered with oilcloth in the fancier establishments, backless benches for seats. And the menu served there was identical to the Maine diet: salt pork, beans, bread and molasses, dried apples, flapjacks, and a potent black brew politely called "tea."

A corpulent male cook reigned supreme in this department. He usually had a few flunkies from China, but he too came from Maine and brought with him the time-honored tradition of silence in the cookhouse—a tradition stronger than any written regulation. The cook enforced it. Experience had shown that exception would be taken at a loggers' table to the most innocuous remark; disagreement led to argument, argument to doubled fists, fists to a free-for-all. So the rule of silence prevailed, and any cook worth his salt unhesitatingly slapped a bruiser off his bench for so much as commending the brown bread or prophesying a shower.

The entire logging setup was geared to oxpower. The bulls were indispensable. As in Maine, they snaked the logs out of the woods, dragged them down the skidways, trucked them to mill and often delivered the finished lumber to the customer. Without them loggers and lumbermen would have been out of business.

On the job they were accosted with all the profanity that ever crept into Christian and satanic dialects; they were threatened and tongue-lashed unmercifully, and touched occasionally with the business end of a goadstick. But off duty they were pampered like city slickers, stabled in better quarters than were the loggers, petted, groomed, guarded and fed the best provender grown in the Sacramento Valley. With three, four, six yoke to a truck, depending on the job, and a dozen or twenty trucks attached to a fair-sized logging camp, the oxen often had numerical superiority as well as status. They even determined the work calendar, and their drivers were the kings of the roost.

"We commenced logging in the spring as soon as snow permitted us to bring in the cattle," recalled an old-timer, "and worked until snow drove them out in the fall. Cattle were worth from $100 to $125, and we combed California for good stuff. All the drivers came from Maine or Canada. They got $125 a month, against $100 for swampers and $75 for others. To be good bull drivers men had also to be good loggers; ordinary drivers weren't worth any wage. I once bought fifty head of cattle. A man appealed for the job of driver. I told him to deliver the bulls and he could get the work. He delivered them all right, but when we took him to Sugar Loaf Mountain and told him to snake a tree down the mountain, he took one look at the skid road and left camp without bothering to wait for a meal."

Skid roads were another western logging innovation to which Maine Yankees had to adjust themselves. Eastern timber was small enough to be dragged over almost any lay of land, given some snow and enough animal power, but massive western butts would settle into soft soil for keeps; twenty yoke of oxen couldn't haul them out. The answer was a corduroy road job that resembled a railroad bed with widely spaced ties and no track.

Behind six or eight yoke of oxen, huge logs were rolled onto the skidway, butt to butt, and loosely linked together to form a train. The skid greaser ran a short distance ahead to splash water on the runway, and a procession was ready to start down the mountain. With a whoop and hullaballoo of "gee-hawing" that could be heard from Tahoe to Carson City, the bull driver went into action.

The oxen leaned, chains clanked, ox yokes wailed. Urged on by the blast of profane commands from their master, the animals strained forward and the logs rumbled and rolled behind. Like a multijointed dragon, the train slithered down the slope; driver walking abreast of the bulls, never faltering in his steady outpouring of curses and encouragement.

And as if the scene called for a touch of the ridiculous, in the short space between the foremost log and the hindquarters of the rear oxen, tripped the skid greaser, spilling water from his bucket and dipper to lubricate the rails, dashing ahead from time to time to refill the pail from the barrels spaced along the trail. For reasons known only to the boss loggers, this job usually fell to a coolie. Dressed in his broadbrimmed basket hat, and going at the task as though the destiny of the logs depended solely upon him, he could turn the tense action into a ritual of comedy.

"Nimbly as a goat," described a witness, "the Chinaman skips around and down the precipitous corners as the logs descend, flinging water here and there, buckets suspended on a shoulder stick, irrigating the skid to ease the downward trip of the logs. And should a break in the linked logs occur, he will gesticulate and swear in evilly excellent English for three steady minutes."

The keenest excitement came on the steep slopes, when the tons of logs started sliding of their own accord, picked up momentum, and leaving behind a trail of smoke from the friction on the skids, threatened to overtake the oxen. Then it was that the skid greaser's nimbleness was put to the test. Come what might, he had to keep the trail wet, and at the same time avoid getting tangled up in the hoofs ahead or bumped by the logs behind.

In a frenzy of motion, he danced down the skidway casting water to left and right, a loose, destructive draw chain clanging about his ankles, logs thundering behind, oxen galloping in front, heedless of the abusive stream of oratory pouring from the bull driver; now addressed as much at him and the logs as at the charging oxen. So effective was the profanity that no record of a train of logs running down greaser and oxen ever found its way into the literature of Sierra logging.

Getting the logs out of the high country was the big problem of the lumbermen. The margin of profit was drastically reduced when a company had to construct a fifty-mile network of winding roads and precipitous skidways before going into efficient production. At best the ox teams were slow and cumbrous.

To speed up delivery of timber, all manner of ingenious systems were tried. At the height of the gold rush around Placerville, vast quantities of lumber were needed for building flumes and canals to bring water into mining towns like Ringgold, Diamond Springs, Missouri Flat and Eldorado City. The nearest timber was on almost inaccessible slopes along the north branch of the Cosumnes River. Miners pooled their ideas and funds, and came up with a funicular railroad that scaled the forty-five degree hillside near Sly Park.

Somewhat to the surprise of the builders, it worked. A log-pond station at the top was fondly named "Hypo"; the lumberyard at the bottom "Depot." With a screeching of cable and the roar of wheels, a great car loaded high with logs careened down one track while the "empty" shot up the other. But the ascending car was seldom empty. Citizens placed such confidence in their invention that they entrusted their lives to it and stood in line for the two-minute upgrade rocket ride from Depot to Hypo, even though it meant climbing down on foot. That tramway set a precedent; thereafter any carrier devised for conveying timber doubled as a roller coaster.

In the East, spring log drives down the rivers had solved major transportation problems, but few of the Sierra streams could be adapted to that system. The canyons were narrow and winding, and sheltered too many snags. The East Carson River, however, filled the bill, and soon became the western counterpart of the Kennebec, though lumbermen quickly learned that flood season wasn't the proper time to trigger a drive; at high water, cross currents would sweep half the cutting onto overflowed swamps and flats where it could never be retrieved. The moment to set off the drive was just after the big thaw that took most of the snow off the mountain—*after* the spring flood when the white water was beginning to recede. Then "let 'er go."

Far back into the mountains, along the high banks of the main river and a dozen tributaries, the loggers stood ready, and as the hooted signal was relayed downstream, trip logs were released and simultaneously enormous piles rumbled into the water. French Canadians and Piute Indians were the drivers, deftly racing across the flotilla, prodding a log away from an obstruction here, breaking loose a jam in the making there, thrusting along a tie-up on the shore, keeping everything in motion: the wood had to be kept moving and moving fast while the flow lasted.

Booms stretched across sloughs and inlets helped; and loggers stationed at strategic points along the shores with poles and peavies struggled with grounded sticks. If the water and the timing were exactly right, the unbroken flow of logs passed down-river, huddled in a channel, covering the surface for fifty miles or more—100,000 cords of wood in one stupendous disgorgement, mixed with logs that would saw into millions upon millions of board feet. It was the most spectacular sight the Carson country ever knew.

But snaking the timber to the river banks, conveying it directly to mills where there were no streams for drives, or carting it over ground too irregular for skid roads was still the slow, expensive part of a logging operation. Complete dependence on the ox truck was what made lumbering so arduous.

In 1867, when Crocker was putting on the pressure for more lumber, Truckee loggers began working on the idea of a chute rig—a natural refinement of the skid road. Their solution was to turn the skid-road logs sideways, fix two parallel strings of them a couple of feet apart with a ground skid embedded between. This formed a rough gutter, and if it were greased well, the logs ought to slide down a mountainside on their own.

It was an immediate success—the greatest innovation yet. The logs plummeted down at a terrifying velocity. Within weeks, lumbermen all over the Sierra were building chutes. From lengths of a few hundred yards, they were extended into a half mile and miles. If carefully engineered, sweeping curves could be worked into the track, and logs might be self-propelled down these chutes for any distance. The speed-up in lumbering operations was remarkable. From the mountains above every lumber center came a steady stream of mighty monsters bowling down the rails at a hundred miles an hour, stirring up clouds of dust and leaving in their wake a cometlike tail of smoke—a treacherous menace to traffic on the highways they crossed.

The chutes of the Truckee Lumber Company were pictured as the wonders of the region. "The mountain tops are vast forests of the choicest trees," expounded an enthralled tourist. "Chutes extend from the tops to the river, and down these the logs glide with such rapidity as to leave a train of fire and smoke, caused by the friction on the bark against the sides. One of these chutes came very near having a tragic history. A log came rushing down just as a carriage containing two gentlemen was crossing the chute. The gentlemen saw the descending monster in time to spring from their seats, but the horses and carriage were crushed in a twinkling."

Many were the accidents caused by these infernal torpedoes of pine and fir. But the logs weren't to be stopped. Sentries were posted at crossings; roads were rerouted; overpasses and underpasses constructed. Traffic be damned, timber kept roaring down faster than anything in the history of chopping.

There had to be a pond or river at the foot of the slide to receive the logs, and they belly-flopped into the water one after another with reports that sounded like a bombardment, and splashings that hurled spray a hundred feet into the air. Occasionally one of them would leap the tracks and plummet into the woods with force enough to tear a swath through the forest for fifty yards. But the tendency to plunge off the chute wasn't enough to discourage daredevil loggers and youngsters from riding them. The most exciting sport known to a generation of Sierra madcaps was riding the logs down the mountains and getting a gratuitous dip at the end of the jaunt.

Then before the novelty of chutes and chute riding had worn off, still another innovation in rapid transit made its appearance. To compensate for nature's oversight in not providing adequate rivers for log drives, waterways had to be created—in the form of flumes. Probably the lumber flumes were merely an expansion of the aqueduct plan that gold towns had for bringing in great volumes of water for hydraulic mining. In any case, they were on the same order.

These mine aqueducts—little more than circuitous wooden troughs—meandered for miles from dry diggings back to mountain headwaters. The big ones spanned canyons on scaffolds higher than the monumental trestles of the Central Pacific, cut through tunnels, took a zigzag course along the flanks of cliffs. The little ones were less ambitious, as a typical Placerville contraption was described—"built, or rather hung, upon rocks; a prop here, a packing there and a brace yonder; here a sawed-off tree formed a post; there a rock formed a stay, while the water rushed and leaped on, on down."

By eliminating some of the curves and making a more substantial supporting frame, the lumbermen would have a water-way, which—they conjectured—would practically put the bull drivers out of business. The advantage of the flume was that it could carry logs or lumber at a comparatively slight incline, and mounted on trestles, could shoot its cargo across gulches and canyons that had never before been traversed by logging traffic. As long as the slant was continuous, adjustment could be made to any kind of topography. Moreover, amazingly little water was required to keep the logs afloat and moving.

For greatest economy of water, most of the flumes were V-shaped, a right angle at the bottom and a wide, three-foot flare at the top, broad enough to hold any ordinary log. Built of two-inch plank, up to thirty inches wide, they were sturdy and reasonably watertight. The stream gushed down the flume at what seemed like half the speed of gravity, and a log swept down even faster, bathed in a cascade of spray. Lumbermen claimed that a log always beat the water to the flat runway at the bottom and had to pause there to wait for the water to catch up. There were short runs and long runs, flumes with straight, sheer drops of not more than a mile, and complexes of flumes with a dozen branches leading fifteen miles from a sawmill back into the tall timber.

Straddling a log for a ride down the flumes wasn't perhaps quite as dangerous a sport as going bareback down the chutes, but it was a lot wetter and, because of the trestle heights, much more thrilling. Some of the more adventurous even tried it standing up. However, as the casualty lists lengthened, management was obliged to declare the flumes off limit. That, of course, made the sport all the more attractive, and instead of embarking at a safe launching gate, it became the fashion to mount the logs from a running start at a low place along the route, where the speed of the floating logs slowed to a crawl of a mere forty or fifty miles an hour.

Keeping small boys out of the flumes was one of the more irksome chores of foremen and employees. "Superintendents shall prevent all persons from riding down the flumes," read

General Rule No. 2 of the Sierra Flume and Lumber Company. "Employees shall not be permitted to ride on any of the flumes, except to make repairs or in case of emergency where the business of the company requires someone to go quickly to the village."

But laws could go hang as far as company officials themselves were concerned. No sooner was the fifteen-mile flume of the Pacific Wood, Lumber and Fluming Company erected than two wealthy directors of the corporation, Senator James G. Fair and mine magnate James Flood, dared each other to take a voyage on it. For crew they impressed into service their logging superintendent, a blushing carpenter unfortunate enough to be standing near the take-off point in a slightly intoxicated condition, and a correspondent from the New York *Tribune* in search of an exciting yarn.

The route commanded some magnificent scenery, for it started high up on Mount Rose, north of Lake Tahoe, crossed valleys and divides on lofty trestles overlooking an expanse of forest and, in sweeping arcs, plunged down to a watery landing at Huffakers ten miles south of Reno. But once the two boats carrying the quintet were launched, the occupants lost interest in scenery—or anything else except survival. The *Tribune* journalist got the story he was looking for.

"I thought if men worth $25,000,000 or $30,000,000 apiece could afford to risk their lives, I could afford to risk mine," he conceded. "The boats were nothing more than pig troughs. Two or three stout men held ours over the flume and told us to jump in the minute it touched the water. We jumped as best we could and away we went like the wind.

"The terrors of that ride can never be blotted from memory. To ride upon the cowcatcher of an engine down a steep grade is simply exhilarating, for you know there is a wide track; but the flume has no element of safety. The grade cannot be regulated. You are wholly at the mercy of the waters. You cannot stop, you cannot lessen your speed, you have nothing to hold on to. You have only to sit still, shut your eyes, say your prayers, take all the water that comes filling your boat, wetting your feet and drenching you like a plunge through the surf and wait for eternity. Compare it to riding down an old-fashioned eaves trough at an angle of forty-five degrees hanging in mid-air without support of roof or house, and extending a distance of fifteen miles.

"At the heaviest grades the water came in so furiously that it was impossible to see where we were going or what was ahead of us. When the water would enable me to look ahead, I could see the trestle here and there for miles, so small and narrow and apparently so fragile that I could compare it to a chalk mark upon which, high in the air, I was running at a rate unknown upon railroads.

"We had been rushing down at a pretty lively rate of speed when the boat suddenly struck something in the bow; a nail or lodged stick of wood. What was the effect? The red-faced carpenter was sent whirling into the flume ten feet ahead. Fair was precipitated on his face, and I found a soft lodgement on Fair's back. But in a second's time, Fair, himself a powerful man, had the carpenter by the scruff of the neck, and had pulled him into the boat. I did not know at this time that Fair had crushed his fingers between the boat and the flume.

"The worst place had very near forty-five degrees inclination. In looking out before we reached it, I thought the only way to get to the bottom was to fall. It seemed as if I would suffocate from the spray. If the truth be spoken, I was scared almost out of reason, but if I was on my way to eternity I wanted to know how fast I went. Every object I placed my eyes on was gone before I could clearly see what it was. Mountains passed like visions and shadows. I felt that I did not weigh a hundred pounds.

"Although the other boat started several minutes later than we did, it was close upon us, and finally struck ours with a terrible crash. Mr. Flood was thrown upon his face and the waters flowed over him.

"This only remains to be said. We made the entire distance in less time than a railroad would take, and a portion of the distance we went faster than any railroad train ever went.

Fair said we went at least a mile a minute. We were a wet lot when we reached the terminus of the flume, and more dead than alive. The next day neither Flood nor Fair was able to leave his bed. For myself I have only the strength to say I have had enough of flumes."

Besides being difficult to navigate, the flumes were expensive to build, expensive to keep in repair and expensive to man, so before lumbermen were through ribbing the periphery of the Sierra with them, they were looking for less costly conveyances and were constructing narrow-gauge railroads into the mountains. The era of mechanization was coming in. In addition to locomotives, there were now wheezing single-cylindered donkey engines, powerful capstans and cables for doing some of the rough work; and tinkerers were playing with mechanical buckers.

Lumbering reached its heyday in the seventies and eighties, but none of the modern inventions could entirely replace the oxen. New devices for hauling and transporting merely supplemented the old. Ox trucks, skid roads and chutes were not yet dispensable.

In 1876 the general superintendent of the great Sierra Flume and Lumber Company, that could boast of all the latest mechanical improvements, was still pleading with his subordinates to favor the bulls with "good stabling, good feed, kind and humane treatment," and announced that his directors were so distressed by reports of oxen being overworked or mistreated that a hospital for the fagged-out beasts was being established at Deer Creek Meadows.

The length and accessible breadth of the Sierra was echoing with ax blows, the crashing of trees and the hoot of locomotive whistles—in the Kern River country to the south, along the Kings River, the basin of the Merced, the Tuolumne, the Truckee and the Feather. The demand for lumber was greater than ever.

Hardly had the Central Pacific snowsheds been completed when it was discovered how combustible they were. The long, slanted enclosures formed perfect chimneys. Miles of them

went up in smoke and had to be rebuilt. In mining towns, provision always seemed to be made for voluminous supplies of
water to wash gold from the hills, but never enough to extinguish perennial fires. Cities like Sonora, Columbia, Placerville
and Auburn were repeatedly swept by flames, and before the
embers had cooled, thousands of feet of fresh lumber were being delivered for a new city. On October 26th, 1875, practically
all of sprawling Virginia City disappeared in a mighty conflagration. Timber from Truckee and Tahoe rebuilt it. The demand for Sierra lumber extended farther and farther east across
Nevada, to Cheyenne and Denver. One mill in 1872 filled an
order for 10,000,000 board feet in Salt Lake City.

Meantime, the Sierra had to serve as the fuel bin of the West.
The works of the Comstock region consumed millions of cords.
Every household in Nevada, and a great many in California,
looked to the mountains for fuel. The Central Pacific counted
on cordwood from the Truckee Basin to take the locomotives
to the Rockies. So starved was the desert for both wood and
animal fodder that when one settler far out on the dry plains
was asked what he was going to do with a stack of willows, wire
grass, tules and weeds cut from a slough, he replied, "Oh, I'm
going to take it up to the railroad. If hay is high, I'll sell it for
hay; if wood is high, I'll sell it for wood."

To supply the insatiable and immediate demand for wood,
lumbermen seemed to be intent on shaving the Sierra bald. The
commerce around idyllic Lake Tahoe was typical. In 1863, a
visitor had noted: "This land is covered with colossal specimens of yellow, sugar, pitch and fir pines, which when connected with civilization on the east and west will afford stupendous fortunes for their owners. At present the timber and
lumber capabilities of the borders of Lake Tahoe seem to be
illimitable."

Tahoe had now "connected with civilization," fortunes were
being made, but at the rate the trees were being felled, the
supply no longer looked so "illimitable." A dozen immense
companies were at work there in 1875. Noisy, smoke-clouded
Glenbrook, halfway down the east shore, was the capital,

where three greedy sawmills whined day and night, and two more were going up. Carson and Tahoe Lumbering Company was constructing a narrow-gauge railroad to Spooner Summit, half the distance between Glenbrook and Carson City, and from the summit twelve miles of V-flume already carried lumber down the other side.

M. C. Gardner Company was completing a nine-mile broad-gauge railroad through Lake Valley and extending jetties and breakwaters a quarter-mile out into the lake. Fifty mariners and loggers were employed on a trio of steamers that towed rafts of logs to Glenbrook from operations at other points on the lake. Tens of thousands of acres of virgin timber were in the path of the axmen. The whole region was going sadly commercial.

The story of one lumberman was not very different from the story of twenty others. They were all crowding one another for contracts and most of them had seen the industry grow from modest family efforts into Gargantuan commerce. Jim Gardner, son of lumber baron M. C., had lived through all the stages.

"During the seventies was the heaviest period in the lumber business," he recounted. "My father was in logging for twenty-one years around the lake, and Gardner Mountain back of Tallac is named after him. They first used portable mills for all the logs cut away from the lake, such as the summit between Glenbrook and Carson, and the range east. When one piece of ground was cleared, they would move the mill and camp to the next stretch of timber, until they finally got all the timber off excepting that lying around the lake. Then was when the real logging commenced.

"They couldn't handle the lumber with mule teams fast enough, so a narrow-gauge railroad was built from Glenbrook to the summit; and from there to Carson City a flume carried the lumber and wood. It was some railroad. It had a very steep grade and took two engines for six cars of lumber, and the cars were usually covered with tourists.

"The flume dump was on the Gardner place at Carson, and I have seen as many as seventy thousand cords of wood in one pile and millions of feet of lumber of all dimensions. There were four railroad tracks and two hundred Chinese to handle the lumber. That was the way it went to market. All the timber on the east side of the lake and around Tallac went to sawmills at Glenbrook and then by rail and flume to Carson.

"After finishing the contracts on the summits around Glenbrook and Spooner's Station, my father took the big contract to cut all the timber from Rowlands to Tallac, and for twelve miles back from the lake to Myers Station on the Placerville road. It took him six years to do it. He bought a big broadgauge engine and nine flatcars; loaded the locomotive on two trucks coupled together and hauled it to Glenbrook from Carson. It took six weeks to get it fourteen miles. On straight roads they pulled it along with oxen, but when it came to short curves and the summit, they had to use powerful chain blocks. At Glenbrook the engine was transferred to barges and towed to the grove near Tallac. All of one summer was spent to get the locomotive, the cars and rails to Tallac.

"Piles were driven in the lake at the grove, which was the landing place for the logs to be dumped from the cars into the lake, and the skidway to roll them off the cars was the length of nine flatcars, and as high as the cars; so that all they had to do was knock down the iron straps which bound the logs on, and they rolled into the lake. It took ten minutes to unload the whole train. There was a man for each car, as the nine logging trucks were strung along the track for almost two miles. The breakwater held six hundred carloads and there was an average of seventy-two carloads daily. The two steamers that towed the rafts of logs across the lake to Glenbrook were the *Emerald* and the *Truckee*.

"People thought the trees would last forever—or didn't care. When a fire started in the woods, it simply burned out. If the Forest Service hadn't come along when it did, the lake would have been ruined."

The Lake Tahoe setting came very near to total destruction. Gardner was right: people didn't care very much. Imaginative agrarians even wanted to hurry along the forest destruction;

they fancied that the cleared slopes around the emerald waters could be turned into grain-producing farm land. There was scenery to spare in the Sierra—too much of it.

For a quarter of a century the popular attitude seemed to be that the wilderness was all very interesting and beautiful; it should be enjoyed while it lasted, but it had to go. Stripping the mountains of trees was inevitable. The natural laws of economy couldn't be stayed just for the sake of preserving a pretty view. Lumber was desperately needed to promote industrial progress. Progress came first.

Only here and there were disputatious voices raised. "We have been too readily inclined to suppose that all our forests are limitless in extent and inexhaustible in character," suggested the *Overland Monthly*. "This erroneous and unjustified presumption has caused us to be exceedingly prodigal. No effort has been made to economize; but a willful waste has been allowed to progress, regardless of consequences. The inroads already made into some of our redwood forests have proven that their durability is not in accordance with our fabulous estimates. When we confine ourselves to facts and figures, its fallacy is proven beyond the shadow of a doubt, and we readily understand how probable it is that these magnificent forests will soon be numbered with the things of the past."

Through the seventies, the eighties and the nineties, the mills at Glenbrook continued to turn out their millions of feet of lumber every year. In May, 1900, John Muir expressed his concern over what was happening at Lake Tahoe—a mild protest considering his usual bite. "The woods resound with the outlandish noise of loggers and choppers and screaming mills at Lake Tahoe," he wrote. "One of the lumber companies at work here has contracted with mine owners to supply 36,000,000 feet of lumber and 60,000 cords of wood this season. The destructive action of men in clearing away the forests has not as yet affected any very marked change in general views . . . but the business is being pushed so fervently from year to year, almost the entire basin must be stripped ere long of one of its most attractive features."

The sabotage at Tahoe was only a sample of the destruction common to the whole western fringe of the range. By the turn of the century people were beginning to take an appraising look; public opinion was changing; lumbermen were getting a bad reputation. No longer were alarmists and naturalists the only ones to use such phrases as "the wanton waste of the forest," "the ravaging of nature," and "the rape of the woods." The timber barons were being put on the defensive, and knew it.

In the heart of the San Joaquin basin the Madera Sugar Pine Company had the longest flume system in the whole Sierra lumber belt—a sixty-mile waterway; an extensive rail network was added in 1899, but the company didn't brag too much about it, for fear of the "rape" charge. Instead they focused propaganda on the beauty and majesty of a little plot of trees near company headquarters at Sugar Pine, which was to be preserved exactly as it stood; and put in a bid for popular sufferance by publicizing a rhapsodic description of one noble pine six feet in diameter and 200 feet tall that was to remain intact—without referring to the thousands of similar trees to be made into shingles, flooring, clapboards and joists.

The West Side Flume and Lumber Company went further in promoting public relations. It had purchased many square miles of magnificent territory on the northern edge of Yosemite—at about three dollars an acre—and built a narrow-gauge railway running for fourteen miles into the virgin forests of sugar and white pine. The company had a payroll of 1,000 men and a plant capable of turning out 40,000,000 feet of lumber a year.

The barons were frankly worried about citizen reaction to the devastation they intended to effect. So on one fine spring weekend in 1900, in a grand gesture of good will, they invited 1,200 guests from San Francisco and Tuolumne County to a forest festival. The mob was taken on a free ride over the breath-taking fourteen-mile route, treated to a luxurious outdoor collation, given a demonstration of how a ripe old tree should be felled and finally entertained at a fancy ball at Carters.

The stratagem was so successful that before the weekend was over 1,200 key California citizens had signed their names to a resolution asserting that "the exact information conveyed to us by this object lesson . . . renews our faith in the undeveloped riches of our mountain districts as one of the many opportunities of employing local capital . . . . The courage and enterprise of our hosts . . . justifies the confidence and hearty support of the citizens of our State."

Not quite so fortunate was the Duluth, Minnesota, capitalist and speculator R. P. Whiteside, who purchased some 8,000 acres adjacent to Calaveras Big Trees, and on April 1st, 1900, received title to 2,320 additional acres, including the Big Tree grove itself. Those giant sequoias were the most celebrated timber in the world. The stand had first been sighted by white men in 1841 and had since been visited by scientists, naturalists and eminent writers from every part of the world.

Seedlings from Calaveras were sprouting in English gardens. Cross sections and pie pieces of *sequoia gigantea* had been displayed in many of the capitals of the world, and the foot-thick bark of one colossal specimen had been laboriously stripped off to a height of 116 feet, shipped East and reassembled—first in New York and then in England's Crystal Palace —to convince the incredulous that such monsters actually did exist.

William Brewer visited the grove in 1861 and was fascinated. He counted ninety of the trees and lived with them for two days, counting rings and making measurements. One felled giant, he discovered, had an age of 1,255 years—"over eight hundred years old when Columbus set out on his voyage of discovery." On a single stump, twenty-four feet in diameter, a house had been built.

"The largest trees have fallen," reported Brewer. "The 'Father of the Forest' is prostrate—116 feet around it and probably 400 feet high. It lies like a wall fifteen to twenty feet high. A carriage might be driven on the trunk. One prostrate tree was hollow; it had burned out and the cavity was large enough for a man to ride through eighty feet of the trunk on horseback! . . . A tree felled a few years ago took four men twenty-seven days to get it down."

These were the trees that Whiteside planned to convert into lumber.

For nearly fifty years they had belonged to James J. Sperry, who fully appreciated their significance and repeatedly tried to sell them to the federal government for preservation. The government wasn't interested. Miffed by Washington's cold shoulder, he agreed on December 28, 1899, to sell them to Whiteside for $100,000, the new owner to take possession on the following April 1st. News of the transaction was casually leaked to the press, and the fun started. Whiteside's men were pictured sharpening their axes; in three months the giant sequoias would start falling.

The fledgling Sierra Club, presided over by John Muir, exploded. A scattering of women's societies and service clubs pledged allegiance to the cause of saving the Big Trees. On the night of January 22nd, before an audience that filled San Francisco's Metropolitan Temple, President David Starr Jordan, of Stanford University, made an impassioned appeal. He described the Calaveras grove as the noblest forest in the world and declared it was "more the duty of the nation to preserve its forests than to foster commerce."

Washington was showered with petitions from every kind of organization the Sierra Club could spur to action. Women by the hundreds pestered Congressmen with letters, telegrams and urgent requests for interviews. Venerable John Bidwell, the original discoverer of the trees and now one of California's leading spokesmen on matters political and economic, declared that "the Calaveras Big Tree Groves must be saved at all hazards. They are among the greatest wonders of the world. . . . The present havoc going on by the lumbermen and shakemen threatens, at no distant day, the entire destruction of the Sierra Nevada forests."

On the other side of the country, Senator George F. Hoar of

Massachusetts, who had received a barrage of communications from California women, sniffed: "I think the State of California ought to have intelligence and public spirit enough to save her own wonderful trees. I do not think Massachusetts would ask any help of the United States Government if *she* had them." Nevertheless, the Senator agreed to do what he could to help.

Stanford's professor-naturalist, W. R. Dudley, an articulate Sierra Club supporter, angrily suggested that "it would be only proper at this stage of the proceedings to exercise the power of eminent domain over the entire eight thousand Whiteside acres and thus expedite the capitalist's early return to Duluth."

Three weeks before the massacre of the Big Trees was scheduled to start, President McKinley signed a Congressional resolution calling for the Secretary of the Interior "at the earliest practicable date to open negotations for, and, if possible, procure . . . the lands occupied by the said grove of trees." But when negotiations were started, Whiteside's price had jumped to almost $1,000,000. The Secretary backed away.

But the clamor had been loud enough to discourage Whiteside from immediately putting his axmen to work. For decades conservationists and the Sierra Club were kept on edge, periodically threatened with the demolition of the Calaveras Grove —until the State finally followed Senator Hoar's advice and secured the trees as a public park.

Although save-the-forest campaigners weren't successful in wresting the sequoias from private ownership in 1900, the episode dramatized for the benefit of all the Sierra lumber barons the new appreciation of scenic wealth. The lumbermen were served notice that the people were not going to permit forever the indiscriminate ravaging of timberlands.

Logging railroads into the mountains lengthened and the locomotives got bigger and heavier; steam wagons that could outpull a locomotive came into fashion, then chain-rigged steamers, steam tractors with giant iron wheels, gasoline log trucks with hard-rubber tires, duplex loading machines, mechanical buckers, spar loaders, heel-boom loaders, experimental tractors with curious belts of steel grinding around forward and rear axles, caterpillars that finally replaced the bulls and all other animals, highline flyers, trucks, trucks and ever larger trucks.

Logging came of age. It was still a big, disorderly, clumsy, chaotic business, but it was efficient, scientific and not so final. The harvesting of timber wasn't done as though the forest floor was being bared for all time. The lumbermen would be coming back to these slopes for another harvest in a generation or two.

X

MOUNTAIN MEADOWS
CHURNED TO DUST

The lumbermen had to put up with a great deal of public censure, but their disfavor was slight compared to the loathing spent on the sheepmen. The most contemptuous scorn was reserved for the herders. They were shunned in the valleys, detested in the foothills, abominated in the mountains.

Clouds of low-hanging dust, spotted here and there across

the valley, were the first signs of the coming of the sheep. From a distance the clouds looked like truncated dust devils that didn't twist and rise according to natural law. Yet they weren't quite motionless. They crept ominously along the ground, advancing so slowly that the swirl of gray could take half an hour to pass a landmark.

The hill folk, the homesteaders and the ranchmen were familiar with these harbingers. Shrouded under every cloud, they knew, was a mass of 1,000—1,500—perhaps as many as 2,000 sheep. In May and early June the flocks came on like a plague, gobbling up every blade of grass, every shrub, every green thing in their path, and leaving behind a trail of churned, close-cropped turf that wouldn't turn green again until the November rains.

To anyone not connected with the business, the hobo flocks were a scourge. Their spring migration signaled the end of the lambing season and the end of the shearing in the valley corrals. After a winter on the range, they were on their way to the canyon pastures and the mountain meadows to steal a summer sustenance. En route they snipped all the greenery in sight, disrupted traffic, covered everything with a layer of dust and left behind them a slippery trail of droppings.

They advanced upon a village with a monotonous tinkling of bells, the piteous bleating of lambs and the soprano blatting of ewes, the barking of dogs and the shouts of herders: "Ho-o-o-o-o-oi, ho-o-o-o-o-oi, ho-o-o-o-oi, eo-o-o-o-o," like so many Indians on a scalping expedition.

One raucous invasion could be taken and dismissed, but half a day behind, another flock would be coming; another and another. In late spring all the thoroughfares into the Sierra, from Tehachapi to Tuolumne were clogged with half-starved sheep. They swept into the mountains from the east as well as the west, from both the Nevada side and from San Joaquin Valley.

For half a century, between the Civil War days and into the early 1900's, sheep raising was the leading agricultural nuisance of California. It was big business, an enormously profitable business in which a good season could bring a fortune; and that fortune might be doubled every third year. But it was dependent on cheap feed or on free government land, and totally dependent on public tolerance.

The Spanish padres were the first to discover the virtues of California sheep pasturage. Tending flocks was good employment for the Indians and Mexicans drawn to the mission compounds. Gay serapes, blankets and quantities of coarse woolen cloth were among the products fashioned by the proselyte craftsmen. In the heyday of mission industry, around 1825, more than a million sheep grazed on the broad acres within sight of the chapel crosses between San Diego and San Francisco, and there were close to another million on private ranches. But the wool was poor and thin. Spain had not been anxious to encourage an industry that might bring rivalry to her own exports in wool, and did little to improve the breed. Mexico did less.

With the desegregation of the missions in 1833, the flocks were utterly disintegrated. Less than a decade after that event, the padres could account for scarcely 150,000. Thousands of lean black "mustangs," so wild that they had to be herded on horseback, were driven in from Mexico. They were prolific, but they had few other commendable qualities; normally they bore twins, frequently triplets, sometimes as many as six or seven at a birth; but the wool was coarse and light, the mutton strong. Rams imported from China did not seem to better the stock.

Then, in 1853, three hundred hybrids arrived from New England, driven at the rate of seven miles a day across the plains, the desert and the mountains, by an enterprising Yankee named William Hollister. The trip took nearly a year and a half. Hollister had heard about the belly-deep grasses in the mountain range and dreamed of a fortune in farming, fatter than the fortunes of the Argonauts. And he quickly proved that there was nothing farfetched about his dream.

By ship and over the half-finished Panama Railroad, Solomon Jewett, another New Englander, brought in a second flock the following year. The business was a success from the start, and dozens of other Easterners soon entered the competition. Twelve dollars for a well-fatted mutton was a fair price at any market, while prize rams were knocked down at auction for $500 or $1,000. A sheepman who didn't make 4 per cent a month on his investment was a poor manager.

The Mexicans had raised sheep primarily for meat; the Yankees saw that the real money was going to be in wool. Cotswolds and Leicesters, as well as Merinos were brought in, and all three were crossed with those prolific Mexican mustangs. Within two decades California was supporting a $6,000,000 woolen industry. A flock almost doubled in size every year. Sheep were shorn in April and again in October, and they averaged a yield of six pounds a shearing. In 1871, 22,000,000 pounds of wool were shipped to the East or to the mills in San Francisco.

Those were the good days of sheepherding in the valleys and Sierra foothills; it was an honorable profession, and a lucrative one. There was plenty of pasturage on which grazing rights went with mere occupancy, and nobody challenged the herder who got there first. It was too good to last. Flocks were inordinately fecund. They were divided and subdivided. Still there were too many sheep for the keepers. Herders were desperately needed. The best in the world were those of the Rhone Valley and the Pyrenees, so the call went out to France, Spain and Portugal. Suddenly the sheep lands were overrun with little dark silent men who cared not a whit about land rights, prerogatives and American amenities.

For twenty-five dollars a month and the prospect of a small bonus for bringing a flock back from pasture plump and intact at the end of a season, Frenchmen and Basques, Portuguese and Mexicans took over as herdsmen. The respected owners of vast flocks relinquished their status as shepherds and became managers and magnates. They recognized that the foreigners knew more about handling sheep than they did, and left them to their own devices in the search for rich pasturage. As in the

Pyrenees and the Alps, the new herders headed for the high country.

That was when the sheepmen began to lose caste. Contempt followed the aliens wherever they went. They were joined by down-and-outers from the mines, scoundrels who needed to vanish from sight for a few months, yokels and pariahs from the East looking for an easy job. Together they brought lasting defamation upon themselves. Probably half of them were honest, competent herders, but there were enough who deliberately invaded alfalfa fields, added untended bands to their own, let campfires sweep across private property, to discredit all their fellows.

"The sheepherder is less respected than any other man, save John Chinaman," charged an unsympathetic San Francisco critic, just back from the mountains. "Who celebrates the praises of the Pacific shepherd? So bad a savor has fallen upon his business that even the word "shepherd" promises to be eliminated from conversation. A man may have broken stones for the Commonwealth; he may have presided at a political ward meeting; but if ever he falls so low as to be obliged to follow the sheep in this fat country, it would be better not to mention the matter to his acquaintances.

"Imagine our dyspeptic and red-hot generation loafing over the golden sunny hills of California after a flock of silly sheep! It is easy to see what cut of men would graduate into the business. None but the riffraff are there—vagrant miners who gamble off their wages as soon as they draw them; runaway sailors who sell their blankets for a pillowcase of biscuits and then go for two days without anything to eat; vagabond soldiers who fall asleep on their posts and let the coyotes pull away a sheep . . . college-bred men who are now gathering their mystical and melancholy crop of wild oats at the same time they watch the sheep—comrades of the wolf and the owl."

For the most part the foreigners were the professionals; the Yankee rabble the hangers-on and the helpers. Never was any other American occupation beset with such rancor. Owners themselves were disdainful of the herders, and they of their subordinates. Sheep attendants had no use for Indian shearers and the Indians hated the wool weighers and the crusty vansmen. Frenchmen despised the Portuguese and both united in common hatred of Basques. The misfits from the East scorned all the others and were scorned in turn. Then, regardless of national origin, every herder loathed those of like calling, for they were always in competition for the best feeding grounds, always exchanging misinformation on the location of mountain meadows and the shortest routes to them.

But on the night after the last of the spring shearing was done at the home ranch, all these glowering characters put aside their grievances and joined in a noisy fiesta, with too much wine, too much barbecued mutton, too many *señoritas* of uncertain virtue, too much discordant strumming of many tunes from many lands.

A herder jigged and danced until dawn, then gathered up his assorted grudges again, packed a string of burros with sacks of beans, potatoes, onions and sourdough, slabs of bacon, gallons of whisky, salt for the sheep, strychnine for the bears and coyotes, saddlebags stuffed with a miscellany of rice, garlic, sugar, coffee and raisins. He strapped on the pots and pans, a medicine chest, his bedding, tent and shotgun; picked up his long crooked staff, and was off to the Sierra with a couple of thousand sheep and a dog for company. If he was lucky, the rancher also assigned him half a dozen Mexicans to help drive the sheep to the first mountain encampment, and a disreputable assistant to stay with him for the season. Under the cloud of dust the slow race to the mountains started.

In all the company the dog was the least dispensable, for a sheepherder without his mutt was as helpless as a hack driver without reins. To be sure, there were a few recognized leaders among the flock; wethers and bellwethers, each with his own designated place at the head, middle, sides or rear, to make a closely knit animal unit; but even the most dependable leader looked to the dogs for orders, as the dogs looked to the masters for theirs.

One long-drawn-out *"Eo-o-o-o-o-o"* and the dog bounded off, running low to the ground, bringing in the flock from the right. *"Eo-o-o-o-o-o-o.* Hey, there, 'nuf. Come 'ere. 'Ere. Damn ye, 'ere. Way over there now. Whoa. Stop. Hold on. Way out. Way out. Curse ye. Come here. Out there. After them. *Eo-o-o-o-o.* Way back there. Heel 'em. *Hup, hup. Hup* there, *hup.* Way out there. 'Way round them."

But the really proficient herder kept his mouth shut on the road. He didn't need to keep singing out, for the dog at his heels understood his every motion. A lift of the crook meant one thing, a sweeping wave of the left hand another, a snap of the fingers or stamp of the heel sent the dog tearing into action. Once a herder and his dog learned to communicate, they kept up an endless sign conversation.

The idea while in transit was to keep the flock uncrowded but compact, roughly in a triangle a hundred yards at the base and about the same in length; open enough so that the young lambs wouldn't get trampled, close enough to avoid wandering and straggling. The dog sensed exactly the right formation and was as eager as his master to keep it. The tireless mutt bounded onto every stump or boulder in the path for a quick look over the mass, or, lacking such vantage points, made flying leaps in mid-run to check for signs of bunching or spreading.

On signal, an experienced dog trotted out leisurely to left or right, circling widely to bring up the farthest stragglers, but so wise were the sheep to the regimen that before he approached, they were moving back into place. A single gesture sent a collie ahead to stand in a road fork or to guard the sheer edge of a gulch down which a detachment might take it into their heads to stampede.

When a bellwether balked at an imaginary menace in the road, halting the flock and suddenly bringing the sheep together in a solid smothering panic, instantly the dog understood and charged ahead to annihilate the bogey, or even leaped upon the backs of the sheep to break up the jam, nipping at tails, making his authoritative bark heard above the bedlam of blatting. One dog could bring more order to the ranks of a thousand sheep than a squad of fleet-footed Mexicans, Indians or college-bred scamps.

Speeding coaches and lines of freighters had to be circumvented. Invariably they brought confusion, divided the flocks and inspired little stampedes—sometimes with a purpose. So hated were the sheep and the sheepherders that a driver did his level best to convey his sentiments. A herder quickly learned to ignore abuse and accept in silence the profane slander cast at him from the high wagon seats or from mounted riders. Nothing was to be gained by talking back.

"Keep 'em moving. Keep 'em moving," was the warning from every sour-faced *ranchero* en route. "There's gunshot waiting for any one of them God-damned hoofers that crosses into my orchard."

And many an evening as the herders were setting up their camp for the night at an isolated spot, with the sheep already bedded down, an irate rancher galloped up to demand who had given them the liberty of the place: "Out. Move on. Move on. Off with you."

There was no choice but to douse the fire, pull up stakes, arouse the sheep and wander on in the night to another uncertain encampment.

But the most difficult test came when the flock was finally allowed to scramble off the road into the bush on the way to the first mountain pasturage. The trail usually led along the shoulder of a canyon. Here at last was an abundance of tempting green feed. The crawling pace slackened to immobility. The sheep, half-crazed from hunger, spread out, each seeking a private forage spot and restlessly abandoning it to race for another the moment her privacy was violated.

Lambs, lost and separated from their mothers, bleated for attention, only to be ignored. The dog was everywhere at once, trying to press the wanderers back into the fold, and even the herders had to join in beating the brush to untangle sheep from chaparral pockets in which they fancied they were trapped.

A clearing farther up the mountain had to be reached before sundown. In a confusion of cussing, incessant chasing, shouting and barking, the procession somehow was pushed forward, and by nightfall a thousand sheep were quietly grazing in a lush meadow. Bone-tired, the herders gathered sticks for a campfire. The burros were unpacked and enough grub pulled out of the sacks for a lean supper. Any notion of setting up tents for the night was discarded. Before the head herder had made a last round of the sheep with his dog, the helpers were rolled in their blankets by the fire, dead to the mountain world. Next morning they were dismissed and could saunter back to the ranch at their own pace to hire out for another run.

Week by week as the snow blanket in the upper mountains disappeared, the flock was moved higher. A meadow with heavy grass a foot and a half high might last for two weeks or a month before it was cropped clean. Temporary headquarters were either a tent or a rough shed of shakes and boughs. With its campfire scullery, the arrangement was sloppy and unsanitary, or it could be as tidy as an old maid's kitchen, depending on the keeper. In the luxury of wilderness the herder and his helper might be alone with their dogs for weeks on end, content and a little crazy with the boredom—whittling for amusement, carving fancy designs on a new staff, hunting occasionally, wandering aimlessly in the hills, watching, waiting, trying to outwit the coyotes and the bears, even piping tunes on an improvised flute, as was expected of a shepherd.

Every two or three weeks there came from the outside world a donkeyload of news and beans. Great day! And the herder might not even be in camp to receive it. All manner of excuses were invented for the helper to take a trip to the valley for a newspaper or another gallon of whisky. Sourdough was baked in the Dutch oven every third day. There were ducks, grouse and squirrels for the shooting, but flapjacks and salt pork were the staples—flapjacks, salt pork and mutton stew. The stew was like leaven, with a few fresh potatoes and onions, another cut of mutton or new chunks of dough tossed into the pot every few days.

Into one of these camps stumbled Professor Joseph Le Conte in 1870, with ten famished students from the University of California. They were on a history-making jaunt across the Sierra, but at this point were exhausted and on short rations, with their food supply all but depleted. They had plenty of pocket money to purchase a sheep and had tramped far out of their way for the sole purpose of securing one.

They arrived at the camp to find the sheep unattended, the herder nowhere in sight. Their "hello-ing" came back in echoes from the mountainsides, but it failed to bring the herder. Meantime a couple of inquisitive sophomores were poking into the tent and rummaging around the scullery. Half-buried in a mound of hot coals was a kettle. The lid came off, and there was a full pot of savory stew ready for serving.

The struggle with restraining consciences was not very resolute. Within ten minutes they were scraping the bottom of the kettle, lounging in contentment and agreeing that never before had anyone created such delectable mutton stew. They were still expressing their sentiments when the herder stole up on the uninvited guests from behind. Warily he took in the compliments.

The all too cultivated apologies from the professor were superfluous. "More pleased than not," allowed the cook laconically, trying to hide his embarrassment. So long had it been since he last saw a human being, he had all but lost his gift of speech. Silently he set about preparing another supper for himself, grinning with delight that someone appreciated his cuisine. He was even too shy to refuse the bills which the professor counted out for the meal—and for another fat lamb to roast for breakfast.

"There are thousands of sheep in this region," observed Le Conte. "We expect to live on mutton until we cross the Sierra."

Such rustlers were the least concern of the sheep tenders. Miners, prospectors and mountain explorers all had an appetite for spring lamb, and they seldom went through the formality of paying cash for it. In the mountains outwitting the herders was a sport like robbing the roost at home. Any means of taking advantage of them was fair game. Appropriating a sheep was no more associated with larceny than taking a deer in season.

"Of course, we despised the sheep and the sheepmen," confessed an early Sierra Club mountaineer, "but we learned not to scorn the advent of a 'stray sheep,' which it was our bounden duty to shoot, in order to save it from a hungry bear. Thus did we prey upon the beasts of the wilderness, and send some poor bruin supperless to his lair."

Between the human and the animal predators, there was no such thing as armistice for the conscientious herder. Most persistent among the beasts were the coyotes. Just out of sight in the chaparral, they pursued the flock wherever it was driven, waiting with infinite patience to pounce on a straggler, to leap from cover when the herder was off guard, to take advantage of the moment when the dog was out of sight. They sneaked in at dawn, prowled the pasture for strays at dusk, nosed around the corral at night.

They were too wary to make a good target for a rifle. Here again the dog was the most reliable fender. A cautious old miner, turned herdsman, swore by his black bitch "Todd." "I taught her to fetch up feeble lambs in the rear of the band," he claimed, "and one evening I sent Todd back for the usual roundup. She didn't come back—didn't show up all night.

"So next morning I went looking for the dog, as well as the lambs, hardly expecting to find either, because there were coyotes all around. But there at the end of the meadow lay Todd with a pair of twins curled up against her belly, and an impudent young coyote stretched out on the ground not fifty feet away. It slunk away soon as I came up. I started to scold the dog, but she just wagged her tail. She was trying to tell me that a single lamb she could have brought back in her mouth, but two she couldn't. She knew that the coyote would snatch up the one left behind, so she just lay down and guarded both of them through the night."

Bobcats, cougars and bears took their toll, too. Of the three, the bears were the worst—audacious, dangerous creatures;

more defiant than coyotes, for once a grizzly or black bear acquired a taste for mutton, he insisted on it for a steady diet,
and invariably after catching a prize, bruin returned the following night with his nephews. Corrals had to be erected to
enclose the sheep, fires kept burning from dusk to dawn, and
the remains of sheep already mutilated by the marauders, liberally sprinkled with strychnine.

Occasionally no means of extermination proved effective.
Dogs were cowed, bonfires defied, corral walls broken down
and herders paralyzed with terror. The only recourse was to
move camp, and chances were that even then the bears would
follow.

At Yosemite Valley in August, 1869, bears made repeated
raids on a flock of sheep guarded by two Portuguese veterans—
Joe and Antone. With increasing boldness and in increasing
numbers, the bears came on night after night to crash through
the wall of the corral and slaughter mercilessly. Shotgun ammunition was exhausted. Joe and Antone had tried all the tricks
they knew to ward off the plunderers, and none of them
worked. From close scrapes with the beasts, both were panic-
stricken. With the bears it was no longer a matter of sly prey-
ing: they appeared to have decided that a dozen sheep a night
was their rightful assessment, and resented any harassment
while collecting it.

Tagged by her two cubs, a shaggy prowler descended upon
the camp early one evening just as the sheep were being
driven into the corral. Arrogantly she moved toward the flock,
without a glance at the herders. Joe made for the nearest tree.
Antone lost his head; he forgot that he was afraid. The bra-
zenness of the bear in coming by daylight was more than he
could take.

"I not going to let bears eat my sheeps before dark," he
screamed at Joe hysterically.

Raising his staff, Antone charged, and his dog charged with
him. The cubs scrambled up a tree. The brute stopped in her
tracks, unaccustomed to such human antics. Indignantly she

reared up, ready to deal with haughty little Antone in one swipe of her mighty paws.

Fire sparked her eyes, and she made a grunting noise that brought the assailant to his senses. He paused a few feet from the towering animal, then turned and fled for a tree, with the bear at his heels. But no handy tree was in sight. In a bound he leaped to the roof of their flimsy hut.

The bear rose up, clawing furiously at the eaves, threatening to join the fugitive. In mortal horror Antone cringed on the far side of the roof. He knew that the whole building would collapse under the weight of the animal, and he didn't like the thought of a wrestling match in the wreckage.

Perhaps it was the dog nipping at her shanks, perhaps the bear suspected that some kind of trap was being set for her. In disdain she snorted, lowered her bulk and made a feint at the dog. Summoning her cubs, she leisurely shuffled into the corral, snatched a sheep and made off into the woods.

That night bonfires bigger than ever kept the camp and its surroundings brilliantly lighted. But as if to demonstrate who were the real lords of Yosemite, the same marauder returned before midnight, accompanied by a great male. Fearlessly they stalked between two of the fires, broke into the corral, killed a pair of sheep and smothered ten, while the terrified shepherds watched from a treetop.

It was still August, a month before flocks were normally taken back to the valley, but at dawn Joe and Antone packed up and headed the remnants of the fold toward the lowlands.

Often sheep could be their own worst enemies, with their crazy stampedes, their smothering huddles, their taking flight at imaginary devils. Bugaboo of all the herders was the scatterbrained nature of their charges. A stone or shadow in the path could send a thousand sheep racing off in all directions. One rattlepated ewe could lead scores to disaster before a dog was able to halt the rush. Keepers had seen half a flock witlessly plunge over a Sierra cliff, after a leader had taken it into her head to make the fatal leap. They had seen thirst-crazed bands refuse to drink at a stream where men did not hesitate to fill their own canteens. To prevent crowding, a staff was often thrust across the entrance of a corral, so that the sheep would have to leap over it and move in more slowly. They had seen the comedy of sheep jumping higher and higher over the spot long after the staff had been removed.

Good, faithful herders made allowances for the character of their flocks. They learned to expect the unexpected and be ready for it. Many a shepherd developed a great affection for his wards. "There are few prettier sights than a troop of young lambs," sentimentalized an old hand who had survived the bears and the boredom and exchanged his crook for a pen. "With the true gregarious instinct of their species, they range in flocks or gangs and are fuller of life, animation, agility and grace than any mortal thing in earth.

"To see a snow-white squadron, two to three hundred strong, suddenly make a dash from a state of repose, and scamper like mad race horses along the edge of a precipitous bluff, until the wild gallop of their twinkling feet is lost in the distance! The green herder rises up from his couch on the green grass and girds his loins preparatory to going after the runaway rascals, when, *presto!* here they come again, leaping and glancing and darting and stamping, right back to the place from which they started, and suddenly stop and look with wonderful, inquiring eyes upon the astonished herder; and before he knows what to make of it, they are off on the same racket again, kicking and flinging and capering and pushing each other purposely to the edge of the bluff. There may be prettier sights in the animal world, but we have yet to see them."

An understanding of sheep wasn't anything that could be acquired. It had to be born in a shepherd. The public be damned! A good herder took pride in his calling and loved the sheep. John Muir was the exception. He took delight in judging them in terms of human frailties. He loved the mountains and hated the sheep.

Muir's prejudice undoubtedly was stimulated by the young Irishman from whom he took over his first flock. "I have tried many kinds of work," the Irish lad informed him, "but this of chasing sheep is the worst of all." He cursed the sheep for the way they roamed over the hills in disordered, discontented companies, excoriated the whole business and assured John that he had indeed chosen the wrong occupation. "All you have to do," he instructed Muir derisively, "is open the corral in the morning and run after the sheep like a coyote all day and try to keep in sight of them. They will show you the range."

The Scotsman adopted the Irish cynicism and retained it the rest of his life. To him sheep became his "mutton family," "hoofed locusts," "poor, helpless, hungry, misbegotten, semi-manufactured creatures born out of time and place, made less by God than by man." Even newborn lambs failed to arouse a spark of sympathy or to stir a protective emotion. They were merely "thick-legged, wrinkled duplicates of their mongrel, misarranged parents"—unhappy beasts "born to wretchedness and unmitigated degradation."

The conduct of the contemptible scavengers was forever interrupting his contemplation, his reading and his naps on beds of lupine and poppies. In his rapture over a dramatic sunset one evening, he had forgotten the silly sheep until he was rudely reminded of realities by their stampeding. "They galloped with a noise like thunder from the slopes and gulches," he related, "driving headlong for the center of the flock, and in a few seconds the whole eighteen hundred were squeezed and felted into a solid circular cake of mutton and wool." He warmly cussed out the flock for its reaction to a glorious sunset and lamented that it had no separate existence; the body of the flock had to contract and expand like the body of a worm; collectively its legs were like those of a centipede.

If he were pressed for a choice between loyalty to the sheep and loyalty to the animals that preyed on them, he unashamedly took the side of the predators. A sudden rushing sound and a low frightened bleating drew his attention from a Shakespearean play in which he was absorbed. Two coyotes had slipped into the flock while he was worshiping the bard. They were devouring a lamb within a hundred yards of him. He watched the intruders, observed their bushy tails, erect ears and handsome lines—"beautiful animals, cursed by man, but loved by God, their sole fault being that they are fond of mutton." Dutifully he sent his dog Fanny after them, but only to chase them back into the woods.

Again when he spotted a coyote stealing from a thicket and watching for a chance to pounce on a lamb, he felt compelled to protect the flock and frighten the intruder away, but he ruefully confessed: "I did not make allowance for his morning hunger, but almost wished I had not seen him, that he might have had a lamb in peace."

Muir's resentment was sharpened to a cutting edge when he saw his despicable flock gnawing away at whole fields of brilliant flowers in the high mountain meadows. On finding a clump of wild lilies that particularly caught his eye, he went to their defense and spent more time protecting the blossoms than protecting the sheep. "To think that sheep should be allowed in this lily meadow!" he stormed. "Except for my guarded lily gardens, almost every leaf that these hoofed locusts can reach within a radius of a mile or two from camp has been devoured. . . . On through the forest ever higher we go, a cloud of dust dimming the way, thousands of feet trampling leaves and flowers, churning the mountain meadows to dust . . . the woolly locusts . . . Poor, dusty, raggedy, famished creatures, I heartily pity them. . . . Sheep brain must surely be poor stuff. . . . To let sheep trample so divinely fine a place is barbarous."

One summer of sheepherding was all that Muir could stand. He thankfully gave up his flock to become a miller in Yosemite Valley, but he never gave up his loathing of the "hoofed locusts" and the men who tended them. In newspapers, magazines and books he launched attacks against the invaders, harping particularly on the herders' carelessness with fires.

"Our forest belts are being burned and cut down and wasted like a field of unprotected grain," he fretted. "Waste and pure destruction are taking place at a terrible rate. . . .

The ravages, however, of mill fires and mill axes are small as compared with those of the sheepmen's fires. Incredible numbers of sheep are driven to the mountain pastures every summer, and in order to make easy paths and to improve the pastures, running fires are set everywhere to burn off the old logs and underbrush.

"These fires are far more universal and destructive than would be guessed. They sweep through nearly the entire forest belt of the range from one extremity to the other. . . . Indians burn off underbrush to facilitate deer hunting. Campers of all kinds often permit fires to run, so also do millmen, but the fires of sheepmen probably form more than 90 per cent of all destructive fires that sweep the woods."

It was Muir, more than any other, who led the fight to have these mutton-chasing firebugs and the flocks driven out of the Sierra. In a small way the battle started when Yosemite was set aside as a state park in 1864, but more than thirty years passed before the sheepmen began to feel the real pinch. By then a wide block of the range had become federal forest reserve; grazing was closely restricted and rangers, detailed from army units, patrolled the hundreds of thousands of wilderness acres.

Yet laws and armed guards couldn't keep the sheep and herders out. The statutes were contested, the authority of the rangers defied. Sheep raisers were desperate: there was not enough feed in all the dry valleys of California for the millions of sheep, and grazing on irrigated lands couldn't be made to pay.

As far as the mutton and wool magnates were concerned, it had to be business as usual. Herders were assigned their flocks and encouraged to steal into the mountains as best they could—"Stay out of sight of the homesteaders. Keep yer mouth shut about where yer headin' for. Cross the line at night. The rangers don't patrol then. Pack six burros with grub, instead of four, so that your camp tender won't have to come out so often and run the chance of being spotted." Evading the rangers became a fine art.

Bells were removed from the lead sheep as the flock approached the "line." By devious routes they were driven in under cover of darkness. They openly worked their way into the reserves earlier in the season before the rangers went on duty. They struck out for more remote meadows. Spies studied the trails and schedules of rangers, and flocks were taken in piecemeal behind their backs. Ranchers budgeted funds for whisky and bribes, and the recipients co-operated in staying out of sight. By hook or crook, sheep continued to summer in the Sierra salad bowls, and John Muir continued to fight.

"Where are all the wonderful gardens you wrote so much about?" inquired an editor of *Century* magazine, whom Muir was conducting on a tour of Yosemite.

"Woe's me," the guide had to reply. "Uncountable sheep have eaten and trampled them out of existence. They have consumed every green leaf, not sparing even the young conifers. They rake and dibble the loose soil of the mountainsides for the spring floods to wash away, and at last have left the ground barren."

Muir had allies in prominent men like Professor William R. Dudley of Stanford University who went on an annual pilgrimage into the mountains. Dudley made a trip with a specific purpose in 1898. He wanted to see for himself whether or not the naturalist was exaggerating reports of the devastation. This was a bad year. It was extremely dry and new forest fires were breaking out daily. The army lads who had been patrolling the heights in previous years were off to Manila and their places were taken by inexperienced agents of the Interior Department. The Kern River region was a good one for Dudley's investigation because he knew the country well. He went there first and was appalled at what he found.

High meadows and mountain river flats, where he had previously seen high grass, had been cropped until the very sod was gone. He learned that some 200,000 sheep had swarmed over the divide through the Tule River region alone. Up to elevations of 10,000 and 12,000 feet he tramped, and nowhere could he find areas that had not been "harrowed to dust by alien hoofs." Difficult benches had been scaled and every plant or leaf devoured. Meadows wet and dry were gnawed to the ground. Open spaces showing a little grass were being guarded by French and Portuguese herders with shotguns. "No one can imagine the destruction the creatures have wrought in these, the wilds and fastnesses of our continent," he reported.

The next year a celebrated conservationist and civil engineer, Dr. Marsden Manson, who had studied areas denuded by sheep as far afield as the Caucasus, the Pyrénees, the Apennines and the Atlas Mountains, made a survey of Lake Tahoe and Yosemite regions. His summary echoed the sentiments of Professor Dudley.

"The crowding of vast herds of sheep, followed by the fires of the sheepherder have been active agents in converting vast areas into deserts," he admonished. "Descendants of the shepherds who devastated the fair land of Isabella are found at the same work in our mountain pastures, equally disregarding the laws of nature. Even in that area sacredly set aside as the Yosemite Reservation, the threat is openly made by the marauding sheepherders who have devastated Spain and Portugal, that they would burn the Government out. Where 8,000 sheep might be pastured without injury, there are 40,000. All the wealth made upon wool and mutton in the entire state since 1849 could not restore the pristine condition. If unheeded for a generation more, it will not be within the power of the human race to stay the destructive forces which have been turned loose."

In a special message to Congress on December 3rd, 1901, Roosevelt took up the theme and eloquently deplored the wanton waste of western forests—"above all by sheep." "The forest reserves must be set apart forever for the use and benefit of our people as a whole, not sacrificed to the shortsighted greed of a few."

Against such talk the sheepmen didn't stand a chance. They had always been unpopular; now they were being portrayed as renegades upsetting the economy of the West. It took years to rout the surreptitious herders, and longer still to thin out the flocks so that grass cropping complied with reasonable standards of conservation. Nearly a decade after pasturing of sheep in specified public lands of the Sierra became a criminal offense, an estimated 34,000 were still there.

But the herders slowly lost the struggle. The spring migrations were less massive, the clouds of dust less frequent. Where sheep had been numbered in tens of thousands, they were reduced to token flocks of hundreds. The enormous wool vans that had long plied between the San Joaquin Valley and the coast disappeared, and the price of a leg of lamb in the local market doubled. Mutton and wool magnates discovered that their valley ranches raised equally good cattle, grapes or tomatoes. But the break came hard.

The best breeds of sheep had come from the East, and a few of them headed back in that direction—on the hoof. The journey of Don José Jesús Lopez was only an example. His flocks were no longer welcome in the Kern River and Sequoia country north of Tehachapi, but there was still good feed in the Rockies. Sheep were wanted at Cheyenne. Don José had developed an extensive range at Fort Tejon. His whole life had been devoted to breeding finer and larger flocks. He wasn't going to see his years of labor entirely destroyed through the whim of a few nature lovers.

Off to Cheyenne he started with 10,000 of his prize animals —a trek of over 1,200 miles. With a few hired men and a wagon train he set out over the Southern Sierra, crossed the margin of the Mojave Desert and went on into Owens Valley. At Lone Pine, under the brow of Mount Whitney, he rested the flocks for a few days, then slowly crept along the Eastern Sierra foothills and crossed the White Mountains over the old Immigrant Trail to Deep Springs Valley. His troubles began there.

It was a time of drought. Water was low everywhere. A cattleman named Piper had annexed a range that stretched to the horizon, and cattlemen were notoriously loath to concede anything to a shepherd, notably watering privileges. But Piper appreciated Don José's plight; the sheep couldn't possibly survive the long march ahead without water. After a galling session of bargaining, Don José was granted permission to let his flock drink its fill at the cattle troughs. The sheep were driven to the water. The fastidious creatures sniffed and turned away. They refused to drink, despite the fact that they had passed over a mountain range, crossed a long arid stretch of sandy, alkaline plain and had not seen a stream since leaving Owens Valley.

Don José moved on, hoping to find water at Pigeon Springs, several miles ahead. There he found only a dry, mud-cracked hole. The fagged, footsore sheep were pushed on that night to Lida Valley where a reservoir had been dammed for a mine. It too was tainted. Even when sheep were shoved into the pond, they would struggle about in it, but refuse to swallow a drop.

In desperation, scouts were sent ahead with shovels to dig a puddle at a place called Stonewall, while the flock with heaving flanks and shrunken bellies took the distance at a slower pace. Halfway to Stonewall, Don José met the men returning. They reported only a dribble of seepage from cracks, nothing to dig for.

Stone Cabin, a slow journey of three days into the desert, was the next possibility. Plotting a course by the stars, they set out, traveling only at night. One hot day followed another. Huddled in heaps with heads tucked under the bellies of the nearest sufferer, the sheep lay on the scorched desert throughout the daylight hours, and at dusk struggled to their feet and were driven on.

On the third day a thirst-crazed band wandered off into the desert with Don José in pursuit. He too had been without water for twenty-four hours and was found unconscious by his men late in the afternoon. They revived him and somehow reached Stone Cabin and its well of sweet water before midnight. Silently the sheep drank. The count was still 10,000. They had traveled an incredible 130 miles without water.

Northward across Nevada and into Idaho territory the flock drifted, until they came to a ford in the Snake River. The stream was on rampage. A width of sixty feet had to be crossed and it was all white water. Moreover, the ford bordered the Bannock Reservation. Permission to cross it had to be obtained before they could proceed. Sheep and herders were at the mercy of the Indians.

The white agent in charge threw up his hands, expressed his regrets that he could not intercede and refused to take responsibility for any trouble that the Bannocks were likely to make.

Don José went directly to the Chief, presented his predicament man to man, and quickly came to terms. He was given twenty-four hours in which to pass through the Reservation; the Chief would accept two and a half dollars in tribute, and ten Indians were to be paid a dollar and a half each in silver for helping to ferry the sheep across the swollen river; the wagons would be floated over without charge.

It was a better bargain than Don José had dreamed he could strike. But on his return to the ford, he was utterly confounded to find that no less than 300 warriors had taken possession of the sheep camp and were feasting on his supplies.

The Chief raised a reassuring wolf call. Instantly 300 braves dropped the sacks they were pilfering, stripped themselves, and with a whoop plunged into the icy flood. Shouting and beating the water with their hands, they formed double life lines across the torrent—a human chute. Herders worked the sheep toward the heads of the lines and tossed one sheep after another into the chest-deep water between the Indians.

No sooner would a sheep hit the water than long arms shot forward to clutch the shaggy wool and swish the animal down the line. Crowding head to rump, the sheep were passed along the surface of the water as though they were carried on a sluice. Ten thousand sheep were heaved across the Snake in half an hour.

Don José returned to the Chief to point out that he had agreed to pay for the assistance of ten Indians, not 300.

"Only for ten you pay," he reiterated, laughing at Don José's concern. He summoned the favored ten to receive their silver, while 290 other naked Bannocks were swimming the wagons over as if it were all a game.

A few weeks later, 10,000 sheep were delivered to a new owner in Cheyenne, and Don José, like hundreds of other unemployed herders, returned to an empty sheep ranch to start all over again at a less reprehensible trade.

XI

NO NEED OF ALPS
AND ITALYS HERE

Paradox of paradoxes, within a decade after Easterners had fought their way over the abominable Sierra, cursing the wilderness and blaspheming its Creator, they were back in the same mountains exalting the scenery and praising God for the marvels of His handiwork.

No one cussed more vehemently than suave "Old Block"

Alonzo Delano from New York. He came overland in 1849, grubbed placers of the Yuba and Feather Rivers with indifferent success, and then turned to financial and literary pursuits more in keeping with his natural refinement. Like thousands of other prospectors, Old Block had seen enough rugged cliffs and gorges to last him a lifetime. He settled down in Grass Valley and swore that he never again wanted to see a mountain.

Yet by 1854 he could resist the lure of the High Sierra no longer. "Off to the Mountains," tattled the Grass Valley *Telegraph* on July 13th. "Quite a party started out this morning for a trip to the Sierra Nevada. Madame Lola Montez, Old Block, Dr. Delevan and others are of the company. It is their intention to be absent about two or three weeks."

Together the catty *Telegraph* and kittenish dancer-actress Lola spoiled that cozy pack trip. Neither had a co-operative attitude. The *Telegraph* item raised all the local eyebrows; Lola raised havoc with the itinerary. The would-be nature lovers got as far as the summit of Donner Pass, where they bedded down for the night on the bleak rocks. For Madame Montez the untidy meal service, the lumpy mattress and the blustering winds took all the romance out of mountaineering. Roughing it wasn't at all the way Old Block had pictured it to her. In embarrassed silence the excursionists showed up at Grass Valley a few days after they had left.

The fiasco, however, didn't dampen Delano's rejuvenated enthusiasm for Sierra wilds. Every summer after that he returned to the heights for a month or more—in the proper company of his wife—to draft ecstatic essays on the glamor of the mountains. "Poor dweller of the burning valley, thou slave of business and the almighty dollar," he stumped, "you need rest for your weary brain and recreation for both soul and body. Ninety-two, ninety-four, ninety-six, ninety-eight—by heaven! Ninety-nine, Fahrenheit. Who can stand it without fretting and sweating?

"I wonder why city folks of the valley will endure the scorching sun of July and August when a charming ride of twelve hours will place them in the cool, invigorating and delightful air of Webber Lake, where that charming sheet of clear, sparkling water invites a soul upon its placid bosom, where the sublime scenery of the snow-capped hills elevates the soul and chases away the busy cares of life.

"No need of Alps and Italys here. We have them of our own. Get upon the grand old hills of California. My word for it, you will come back recuperated, revived and charmed. Before, behind—all around—one grand mass of bold mountains, inspiring one at once with awe for the Almighty Power which would raise these mighty hills and hold the earth in the hollow of His hands. Glory be to God. Amen."

The Webber Lake which Old Block endorsed so headily was a circular dot of blue water in Henness Pass twenty miles north of Donner Gap. It was little more than a mile in diameter and about 7,000 feet in altitude. There in 1860, Dr. David G. Webber, a benevolent physician from New York and Chicago, had erected one of the first Sierra resorts; not with the idea of gouging vacationists, or even making ends meet. Money didn't interest the doctor. He was a confirmed philanthropist, a genial old widower whose hobby all his life had been rescuing indigent youngsters, adopting them and giving them an education. By the time he reached California in 1849 he had a "family" of at least fifty scattered through the states.

Though Webber Hotel would have been just about large enough to house his wards, it wasn't built for them. He conceived of it more as a sanitarium where healthy Californians could get away from the mad world and find temporary redemption in the idyllic environment of blue water, upland meadows, tamarack forest and craggy, snow-capped mountains.

The doctor was neither crank nor crackpot. He had no spurious sophistry to sell. He was just a nice old gentleman. Providing sheer, undiluted pleasure in the great outdoors, without any strings attached, was his sole purpose in operating Webber Hotel. He maintained a stable of fine saddle horses and a flotilla of boats and sailing craft. His buggy roads and saddle trails ran for miles back into the mountains. There were guides to take sportsmen on grizzly or deer hunts and on tramps to mountain tops. Three times a week, from the end of May to the first of November, his four-horse stagecoach plied between the hotel and Truckee to bring in new corps of nature lovers. He even stocked the lake with trout and provided such superb fishing that his guests indulged in it day and night—spear fishing with pine-knot flares at night; casting from dawn to dark.

Dr. Webber didn't need to advertise his establishment. The public and the press did it free of charge. "Webber Lake is decidedly the most enjoyable and cheapest pleasure resort in California," plugged the Sacramento *Bee*. "Stay one day only at Webber and perhaps you will pronounce it dull," warned San Francisco's *Alta*. "Stay a week and you will wish to prolong your visit a month. Stay a month and you will certainly pass the heated season there year after year."

The doctor set a high standard, but surprisingly enough, it could be matched at a considerable number of other hideaways scattered here and there through the mountains, along the shores of high lakes, at the foot of frothing falls, in the Big Trees, at panoramic outlooks. These modest hostelries sprang up like a fad in the sixties and seventies. Likely as not, the proprietor was a man who had fallen fanatically in love with the landscape, and wanted to share it with others, even though the clientele he drew would never begin to amortize the investment made in Victorian piazzas, boats, trails and gazebos. In the age of Queen Victoria the Sierra offered the perfect asylum for professional nature lovers.

Occasionally the high-minded escapist who erected a cramped public house too near the beaten path got more trade than he bargained for. In a matter of days after his shingle appeared, he could be swamped, and the quiet retreat he had planned turned into a grand concourse; all California would seem to be converging upon him, and revenue poured in so fast that he could afford to abandon his obsession with nature and become the capitalist.

That was what happened to the innkeeper at Strawberry on

the Placerville-Carson road. His reputation for fine food and lots of it, spread like the pox. Came the Washoe gold rush, and Strawberry's quiet little hostelry was overrun, as journalist J. Ross Browne discovered to his chagrin in 1860.

"We found the barroom packed as closely as it could be without bursting out some of the walls," he lamented, "and of all the motley gangs that ever happened together within a space of twenty feet, this certainly was the most extraordinary: dilapidated gentlemen with slouched hats and big boots, Jew peddlers dripping wet, red-shirted miners, teamsters, *vaqueros,* packers and traders all swearing horribly at nothing. . . . But chiefly remarkable in the crowd was the regiment of light infantry pressed in double file against the dining-room door, awaiting the fourth or fifth charge at the table.

"At the first tinkle of the bell, the door was burst open with a tremendous crash, and for a moment no battle scene in Waterloo could have equaled the terrific onslaught of the gallant troops of Strawberry. The whole house actually tottered and trembled at the concussion. Long before the main body had assaulted the table, the din of arms was heard above the general uproar; the deafening clatter of plates, knives and forks, and the dreadful battle cry of 'Waiter! Waiter! Pork and beans! Coffee, Waiter! Beefsteak! Sausages! Potatoes! Ham and eggs!—quick, Waiter, for God's sake!'

"It was a scene of destruction and carnage long to be remember bered. When the table was vacated it presented a shocking picture of desolation. Whole dishes were swept of their contents; knives, forks, plates and spoons lay in a confused mass among the bones and mutilated remnants of the dead; chunks of bread and hot biscuit were scattered broadside, and mince pies were gored into fragments; teacups and saucers were capsized; and the waiters, hot, red and steaming, were panting and swearing after their superhuman labors.

"Half an hour more and the battlefield was again cleared for action. I joined the invaders this time. As the bell sounded, we broke! I rushed through the struggling mass, fixed my eye on a chair, threw out my hands frantically to seize it, but, alas! it was already captured.

"I got a seat at the next onslaught. Pork and beans, cabbage, beefsteak, sausages, pies, tarts, coffee and tea, eggs, and so forth—these are only a few of the luxuries furnished by the enterprising proprietor of the Strawberry."

Browne had arrived too late to reserve a bed in the upstairs dormitory "where two hundred and fifty tired wayfarers were already snoring in double-slotted bunks," but for a small gratuity the landlord favored him with a "layout" on the parlor floor. Browne had scarcely retired to the warmth of his own blankets on the bare floor when he discovered the duplicity of the proprietor. One by one, forty others, according to his count, crept in to share the same floor, and in all the confusion his nearest roommate succeeded next morning in walking off in Browne's only pair of dirty socks before the owner could get them on.

The journalist moved on to Lake House, the only hotel near Lake Tahoe in 1860, and Lake House, too, had gone commercial. "A tolerably good-sized shanty," was the highest praise Browne could give it. "The host did more scolding, swearing, gouging and general hotel work in the brief space of half an hour than any man I ever saw. He seemed to be quite worn out with his run of customers—from a hundred to three hundred a night, and nowhere to stow them—all cussin' at him for not keeping provisions. I was not sorry to get clear of the Lake House, its filth and its troubles."

But Tahoe, like a dozen other neighboring lakes, would soon be able to accommodate pleasuring parties in boarding houses every bit as fine as Dr. Webber's on Lake Webber. The tourists were coming, and coming in legions. Roving reporters, such as Old Block, Mark Twain, and John Muir, started turning out essays on the beauty of Lake Tahoe almost as fast as hotels could be brought into existence. During the next decade no less than a dozen sprawling edifices began to give the shores an air of the real summer resort—in stark contrast to the whining sawmills at Glenbrook. The lake was dotted with sails, row-boats and steamers. Flags, bunting and Chinese lanterns decorated the landings and hotel lawns.

Cardwell's Grand Central Hotel set the standard there, with large, handsomely furnished rooms for 160 "discriminating guests." The management advertised boats, horses and carriages, a bowling alley, bathrooms, broad porches, croquet grounds, a laundry, "a cozy little bar at some distance from the hotel,"—all that could "tend to the rational enjoyment of lake tourists."

"Sail around the lake," exclaimed a satisfied customer, "and, my word for it, you will relish the elegant dinner which Cardwell has in readiness upon your return. The tables of the Grand Central are laden with every luxury which appetite can crave. There are few examples on the coast of greater hotel enterprise than is here displayed."

As an indication of how the publicity about the Sierra, Lake Tahoe and the Grand Central was getting around, on one night Cardwell's hotel register showed addresses from San Francisco; Chicago; Buffalo; Syracuse; Cincinnati; Virginia; Danvers, Massachusetts; New Carlisle, Pennsylvania; New York; and Tugwell, England. But this was an establishment for the elite; miners and lumberjacks weren't admitted and it was appallingly expensive. For his better accommodations Cardwell had the gall to ask twenty dollars a week—American plan.

To most of the nation, the indelible symbols for California were still gold, the lumber baron, a tide of raw humanity and the great wastes of unwatered desert; yet among the literate and the genteel the symbol of magnificent mountain country was also getting recognition. The new symbol was even masqueraded on the floor of the Senate in Washington on May 17th, 1864.

That day the Senate had a particularly heavy agenda. Up for prior consideration was a resolution on the mounting public debt. Action had to be taken on an appropriations bill for the next fiscal year. Held over from the day before and promising acrimonious debate was a snarl over equalization of pay for

Union soldiers. Moreover, a depressive cloud was hanging over Congress. The war news from Spotsylvania was grim and a great many legislators were worried about the capabilities of a general named Ulysses S. Grant, whom President Lincoln had recently appointed Commander in Chief.

So this was the morning on which Senator John Conness of California chose to call up Senate Bill No. 203, just reported— without amendment or enthusiasm—from the Committee on Public Lands. No. 203 would grant to the State of California "for public pleasuring, resort and recreation, a certain cleft or gorge in the granite peak of the Sierra Nevada Mountains, known as 'Yosemite Valley,' as well as another tract known as the 'Mariposa Big Tree Grove'—both to be held by the State 'inalienable for all time.'"

Nothing could have been further removed from the crises of the hour. While the Senate was overburdened with problems of war and finance to buoy up a foundering republic, the Senator from California wanted to take time out to discuss California scenery and pleasuring.

Conness had the floor. "I will state to the Senate," he began ponderously, "that this bill proposes to make a grant of certain premises located in the Sierra Nevada Mountains, to the State of California, that are for all purposes worthless, but which constitute some of the grandest wonders of the world. It is a matter involving no appropriation whatever. The property is of no value to the government. The trees contained in that grove have no parallel, perhaps, in the world. They—"

Somehow, Senator Lafayette Foster of Connecticut managed to break in with a question: "I should like to ask the Senator from California whether the State of California—"

Foster's query was cut short by an impatient announcement from the dais: "The chair must interrupt the Senator to call up the special order of the day, the time fixed for its consideration having arrived."

"I hope it can lie over for the present," pleaded Conness, as though his mysterious cleft or gorge and the big trees were fully as important as the War between the States.

"Let it go over informally for a few minutes," interceded Senator Henry Wilson of Massachusetts, with a trace of sarcasm.

The chair eyed the clock, tried to hide his irritation and granted the request.

Once more the Senator from Connecticut was recognized. In essence he wanted to know why, in heaven's name, such a bill was coming before the Senate, who had proposed it and why.

"I shall state to the Senator from Connecticut and to the Senate," replied Conness, regaining his composure, "that the application comes to us from various gentlemen in California, gentlemen of fortune, of taste and refinement."

"It struck me as being a rather singular grant," Foster fired back tartly, "unprecedented so far as my recollection goes."

"There is no parallel," Conness smugly answered, "and can be no parallel for this measure, for elsewhere there is not on earth just such a condition of things. The Mariposa Big Tree Grove is really the wonder of the world, containing those magnificent monarchs of the forest that are thirty to forty feet in diameter."

"How old?" needled Senator Garrett Davis of Kentucky, as a ripple of laughter passed through the chamber.

"Well, sir, they are estimated to reach an age of three thousand years," Conness answered in dead earnestness. He waited for the smiles to wilt and for the commotion to subside. He felt a little unsure of himself. Of course, he had never seen Yosemite, knew of the place only by hearsay, and didn't want to be pressed into admitting it. But he could talk eloquently about the Big Trees. So far as he was concerned, the trees were more of a show than the cleft, anyway.

"There are two such groves in the State," he continued. "One is known as the Mariposa Grove, the other as the Calaveras Grove. From the Calaveras Grove some sections of a fallen tree were cut during and pending the great World's Fair that was held in London some years ago. One joint of the tree was sectionized and transported to that country and set up there. The

English who saw it declared it to be a Yankee invention, made from beginning to end; that it was an utter untruth that such trees grew in this country; that it could not be; and although the section was transported there at an expense of several thousand dollars, we were not able to convince them that it was a specimen of American growth. They would not believe us. The purpose of this bill is to preserve one of these groves from devastation and injury. The necessity of taking early possession and care of these great wonders can easily be seen and understood."

Conness wasn't entirely convincing. All too evidently some of his fellow congressmen sympathized with the British.

"I am at a loss to understand," quipped Foster of Connecticut with a straight face, "what it was I was so unfortunate to say, which led the Senator to suppose that I doubted him."

In a flurry of asides, Senate Bill No. 203 was voted through. If no federal expenditure was involved, reasoned the legislators, if the property was as worthless as Conness claimed, nothing was to be lost in giving California the darned cleft and the outsized trees. With the entertainment of the morning over, the Senate could now return to the business of winning a war and salvaging a nation.

The United States Senators were not alone in their irreverent attitude toward the wonders of Yosemite. Even in California much the same indifference prevailed. Very few people had seen the valley in 1864. Although members of the Walker expedition had undoubtedly looked down into the canyon as early as 1833, its actual discovery was made little more than a decade before Conness brought it to the attention of the Senate, and that discovery was entirely accidental—the by-product of a retaliatory foray against a minor tribe of Indians, the Yosemites, who had been raiding the mining communities in the Mariposa hills.

The principals in the dramatic discovery were Major James D. Savage and a young medic named Lafayette H. Bunnell. Dr. Bunnell went along mostly for the adventure; Savage was commanding officer of the Mariposa Battalion. For several years the Major had run a chain of Indian trading posts west of Yosemite and been on the friendliest of terms with all the tribes in the area. In fact, the chiefs had been so impressed with his talents as merchant and peacemaker, that they had bestowed upon him bride after bride, until he had a harem of five wives. But the influx of Yankee gold scroungers bitterly antagonized the Indians; Savage lost caste, too, and eventually his posts were included in the raids.

The double cross worked both ways, and late in March, 1851, it was Savage who led the column of volunteers up the valley of the Merced, bent on capturing or exterminating the whole tribe of wily Yosemites. Never before had the Indian stronghold been invaded by white men, except perhaps by a stray hunter or prospector.

Guided by an amiable Indian, the file was strung out along the trail for half a mile late one afternoon. Through the five-foot drifts of snow, the going was hard. Major Savage elected to serve as rear guard. Bunnell, more poet than soldier, was riding by himself well ahead of the Major, enjoying the solitude and the scenery.

Suddenly the doctor caught sight of an incredible magnificence of cliff ahead. He drew up his horse, overwhelmed by the spectacle. For a better view he reined the horse off the trail to a higher elevation and sat in the saddle gaping in wonder.

The scene made such a profound impression on him that years later he could recall every detail: "The face of that immense cliff was shadowed by the declining sun. The grandeur was but softened by the haze that hung over the valley—light as gossamer—and by the clouds that partially dimmed the higher cliffs and mountains. This obscurity of vision but increased the awe with which I beheld it, and, as I looked, a peculiar exalted sensation seemed to fill my whole being, and I found my eyes in tears with emotion. The shadows fast clothing all before me and the vapory clouds at the head of the valley leaving the view beyond still undefined, gave a wierdness to the scene that made it so impressive; and the conviction that it was utterly indescribable added strength to the emotion."

The reverie of the first white man to appreciate the majestic beauty of El Capitan was rudely interrupted by Major Savage, bringing up the rear. "Better wake up from that dream or you may lose your hair," he shouted, not so much as glancing at the cliff. "Some of the murdering devils may be lurking along the trail to pick off stragglers."

Shaken by what seemed to him like a celestial vision, Bunnell pulled back onto the trail and retorted: "If my hair is now required, I can depart in peace, for I have seen the power and glory of a Supreme Being."

"Hold up, Doc!" scoffed the Major. "You're soaring too high. Better mind this devilish trail or we shall go soaring off some of these slippery rocks."

The doctor still hadn't quite regained his terrestrial bearings when he dismounted at the Battalion bivouac an hour later, and he detected among some of his fellow volunteers a similar detachment. Even their language was subdued. They all seemed to be concerned about what to call the place. As its discoverers, they maintained it was their right and duty to name the valley. Drawing from a limited acquaintance with the Scriptures, mythology and foreign parts, they tossed one suggestion after another at Bunnell, whom they regarded as the natural interlocutor.

"Why go to a foreign country for a name?" begged the doctor. "What's wrong with an Indian name? Let's call it Yosemity.' "

"Devil take the Indians," objected a Mariposa gold digger. "Why should we honor those vagabond murderers?"

"Let's call it 'Paradise Valley'!" someone called.

"Hear ye! Hear ye!" barked a tall Texan, John O'Neal, bluntly displacing Bunnell as functionary. "A vote will now be taken to decide what name shall be given to this valley. How many ballots for 'Yosemity'?"

Almost unanimously the choice was "Yosemity." Though liberties were taken with its spelling, Bunnell's name stuck from the start.

But the Yosemite wars lasted much longer than Savage, the doctor or anyone else anticipated. More than two years elapsed before the last of the tribesmen were herded out of the valley. They hid in caves; they retreated to higher mountains; they surrendered only to sneak away and fight again. The Yosemites loved their valley passionately and refused to yield it. They fought by hurling down barrages of stones from cliff hide-outs; they fought from ambush; they showered their tormentors with arrows.

"My people do not want anything from the Great White Father," declaimed Chief Tenaya proudly in one of his periods of recurrent captivity. "The Great Spirit is our father and he has always supplied us with all we need. Our women are able to do our work. Go then. Let us remain in the mountains where we were born; where the ashes of our fathers have been given to the winds."

Tenaya's pathetic appeal was ignored. By midsummer of 1853 his ashes, too, had been given to the winds and his people decimated. Yosemite belonged to the white men. And in the process of trying to smoke out the Indians, the Yankee vanquishers had discovered scenic wonders like Bridal Veil Fall, Cathedral Rocks, Vernal and Nevada Falls, Clouds Rest, Mirror Lake, Half Dome and Glacier Point—though the naming was left to less bellicose excursionists.

Yet even after Yosemite had been made safe for sight-seers there was no rush to take advantage of the great scenic discovery. Late in the summer of 1853 a few prospectors nosed into the canyons; they were impressed neither by the vistas nor the lode. In 1854 no one at all ventured in, though Bunnell and some of the other veterans of the Mariposa Battalion were doing their best to spread the word about the fantastic waterfalls and towering cliffs. Occasionally rumors of a 1,000-foot waterfall were noted in the California press, but editors placed no more credence in the reports than did readers. A thousand feet? Why, famous Niagara was only 164.

One of the rumors, however, did strike the imagination of the prominent San Francisco journalist, James M. Hutchings.

He was thinking of launching a new West Coast periodical and was on the lookout for a spectacular story for his first issue. Naturally, he didn't believe the waterfall rumor; still, if the drop were only a *little* higher than Niagara, he'd have quite a scoop. He made up his mind to go and see for himself.

Hutchings talked an artist and two other adventurous friends into joining him, and they headed for Mariposa. There, to his astonishment, twenty miles from his destination, he could find scarcely anyone who had ever heard of Yosemite and no one who was interested in it. He spent days futilely combing the area for a guide or for someone who would furnish reliable directions. Woodsmen, old hunters and town officials all admitted they couldn't help him. Men who had served in the Mariposa Battalion threw up their hands; they had been led in by Indians. No bribe was big enough to tempt them to try retracing the route. Finally he located two displaced Yosemites who agreed to show the way.

Under the guidance of these homesick Indians, the party reconnoitered the big canyon and Hutchings quickly realized that he had his scoop. He spent five days tramping up and down the valley, then hurried back to civilization to become Yosemite's chief publicist and promoter.

The first issue of Hutchings' *California Magazine* didn't come from the press for another year, but the lead article on "Yo-ham-i-te Valley" brought the journal immediate success. If the word description of this scenic discovery seemed a little overdrawn, the artist's sketches of fantastic rock sculpture and the stupendous falls at least were convincing.

The editor told of the lofty granite mountains, foaming cataracts, placid lakes and evergreen forests. Somewhat handicapped by the lack of authentic nomenclature for the landmarks, he freely invented titles like "Giant's Tower," "Twin Domes," and "Cascade of the Rainbow." Altogether it was a rousing good piece, calculated to stimulate interest in "Yo-ham-it-e" real estate.

Breathlessly he introduced readers to pinnacles "exceeding 3,000 feet in height, now in appearance like a vast projecting tower, now standing boldly out like an immense chimney or column, then like two giant domes; yonder a waterfall of 2,500 feet, and as it rolls over the edge of the precipice, its quivering spray is gilded with the colors of the rainbow . . . a dense forest of lofty pines that by distance look only as weeds or shrubs."

The Giant's Tower was an "immense mountain of perpendicular granite nearly 3,500 feet to the highest place upon it"; beautiful Indian Lake was a favorite resort "for ensnaring the speckled trout"; the great Yo-ham-it-e Falls was "the highest waterfall in the world."

Hutchings acknowledged that the public had perhaps been justified in doubting previous estimates of heights, but there was no longer any reason for skepticism; actual measurements exceeded previous estimates. "They now stand forth as realities—" he assured his readers, "realities which invite the spontaneous admiration of every lover of the sublime and beautiful, who may visit the deep solitude of this interesting and remarkable valley." Any danger from Indians was summarily dismissed. "When we arrived there," he stated, "scarcely an Indian track could be seen. The trails were overgrown with grass, and nothing remained but the whitened bones of animals."

"Before many years shall have passed," predicted Hutchings, "Yo-ham-i-te Valley will become famous as a place of resort . . . where, in the calm solitude of mountain life, the excitements of business may be forgotten; and in the unbroken stillness of this magnificent spot men shall, with deep reverence, commune with the sublime and beautiful."

Hutchings didn't limit his literary exploitation of Yosemite to the *California Magazine.* The thoroughgoing propagandist turned out glowing accounts of the monumental wonders for metropolitan newspapers and back-country gazettes alike. His stories were liberally plagiarized and enlarged upon. Many an eastern editor, with tongue in cheek, published the accounts of fabulous Yosemite as just another illustration of how far Californians would go in braggadocio and burlesque.

Few readers accepted the descriptions at face value, but they did excite a certain amount of curiosity among naturalists and the romanticists.

The valley wasn't yet in any imminent danger of being overrun. It was virtually inaccessible. An expedition had to fight its way through fifty miles of tangled forest and dangerously rough rock country. Guides were difficult to find. And the trip was prohibitively expensive. From San Francisco it involved a steamboat excursion of 125 miles up the Sacramento and San Joaquin Rivers to Stockton, a two-day stage ride through the Sierra foothills and Mariposa County; then the last fifty miles into the wilderness on horseback.

But Hutchings' prediction that Yosemite would quickly develop into a popular resort inspired a few enterprising citizens to action; they wanted to get in early on the tourist shakedown. One group started cutting a toll trail from the South Fork of the Merced into the valley. In anticipation of the hordes that would soon be swarming to the new scenic mecca of America, an *hôtelier* erected a canvas-roofed tavern and hostelry on the route.

Irritated by this mercenary exploitation, Bunnell joined forces with two other trail hounds and started building a free trail from Coulterville. No sooner were the trails broken than a saloon opened its rustic doors in the valley—the first substantial structure. Sheepherders moved in with their flocks and threw together awkward shacks that were frequently shared with sight-seers. A "hotel" went up at the lower end of the valley, and another at the upper—squalid, rickety affairs made of poles, shakes and billowing canvas that would have been an eyesore to a lumber camp.

This was the shape of things in Yosemite Valley in 1864 when the Senate of the United States was prevailed upon to deed the canyon to the State of California. According to a careful tally compiled by Hutchings, exactly 653 white men, including sheepherders and all the Mariposa Battalion volunteers, had been to the valley up to that time.

As a sanctuary "for public pleasuring, resort and recreation," Yosemite was a long time in the making. For a quarter of a century after the Indians were driven out, the only access to the valley was over a perilous trail. Every bed, bottle and bucksaw came in by mule pack, and often the celebrities traveled the same way.

But Hutchings had big bold plans in store for the wonderland. Three weeks before the Senate placed its stamp of approval on Bill No. 203, he gave up his imposing Pine Street residence in San Francisco and moved everything that could travel by mule to the shabby "Upper Hotel" near the foot of Yosemite Falls. Nor did he go as guest; he was taking over as proprietor. Merely writing about his Shangri-La wasn't enough; he wanted to breathe the blessed Yosemite air, to live there, to play host; and his wife would make an agreeable hostess. What Dr. Webber had done at Webber Lake he would do at Yosemite.

Admittedly the Hutchingses knew nothing about innkeeping, and the jerry-built two-story, two-room dormitory they had purchased hardly lent itself to refinements of hospitality. "It's doors and windows were made of cotton cloth," apologized the proprietor. "When our first guests arrived, the ladies were domiciled upstairs and the gentlemen down. This arrangement, we felt, had its inconveniences, as it sometimes separated man and wife, and we determined upon changing it.

"But how? The nearest sawmill was some fifty miles distant and over a mountainous country that was accessible only over steep and zigzagging trails. Bolts of muslin, however, could be packed—and were; rooms were accordingly made of that. Guests, in this way, were provided with apartments, it is true; but unless their lights were carefully disposed, there were also added unintentional shadow pictures, which if contributory of mirthfulness in a maximum degree, gave only a minimum degree of privacy."

As a *restaurateur* Hutchings also had his limitations. He was much more interested in dispensing intimate information about rock fissures, squirrels and *pinus ponderosa* than providing formal table service. Consequently, while he was engrossed in a breakfast discourse on the habits of the horned toad or the life cycle of *sequoia gigantea,* guests frequently were handed sugar for their trout and salt for their strawberries.

Assigning four or five to a bed never disconcerted him. The utmost capacity of his quarters, he estimated, was twenty-eight. One night he had a full house; all twenty-eight places were filled and the guests were sound asleep when eleven stragglers showed up. He welcomed them warmly, and was serving them a late supper when eight more appeared; then another ten, making a grand total of fifty-eight. All the latecomers were fed bountifully and squeezed into beds among the prior occupants.

Yet no one ever lifted a voice in complaint. A fellow-editor from New England, Samuel Bowles, even gave the establishment a guarded endorsement in 1865: "Mr. Hutchings keeps a hotel and can accommodate a dozen or so people very comfortably, and is both enterprising and courteous." What the host had to show his guests more than made up for the lumpy mattresses and greasy potatoes.

"The Yosemite!" sighed Bowles, "As well interpret God in thirty-nine articles as portray it in word of mouth or pen. As well represent castle and cathedral by a stolen frieze or broken column as this assemblage of natural wonder and beauty by photograph or painting. The overpowering sense of the sublime, of awful desolation, of transcending marvelousness and unexpectedness! . . . No one scene in the Alps can match this. . . . It is Niagara magnified. . . . It is the confrontal of God face to face."

Despite his shortcomings as host, Hutchings was a success, and his theatrical display of Yosemite an enormous success. Gradually the muslin privacy yielded to more substantial sheathing. In his backyard he designed an overshot water wheel and built a sawmill; with home-produced lumber he enlarged his hotel, added porches, private rooms and outhouses; constructed stables and hen coops; packed in a fine library of 800 volumes; planted an apple orchard of 150 trees; and started a famous strawberry bed from thirteen plants shipped all the way from the East via Panama at a total cost of forty-five dollars.

By the California Yosemite Commission he was eventually appointed official "Guardian of the Valley." He entertained at his hotel contemporary greats ranging from editor Horace Greeley to geologist Clarence King. His business was the business of letting the world know about his beloved paradise. Three hundred and sixty-nine were drawn to it in 1865, his first full season of operation. Four years later, when the Central Pacific began bringing tourists from the East, his registration jumped to over 1,000. By the 1880's it was advancing toward 5,000.

But for the future of Yosemite and the Sierra, the most important wayfarer ever to dine at Hutchings' table was John Muir. He came in 1868, a disenchanted sheepherder looking for a job. Hutchings put him to work at the sawmill. Muir wasn't much better at turning out lumber than he had been at tending sheep, but he fell in love with Yosemite and soon displaced his employer as the foremost advocate and defender of the mountains.

One after another, Hutchings welcomed three new hotel proprietors to the valley. Competition was the least of his concerns, for keeping open house was an expensive hobby; he was glad to share the costs. Even when a road brought the first carriages and coaches in 1874, "Hutchings House" was hardly a paying proposition.

His objective, regardless of cost, was to bring more admirers to Yosemite. They came. Where he and his family had once been the only year-round residents, by 1880 Yosemite boasted of a village with a blacksmith shop, grocery store, souvenir venders, photographic galleries, artist's studios, a telegraph office, bakery, livery stable, public school, chapel, Wells, Fargo branch and a post office for which James Hutchings himself distributed the mail—at a salary of twelve dollars a year.

As soon as the transcontinental railroad was in operation, the Central Pacific had extended a branch line south to Stockton, Modesto, Copperopolis, Merced and Madera. All these towns were within easy reach of Yosemite, and in tourist season spielers and stage drivers descended upon every out-of-town passenger as he stepped down from the cars, pressing for the privilege of rushing him by the quickest, most scenic route to the world's most magnificent sights. For thirty-five years glib coachmen controlled the traffic to the valley, and their monopoly wouldn't have ended then, if an upstart little railroad, the Yosemite Valley, hadn't horned in to take sight-seers directly to El Portal in 1927.

New attractions to lure tourists and trampers were added annually. Electricity and telephone services were wired in. Hotels advertised luxury services—baths, barbershops, plush bars and a wooden stairway to Vernal Fall. For those who wanted to rough it, there were public camp grounds and dozens of trails leading in all directions—to Little Yosemite, to Glacier Point, to the Upper Yosemite Fall, to Tenaya Lake. And as if natural wonders were not enough, men went to all the trouble of cutting tunnels in the butts of big trees, so that tourists could drive through them—with a photographer tagging close behind to record the event.

It was John Muir's unbounded contempt for sheepherders and lumbermen and what they were doing to Sierra landscape that led to the creation of Yosemite National Park in 1890. The State controlled the valley; he insisted that the federal government should seize the thousands of acres surrounding its rim before the land was completely denuded. In magazine and newspaper articles he damned the woodland vandals until the salvation of the Sierra seemed to become a national crusade and Congress was compelled to respond by declaring that the vast area was "hereby reserved and withdrawn from settlement, occupancy or sale . . . and set apart as reserved forest lands."

But the establishment of a national park, with a state-owned island in its midst, brought almost as many problems as it solved—problems of water rights, land rights and jurisdiction. State employees watched a border fire race out of control into federal land where it wasn't their responsibility. Muir saw that a system of divided authority wasn't going to work, so he started another campaign to re-cede the valley to the United States. Against formidable odds he won that battle, too, and the whole tract became a national park in 1906.

Neither Muir nor his nature-loving disciples had quite fore-seen what the new management would do to the character of Yosemite. For four decades there had been some kindly old gentleman, like James M. Hutchings, to dispense informal counsel, philosophy and wit to sight-seers and greenhorn bush-whackers venturing into the canyon. In a tragic carriage ac-cident the "Guardian of the Valley" was killed under the shadow of El Capitan in the fall of 1902. Now the real guardian was the Secretary of the Interior in Washington, and since he had insufficient funds or personnel with which to police his do-main, he called upon the Department of War.

The genial give-and-take paternalism was abruptly dis-placed by the uncontestable authoritarianism of the United States Army. From the Presidio in San Francisco, two troops of cavalry marched in to set up a military encampment in a mea-dow under Yosemite Falls. Bugles blared at sunrise, taps echoed against the cliffs at night. Tourists turned out en masse to review the guard-post line-up at nine in the morning. In-congruous military exercises became part of the Yosemite show, as though the naturalists had capitulated to the war-riors.

From May to November the "Boys in Blue" were the most conspicuous society in the valley. As military police they took their job seriously, patrolling the public grounds efficiently and officiously, dropping blunt warnings to campfire builders, dressing down out-of-season fishermen, commandeering forbid-den rifles and revolvers. In the spring they engaged in "light burning," setting fire to miles of marginal brush; in the fall they went on twenty-four hour alert as fire fighters; in summer they disappeared in pairs to make war on the sheepherders in the High Sierra, and there they gained the reputation of being the most uncompromising troopers in California history.

The Secretary of the Interior could forbid grazing, but unfortunately he did not have authority to mete out penalties. So the mounties invented their own system of retribution. Flocks were driven out of the park in one direction and offending herders were expelled in another. By the time sheep and their keepers were reassembled days later, the toll in mutton was large enough to serve as a very adequate fine.

But the Boys in Blue were also heroes when it came to searching for lost hikers, rescuing rock climbers from cliffs and administering first aid in emergencies. They built trails and roads, developed new park accessories and annually, on July 4th, provided entertainment that outclassed any scenic attraction. For that great celebration admirers flocked to Yosemite from as far away as Sonora, Chinese Camp and Bootjack.

A booming cannon echoing through the mountains at sunrise set the mood. There were parades, mule-pack races, contests in rapid mounting, horse stunts, hurdle races, baseball games, and finally a glorious display of fireworks. That day of showmanship more than made up for the military pomp that pervaded the park during the rest of the season. Yosemite was under the command of the military until 1914, when the army was at last ousted in favor of civilians—anticipating the early arrival of the National Park Service.

Meantime, with Yosemite in good hands, John Muir had inaugurated an all-out crusade to save the Big Trees in other parts of the Sierra. "Thousands of the finest sequoias have been felled, blasted into manageable dimensions and sawed into lumber by methods destructive almost beyond belief," he decried. One small mill, in a single season, he claimed, had sawed 2,000,000 feet of sequoia lumber and sold it as redwood. He condemned a master of woodland revels for leveling a sequoia simply to make a dance floor from its stump; and deplored the practice of removing bark from trunks for displays in New York, Philadelphia, Paris and London—"as sensible a scheme as skinning our great men to show off their greatness."

"Probably more than three times as many sequoias as are contained in the whole Calaveras Grove have been cut into lumber every year for twenty-six years, without let or hin-

drance and with scarce a word of protest on the part of the public," he upbraided. "Any fool can destroy trees, and few of
the destroyers ever plant any. It took more than three thousand years to make some of the oldest of the sequoias.
Through all the eventful centuries, God has cared for the trees,
saved them from drought, disease, avalanches, and a thousand
storms; but we cannot save them from sawmills and fools; that
is left to the American people."

Muir had strong allies. Above all, he could count on
the great outdoorsman, Theodore Roosevelt. "The progress of
true civilization," echoed T. R. in an address at the University
of California, "is best shown by the increasing thought which
each generation takes for the good of those who are to come
after. You can ruin its forests, you can dig up its streams, you
can hack and scar its surface until its marvelous beauty is gone.
No state can be judged to be really civilized, which in the treatment of its natural resources does not aim to preserve the
beauty of the land in which its people live. An aesthetic as
well as an economic factor is involved in the problem of conservation. Don't mutilate the sequoias. Don't let others
mutilate them."

The appeals were taking effect. In Congressional acts almost
simultaneous to the one that gave Yosemite its first federal
jurisdiction in 1890, General Grant and Sequoia National
Parks were created. Together they contained some 250 square
miles on which stood the oldest, largest trees in the world.
But that was only a start. Muir began telling the world about a
canyon near the headwaters of Kings River "yet greater than
Yosemite," about majestic Kern Canyon and Mount Whitney,
the highest peak in the United States.

Eventually a long procession of mountains and the wildest
expanse of broken mountain land in the nation were added to
the twin parks, Sequoia and Kings Canyon—a reserve five
times greater than the original 250 square miles. It was a major
triumph for Muir and his fellow campaigners.

The credit, too, had to be shared with pioneer mountain
hosts like Dr. Webber and James Hutchings, for actually Un-

cle Sam was merely carrying on from where they left off; playing host to the multitude, doing on a vast scale exactly what the private patrons had undertaken in their experimental way.

In the end the Sierra spectacle turned out to be a much more popular extravaganza than any of the promoters in the 1860's estimated. Within a century the range became one of the nation's favorite recreation grounds. The canyons, upland lakes and highways over the mountains were studded with lodges and motels to welcome the throngs of fans. If a tourist or tramper could get to the parks ahead of the mob, he could have a choice of accommodations ranging from a camp site with a handy faucet to a luxury suite with a tiled bath. In the mountains were hundreds of miles of trails leading to scenic wonderlands, or over the Muir Trail one could ramble for 212 miles along the spine of the range from Yosemite to Mount Whitney Portal.

The State played host at its own parks, the Sierra Club played host on the high trails, hundreds of private landlords played host along the approaches; and in the national parks the United States Government was the most open-handed host of all.

Rescued from the Indians, the miners, the sheepherders and the lumbermen was a wilderness playground and an athletic field of more than 1,500,000 acres that belonged to the people —belonged alike to the troop of Boy Scouts from Boston listening to their echoes in Tokopah Valley, to the family of anglers from Alabama, to the Epworth Leaguers from Missouri sizing up the Big Trees and to the honeymooners from Ukiah brooding over the wonder of Bridal Veil Fall. It would belong to their children and children's children too.

XII

THE DEVIL NEVER GETS ABOVE
TIMBER LINE

Clarence King, celebrated geologist, mountaineer and *bon
vivant*, had an irrepressible urge to plant his feet on the highest
point in the United States, and be the first to do it. Twice in
1864 he had been obliged to retreat from Mount Whitney; the
first time because of short rations, the second because of mis-

calculation, bad weather and the formidable precipices of the east wall.

Now, seven years later, he was at it again and success seemed to be within his grasp. Clouds swirling overhead, where the summit ought to be, reduced visibility at times almost to zero, but King and his companion were confident that they were very near their goal. Bone-tired from the grueling climb, they summoned strength and spirit for the last leg of the assault.

With his superior flair for the dramatic, King himself best described those minutes of suspense: "We began to scale the southeast ridge, climbing from rock to rock, and making our way up steep fields of snow. Precipices, sharp and severe, fell away to east and west of us, but the rough pile above still afforded a way. We had to use extreme caution, for many blocks hung ready to fall at a touch, and the snow where we were forced to work up to it, often gave way, threatening to hurl us down into cavernous hollows.

"When within a few hundred feet of the top, I suddenly fell through, but supporting myself by my arms, looked down into a grotto of rock and ice, and out through a sort of window over the western bluffs and down thousands of feet to the far-away valley of the Kern.

"Carefully and slowly I worked my body out and crept on hands and knees up over steep and treacherous ice crests where a slide would have swept me over a brink of the southern precipice. We kept to the granite as much as possible. . . . Above us but thirty feet rose a crest, beyond which we saw nothing. I dared not think it the summit till we stood there and Mount Whitney was under our feet."

King's sense of triumph was so complete that the scudding clouds which obliterated the view didn't bother him. He had achieved his fondest ambition. Then, by some miracle, breaks appeared in the mist. Gaunt skeletons of the range came through. He could trace the familiar outlines of canyons and rivers below, and most rewarding of all, there was glorious Mount Tyndall six miles to the northwest; the mountain he had climbed almost hand over hand in 1864 and from which he had personally given Mount Whitney its name—in honor of his boss, Josiah Dwight Whitney, the director of the California State Geological Survey.

This was a moment to remember. Once more the clouds closed in. As his calling card, King scratched his name on a half-dollar, cached it on the crest and hurried down the mountain to wire the story of his conquest to the world.

He would have been pleased if the response to the news were a little more generous. Actually not many people gave a rap about Mount Whitney. They still preferred to believe what their geography books taught them; that Mount Shasta was the nation's highest peak. But the few who were stirred by such topographical intelligence readily conceded that the first ascent of Mount Whitney should be ranked at least among the great military victories and great discoveries.

For more than two years King kept his laurels green. In lectures, articles and books he made sure that his achievement was not forgotten. Back East in his home territory he was duly honored and feted, and in 1872, just as the encomium was beginning to taper off, his popularity got another lift from the publication of an exciting book, *Mountaineering in the Sierra Nevada*, which gave a moment-by-moment account of his contests with the high peaks of the West.

But in little California towns like Cerro Gordo and Lone Pine, nestled under the shadows of Mount Whitney, the local boys didn't think much of the acclaim the Eastern city slicker was getting. Too often they had seen him scouting Owens Valley with all his instruments and his arrogance. They resented his attitude, resented the way he promised little favors and never delivered, resented the presumptuousness of an outsider distributing strange names among their mountains. And his superior, Professor Whitney, was no better; in fact they harbored a hearty resentment against the whole survey outfit, particularly because of the preposterous salaries they wangled from the legislature.

With rod and gun the townies had roamed all through the

high mountains on expeditions they considered as glamorous as King's, yet it never occurred to them that they were entitled to honorable mention, even in their county weekly, the Inyo *Independent.* To be sure, they hadn't climbed Mount Whitney; anybody who wanted to take the trouble could do that on a spare weekend.

Just for a lark, on July 27th, 1873, William Goodyear, a former employee of the State Geological Survey and M. W. Belshaw of Cerro Gordo saddled their mules and headed for the peak that had made King so famous. Recalling the hair-raising perils and the brushes with death the geologist had experienced in ascending the mountain, they were prepared for a rough struggle, but somewhat to their amusement, they found no such dangers and few obstacles. It was easy going. No blocks ready to fall at a touch, no cavernous hollows, no grottos. Without difficulty they rode the mules clear to the top.

To the delight of Owens Valley citizenry, Goodyear's report appeared in the Inyo *Independent* a few days later. "I know this peak well," read the testimony, "and cannot be mistaken as to its identity. Since Mr. King's ascent of it, the half dollar which he left on the summit has been found there with his name inscribed on it. This is by no means the highest among the grand cluster of peaks which forms the culminating portion of the Sierra Nevada. But there is some interest in the fact discovered by Mr. Belshaw and myself when we reached the summit—that *this peak is not Mount Whitney.*"

The roars of laughter at King's expense echoed up and down the valley, and for 3,000 miles across the country. Instead of Mount Whitney, the debonair scientist-mountaineer had climbed Mount Langley—an eminence he himself had previously dubbed "Sheep Rock"—and he hadn't known the difference. Perhaps the cloudy weather on the day of his ascent had fooled him, but still it was an inexcusable, appalling error. So no one had yet reached the summit of the United States.

King was in New York. The first inkling he had of the absurd blunder was what he read in a science journal. He was incredulous, yet the case against him was so clearly presented, it could not be refuted. He was irked by the humiliating jibes, but more disturbed by the possibility that he might even now lose out on the chance to be the first to climb Mount Whitney. At the first possible hour he boarded a train for the West.

Meantime, on August 17th three Lone Pine loafers—A. H. Johnson, C. D. Begole and John Lucas—distinguished only for the inordinate amount of time they spent in trolling mountain streams, sauntered out of town ostensibly on another of their fishing expeditions. Even when they returned a few days later, they were in no hurry to report on their catch or their itinerary.

For three weeks they kept the details of their adventure quiet. Then a rumor leaked to the editor of the Inyo *Independent,* and on September 13th, subscribers were let in on the secret. "Mr. Goodyear thought the ascent of the high peak impracticable, or nearly so," noted the squib, "but A. H. Johnson, C. D. Begole and John Lucas of Lone Pine have demonstrated the fact that its summit can be attained. On the 18th of August these three gentlemen were on the summit of Mount Whitney.

"Passing over two deep canyons, and spending the entire day in the labor, they finally succeeded in reaching its highest point; and have the honor of being the first to stand on the greatest elevation in the United States. They gave it the name of Fisherman's Peak, which is better than some of those farfetched, worn-out classical cognomens, but hardly as elevated in character as the loftiest peak in Uncle Samuel's dominions would seem to deserve. The summit is granite and flat topped."

For their feat the three fishermen expected no honors and received none. To them it was a wonderful practical joke on the cocky geologist, and they realized how practical it was when they read in the Inyo *Independent* a week later that Clarence King had recently been seen steaming through Visalia, on the other side of the range, hellbent for the real Mount Whitney. "He had a multitude of instruments with him," joshed the reporter, "and intends, we are told, to settle the status of Mount Whitney. Some of his weapons are so formidable that it would seem that if he does not find the little hillock in the right place and just the right height, he intends to fix it so as to comply with science."

King didn't learn that he had lost the race to the top of the United States until he arrived there just before noon on September 19th and found the undeniable evidence of his defeat in a sardine can. It was a sickening disappointment. He felt cheated. But for the record, he sportingly scrawled on a scrap of paper: "All honor to those who came before me," then stormed down the trail to Lone Pine to give the usurpers a piece of his mind.

He took the three fishermen to task for their "unsporting inclinations" and lambasted them for disgracing the mountain with a terrible title like "Fisherman's Peak." Spitefully the anglers reminded him that among the rights of first ascent was the God-given privilege of naming the mountain anything they damned pleased. King sputtered and fumed, knowing full well that he didn't have a leg to stand on, but he upset himself more than he did Lone Pine.

For a few weeks the naming of the loftiest landmark in mid-continental North America became the *cause célèbre* of the West. The fishermen seemed to be the only ones who were satisfied with the designation, and they were cussedly determined to keep it. Even the Inyo *Independent*, which acclaimed them as "those lucky men whose names are bound to be handed down to posterity," balked at "Fisherman's Peak." "The name will hardly do," decided the editor. "We advise these pioneers to recall it and make up one more becoming."

"Dome of the Continent" was bandied around for a time; almost everyone seemed to favor that—except the fishermen. As a sop for Whitney, it was proposed that the State Geologist's name be transferred to Sheep Rock. "Whatever the name," concluded the *Independent*, "whether 'The Dome' or 'Fisherman's Peak,' either or any is far preferable to 'Whitney.' Whitney has never effected enough, except to draw heavy salaries as State Geologist and assume honors belonging to his abler subordinates, to entitle him to the distinguishment of a transfer. Whitney is a name good enough for a minor peak or an ordinary geological earthquake fraud, but won't bear forced transplanting and give satisfactory results."

The whole issue was thrown into further confusion by other local sons, including William Crapo and Abe Leyda, who belatedly claimed that they had ascended the mountain before the fishermen and therefore had the right to give it a name. At that point the rivalry degenerated into a bout of name-calling.

"We think we smell a skunk and a tadpole," asserted the three in a public statement. "But in studying it over, we have concluded that it is a cross between a skunk and a coyote. We can inform the scientific geologist that he lies, and no one knows it better than himself. The immortal three were not scientists; did not have a barometer, a compass or a Geological Survey Report; and were dirty fishermen, as he insinuates, and ragged, but withal were not as dirty and filthy as he who tries to take the credit of being the first away from us."

By late October the "dirty fishermen" were ready for a compromise. To share the publicity with the county, they agreed to call the mountain "The Dome of Inyo." That was that. It was their final word. But time, the public and the map makers made the ultimate decision. Though "Fisherman's Peak" did appear on a few maps, "Dome of the Continent" and "Dome of Inyo" were as quickly forgotten as the three Lone Pine anglers; and in the end Clarence King had his way. "Mount Whitney" it was and is.

Until about 1864 nobody could get very excited about naming Sierra peaks, climbing them or exploring the rugged terrain in between. In the search for furs, passes and access roads, lumber, Indians, gold, grizzlies and grazing land, much of the range had been worked over—unsystematically and anonymously—but it remained unmapped and unchronicled.

Hunters and trappers had roamed through the mountain wilderness for weeks and months at a stretch, guided by the sun and the general lay of the land; they were good woodsmen, keen and observant, yet the nearest they ever came to publicizing where they had been was in campfire and barroom tales. To sheepherders who explored hundreds of square miles in search of pasturage, it never occurred that the authorities might be interested in a report of their wanderings, and naturally, when they found a lush mountain meadow, they weren't telling anyone about it.

Agents of land and lumber speculators scoured the country in the same secrecy. Fighting units, tracking down hostile Indians, usually traveled with a guide from another tribe; neither officers nor men paid too much heed to the terrain, and like the members of the Mariposa Battalion, were totally incapable of retracing their steps. Good prospectors liked to wander off by themselves; if they found anything worth talking about, they kept quiet, and if they didn't, they kept quiet too, just to mystify their competitors. Many had only the foggiest notion of where they had been, anyway.

But even if all the experience of these mountaineers had been pooled and catalogued, it would have been so interlarded with misinformation, vagary and contradiction that the sum would have been very nearly worthless—no more valuable than Thomas Keough's prosaic account of his summer odyssey in 1864 with ten fellow prospectors from Independence. They were typical of the hundreds of bushwhackers who roamed over passes, peaks and mountain perimeters before the men of science and the sportsmen took over.

"I have heard it said," ruminated Keough, "that the trail over what is now called Kearsarge Pass is an old Indian trail. The fact is our party built that trail to get our animals over the top of the Sierras. It might have been possible for a man to work his way on foot over this pass, but there was no sign of a footpath until we built the track in the summer of 1864, when we started on this prospecting tour. It was a rough trail we built, but it sufficed for our purposes and we got our animals over it."

Having built the trail, however, half the group decided they had had enough of a vacation, and quit. Keough and five companions pushed on down the Kings River and into San Joaquin Valley. It was rough traveling and rougher prospecting. After days of digging they totaled their profits and dis-

covered they had cleared exactly thirty-eight cents. In a fit
of frustration, they hit the trail again, worked back into the
mountains, following the South Fork of the San Joaquin to its
uppermost headwaters. There, just as the last of their grub was
giving out, they discovered rich gold in a barren mountain of
red rock.

But what good was gold to starving men? They turned to
fishing, and the trout refused to bite. They caught rattlesnakes,
skinned and cooked them, but without seasoning the meat was
too revolting to down. Two grouse, roasted whole without being plucked or dressed, was the only food for one day. They
abandoned the red mountain and wandered for almost a week
among the granite cliffs and boulders of Kings Canyon.

"Then we held a council," continued Keough, "and next day
slaughtered one of the horses—an old horse about twenty-five
years old. We made a rack of green willows and jerked a lot of
him, and roasted a lot more in front of a big log fire. After we
got everything ready, we divided up the jerky and roast meat
and struck south.

"We picked our way along with the animals, but the country
kept getting rougher and rougher—deep canyons and precipices, a terribly rough, bouldery country—all bare granite. One
of our party got part way down a cliff where he could neither
get up nor down, and we had to tie our blankets together and
let them down and pull him up. It was a several-thousand-foot
drop down below where he was on the cliff. I never could understand how he got down there.

"For two days we tried to work south. Finally we got into a
canyon full of boulders where we could neither get our horses
one way or the other. They were so worn out and hungry that
we finally killed them. They would have starved to death in
that barren granite. We left our saddles and everything and
took our clothes and necessary blankets and went on foot.

"We lived entirely on horse meat. I don't know how horse
meat might be with a little salt, but it certainly is not very nice
without salt. It was just sweet and sickening, and we tried to
chew it as we traveled along, but the meat would keep swell-

ing up in our mouths like a sponge until we could not work our jaws.

"Traveling without the animals was easier, but the country kept getting even more impassable. In working down one canyon, thousands of feet deep, we had to slide down a water run. Sometimes we would slide thirty feet and fetch up on a bench, throwing our blankets on ahead.

"We camped down in one of those canyons one night and then the next morning started east in the hope of reaching the summit of the Sierra Nevadas at a place where we could go down the easterly cliffs into Owens Valley. By night we reached the summit at a place about eighteen miles from Independence, and the next day worked our way down the east cliff into the valley."

Keough may be saluted as organizer of one of the first Sierra "outings"—circuit pack tripping in the manner of the 1860's. As a gold-grubbing expedition it was a failure; the prospectors would have been better off if they had stayed home, for when the bedraggled group reached Independence, they learned that the five who deserted them at the crest of Kearsarge Pass had accidentally stumbled onto the richest ledge in the area— a strike that was to develop into fabulous Cliff Mine.

The only human beings that Keough and his colleagues encountered that summer on the long trek between Independence and the San Joaquin Valley was a delegation of "exploring scientists," led by a professor who introduced himself as William Brewer of the California Geological Survey Corps. To the men from Independence these men appeared slightly off their rockers, and even after Brewer had explained what they were up to, the mission didn't make much sense. Not in one lifetime could four men, or a dozen, map all the ups and downs of the range, as they talked about it, and show, to boot, what was in and under the rocks.

Brewer and his men had become accustomed to that kind of reaction. In 1860 the legislature had ordered a survey of the entire State under the direction of geologist Josiah Whitney; having investigated the Coastal Range, the southern valleys and the gold-bearing foothills over a period of four years, Whitney's troops were moving into the High Sierra. Included on the State Geologist's team were some of the most competent scientists of the nation—professors from Yale and Harvard, geologists, botanists, zoölogists, topographers, paleontologists; a total of about a dozen, but considering the magnitude of the task, not nearly enough. The legislators had no comprehension of the size of the job and lay observers had less.

In their spare time they were expected also to make million-dollar judgments on the probable value of a gold strike, to discredit mine sharks, swindlers and humbugs, to give learned opinions on a find like the Calaveras skull, and take abuse for debasing Mount Shasta. Unfortunately their conclusions weren't always right, and those that were seldom added to their popularity. Nobody in California appeared to have a good word for the Geological Corps.

Then, too, they were ingenious at making things difficult for themselves by mixing scenic appreciation with science. Confirmed romantics, they fell in love with the mountains and made the mistake of letting the public know it. If the Corps had been commissioned solely to publicize the Sierra, to remove some of the guess-and-by-golly travel in the wilderness, to open the mountains for the mountaineers they would have been heroically commended. They did just that, but the legislature had more commercial objectives in mind.

"Here there is a grassy flat, half a mile wide, which terminates just above a grand rocky amphitheatre," wrote Brewer ecstatically from the base of Mount Lyell where he and Professor Whitney had established camp in an idyllic setting. "Sharp granite peaks rise behind to about 13,000 feet, with great slopes of snow, and pinnacles of granite coming up through, projected sharply against the deep blue sky. It was most picturesque, wild and grand. What an experience!

"Two of us, at least sixty miles from civilization on either side, among the grandest chain of mountains in the United States, whose peaks tower above us—we sleeping in the open air, although 1,000 feet higher than the celebrated hospice of the Great St. Bernard, the frost falling white and thick on our blankets every night.

"The high granite walls of the valley, the Alpine aspect of the vegetation, all conspired to make an impressive scene. Just opposite camp, a large stream of snow water came over the rocks—a series of cascades for 1,000 or 1,500 feet in height— a line of spray and foam. By our side a little rill supplied us with the purest cold water. Such a camp—picturesque, romantic! . . . We turned in early; the bright moon lit up the snowy peaks grandly above the great rocky amphitheatre, while the music of waterfalls lulled us to sleep."

Californians were not impressed with the kind of music the official geologists reported. They were having altogether too good a time. Were the legislators subsidizing a camping party? Members of the Corps climbed and named heights like Mount Silliman, Mount Brewer, Mount Tyndall; they diagramed, described and mapped sweeping areas, introduced naturalists and sportsmen to Sierra mountaineering, but their accomplishments were not appreciated by the legislature. In 1865 funds were cut off and the Geological Survey passed out of existence.

Apathy toward scientific exploration of the mountains set in. It lasted for a quarter of a century. In the seventies and eighties federal geologists fixed the altitudes of some of the peaks from stations in the desert east of the Sierra, mapped the Mono Lake region, and made studies of the glaciers around Mount Lyell; but further investigation of the mountains was left largely to the amateurs, free lancers, the sheepherders and John Muir—mostly Muir. With his sack of bread and an ax, he prowled over the range from one end to the other, and in a steady flow of articles and books let sedentaries know what they were missing.

But during that lapse of twenty-five years, attitudes in the West were changing. After a long period of boisterousness, California was calming down. Culture and civility were taking hold. Men were more reluctant to twit folks who found splendor and inspiration in mountain scenery. Muir had captured an audience. Notably he could count on supporters among the faculties at Stanford and the University of California—important scholars like Joseph N. Le Conte, J. H. Senger, President Jordan; popular educators who shared their hobbies with students and extended their interests beyond laboratories and classrooms. Between the two institutions a whole galaxy of eager mountaineers was forming.

Just before the end of the spring semester at the University of California in 1870, Professor Le Conte, who had been slipping asides about the Sierra into his lectures on natural science, was dumfounded when a group of ten students, without even leading up to the subject, bluntly proposed that he accompany them on a trip to Yosemite and the High Sierra. In the best academic circles, such a familiar relationship was frowned upon. The professor was a man to be held in awe; part of his job was to keep a proper distance from students. This was a presumptuous attempt to break the traditional barrier of formality. But Le Conte was enough of a rebel to accept.

"The party was to go in regular pioneer style," explained the professor, "cooking its own provisions and sleeping under the open sky wherever a convenient place was found; each man was to bestride his own horse, carry his own bedding behind his saddle, and his clothing—with the exception of one change of underwear—on his back. This was, it is true, a little rougher and harder than anything I had ever undertaken; but still I was fond of adventure, and longed to enjoy the glories of Yosemite and the beauties of the Sierra, and more than all, to study mountain structure and mountain sculpture, as exhibited there on a magnificent scale."

In the five-week trip they rode their horses from Oakland to the foothills, toured Yosemite, crossed the mountains to Mono Lake and returned by way of Lake Tahoe and Placerville. It was a glorious holiday, and a summer seminar as well, for the Professor liberally diluted the fun with campfire lectures on such subjects as "Glaciers and Glacial Phenomena" and "Deposits in Carbonate Springs." Through it all, he was able to stave off any compromise of his position and retain a certain amount of dignity.

The expedition was history-making. It established a pattern for organized High Sierra trips that was to be followed for decades; it stimulated enough interest to start similar groups heading for the high mountains; it paved the way for the creation of the Sierra Club.

During the next few years Muir, in his lone wanderings, occasionally encountered these probing mountaineers, parties of three or four, or as many as fifteen or twenty; and though he was doing his best to urge people to pay homage to the Sierra, he seldom seemed overjoyed to see them invading his haunts —"A strange sight the tourists made, mounted on mules or small mustang ponies, winding single file through the solemn woods, in gaudy attire, scaring the wild creatures, and one might fancy that even the great pines would be disturbed and groan aghast."

Whether or not Muir liked it, the mountaineers were coming. In 1872 Mount Ritter was conquered, Mount Whitney the next year, Mount Kaweah in 1881, Banner Peak and Mount Williamson in 1884, Barnard in 1892, Darwin in 1895, University Peak and Mount Stanford—to honor the University of California and its rival across the Bay—in 1896, Split Mountain in 1902, Mount Humphries in 1904.

And by then the Sierra Club was going strong. Professor Senger, a man strong for organized assault of the mountains, in 1886 proposed establishing a library on mountaineering in Yosemite Valley as a start toward stirring interest in a climbers' association. Men of action thought the literary approach a little abstruse. A young journalist, Theodore Solomons, had a better idea. He was dreaming about a trail that would run parallel to the crest of the High Sierra for the full length of the range. By 1890 Professor Senger was putting less emphasis on the library and discussing with faculty and students at Berkeley a plan for organizing a mountain club.

Things moved slowly, but two years later the idea had been expanded to include noncollegians as well as students; Senger had John Muir's endorsement and his pledge of membership. The Sierra Club was chartered on June 17th, 1892, with its designated purpose: "to explore, enjoy and render accessible the mountain ranges of the Pacific Coast; to publish authentic information concerning them; to enlist the support and co-operation of the people and the government in preserving the forests and other natural features of the Sierra Nevada Mountains. . . ."

Leading citizens, lawyers, doctors, professors, journalists and distinguished businessmen were among the 182 charter members, and the club was given real status with John Muir's name as its president. Members went to work on publications, maps, lobbying and trail building, but their real business was climbing mountains. Thousands of jumbled peaks were still unclimbed in 1892, and the Sierrans started to check them off one by one.

Typical of the aggressive spirit was the ascent of the spire on Cathedral Peak by Theodore Solomons and his friend, Charles Bailey, in August 1897. Several mountaineers before them had climbed to the roof of the ragged mountain that looked like a giant broken molar, but no one had claimed conquest of the sheer spur protruding from Cathedral's roof. Solomons had vowed that he would fasten a dishrag banner to the tip of the spire. On reaching the summit proper, however, it was apparent that the only possible way of getting to the tip was by casting a line over it and mounting the rope hand over hand. That accessory had been left at home.

Bailey was ready to call it a day, but Solomons first had to inspect the other side of the spire, to make absolutely sure that there were no finger holds. He peered cautiously around the base of the spur, and the sight was enough to chill his blood. He could see the corner of a narrow ledge from which the opposite side might be scanned, but the only access to it was over a shelf of steeply rounded granite, and both ledge and shelf plunged for hundreds of feet straight down. Once the ledge had been spotted, however, even Bailey wasn't going to be content until it was explored.

"It was not the slope in itself that gave us pause," claimed Solomons, "for had the spire risen from level ground, we would have attacked it without a moment's hesitation. It was the abrupt termination in nether air that won from us a most cordial respect."

The temptation was irresistible. Bailey followed the intrepid Solomons across the rounded granite to the narrow ledge. There was no point in looking down, for nothing but space was there. They looked up, and there to the astonishment of both was a chimney made to order.

"I cannot say that we were exactly pleased," confessed Solomons quite candidly. "I think either of us would rather have found as unbroken a facet of pinnacle on this as on the other side. Then we would have heaved a virtuous sigh and returned with the information that only a cowboy with a lariat and a good pair of biceps need apply. But the chimney seemed put there to make Cathedral Peak accessible—and dangerous.

"Bailey was for giving up. Not that he judged the chimney a difficult climb, but he believed he had no moral right to take the chances its ascent involved. I agreed with Bailey in the sentiment, but was disposed to consider the question as to how much chance there really was. The chimney was a nice width and depth for the employment of knees as a means both of resting and ascending, and there were several joint-crevasses by which the fingers could assist. The height was not great. Any ten-year-old boy who could not wriggle himself up that granite column ought to be spanked!

"The question of a possible fall, I argued with Bailey, need not be considered, if we were to be consistent with ourselves and with the principles of Alpinism; wherever a man works on steep slopes, not to speak of precipitous walls, there is liability of injury or death. The chimney was obviously easy and I decided to go, though Bailey protested."

Solomons went up the chimney with more agility than the boy of ten and Bailey followed as easily. Then on the four-foot-square tip, Solomons calmly produced their lunch—wrapped in a dishcloth; from under his shirt he pulled a light, flexible staff, and while they munched sandwiches, the dishcloth flag fluttered from the heights of Cathedral Peak.

But after the descent Solomons had second thoughts: "I do not care to assume the responsibility of advising others to attempt the summit. There is no difficulty in reaching it, but a fall from the chimney would inevitably prove fatal, and while I have often taken chances of this nature, I will never do so again because I believe such acts are pure folly. Nine hundred and ninety-nine one-thousandths of the total pleasure and profits of mountain climbing may be realized without the slightest danger, and for the sake of the other thousandth part, it is surely an act of immorality to risk one's life."

Although the morality of mountain climbing never became a major issue among the philosophers of the Sierra Club, caution and discretion were from the beginning the basic principles of operation. To give all the members their nine hundred and ninety-nine one-thousandth's worth of pleasure and profit, the proposal was made in 1901 that an outing of several weeks be planned for the whole club.

Lovers of solitude and mountain meditation were horrified; such a mass excursion was as appealing as participation in an army field maneuver. Nevertheless, a majority thought it worth a try. "An excursion of this sort," argued the club secretary, William E. Colby, "if properly conducted, will do an infinite amount of good toward awakening the proper kind of interest in the forests and other natural features of our mountains, and will also tend to create a spirit of good fellowship among our members."

Over a hundred thronged to Tuolumne Meadows that summer. They climbed mountains, explored Yosemite, camped in the open, took their meals at a common field kitchen, assembled around evening campfires and had a wonderful time. "In spite of predictions to the contrary, the outing was a complete success," reported the next issue of the club *Bulletin*, "and one of the most positive proofs of this was the fact that the majority were planning for next year's outing almost before they had reached home. The objections raised by many before the outing started, that being such a large party would be unpleasant, proved entirely without foundation. In fact, the association with so many genial spirits and the valuable instruction obtained from the learned lights of the party, made it a pleasure and a memory never to be forgotten."

Kings Canyon and Mount Brewer were on the itinerary the next year, and in 1903 the club was ready to tackle Mount Whitney. By midmorning of July 12th that year "the largest party ever assembled on a California mountain top" were crouching on the high point of the United States—an invasion of 103. They had spent three days covering the forty miles from Kern along Volcano Creek to Whitney's base. It could have been done in less time, but too many anglers in the crowd were lured from the trail by the golden trout of Volcano Creek. The total catch: 600.

Stuffed with trout, the long line of Sierrans started breaking camp at midnight on the 11th. All were on the trail by four o'clock in the morning and at 8:45 A.M. the vanguard reached the crest that had given Clarence King so much trouble. "We looked out over the great valley to the eastward and to Inyo Range beyond," their scribe recorded. "We plainly distinguished Lone Pine and the meandering lines of the river nearly 11,000 feet below us. But it was to the northwest the grandest view lay—peak after peak and crag after crag—the highest Sierra in all their nobility and grandeur. Near, and perhaps most striking of all, was Mount Williamson, its almost perpendicular side ridged and fluted in rich dark reds and browns, its summit dented and apparently defying all attempts at climbing."

But climb it they did. A group of ten members had to answer that defiance. And two days later, after threading through miles of broken, sharp-edged granite, crossing a sapphire lake on the ice, tramping over vast snow fields, ascending chimneys, zigzagging across slopes of talus, feeling a way up the bold crevice on the face of the towering cliffs, scrambling over more acres of giant boulders, they reached the summit and an outlook "incomparably more grand than from Whitney." Two major mountains in three days, and this was no longer solely a masculine pursuit. Four women had gone along. Dressed in billowing bloomers, bodices and sunbonnets, they made it as easily as the men.

On the strength of these early trips, the Sierra Club became a permanent travel agency for the range, and it has been in business ever since. Arrangements are made annually for hundreds of mountaineers of every class and distinction, tramps and pack trips to near and remote parts of the range, outings that capture some of the flavor of the Keough expedition, the Le Conte trip and even Solomons' test of nerve.

Most of the addicts are content to stay on the trails, and between Tehachapi Pass and the saddle south of Lassen Peak are hundreds of miles of them, with well-marked detours leading to peaks, flats, lakes and lookouts—enough wilderness thoroughfare to last a lifetime of summers on foot or in the saddle. But rock climbing is the ultimate in exploring the heights, and sooner or later every resolute mountaineer is beckoned off the trail in search of that extra one-thousandth part of the sport that Solomons cautioned against, a conquest with an element of danger.

Moments of fear, terror and despair are part and parcel of such adventure, and the most disciplined climber at some point in ascending a challenging mountain for the first time can expect to be confronted with his personal kind of panic; the moment when he sees no way out of a predicament, no way up and no way down.

It came to experienced mountaineer Francis Farquhar while ascending the sheer slopes of unscaled Middle Palisade, high above the Kings River region on August 26th, 1921, with Ansel Hall, Yosemite Park's Naturalist.

"Presently I found myself standing on a ledge to the right of Hall, who was in the main chimney," he wrote. "I had reached the point with difficulty and was now absolutely blocked from further progress upward. The way across the ledge toward Hall did not seem very inviting, and I studied the rocks carefully, with the thought of descending a few feet and rejoining him by a lower route. But the more I looked, the more impossible seemed the descent, and presently I became unnerved and thoroughly scared. The longer I looked at the enormous depth below, the worse I felt. Even the ledge to which I was clinging began to seem insecure. . . . Hall too seemed to be in a situation from which further progress was doubtful. He was only fifteen feet away, but that seemed a long distance to me."

The two had reason for alarm. It was the second peak they had climbed that day, signs of fatigue were beginning to show, and the mountain was proving to be far more challenging than they had expected. Lower ledges were covered with deposits of loose gravel and rocks, making it necessary to climb side by side to escape the other's cascade of debris, and the going became more difficult the higher they went.

But like hundreds of climbers who had experienced the same paralysis, Farquhar pulled himself together, subdued his fears and gave up thinking about the abrupt landscape below him. Confidently he sidled across the ledge to his partner for a brief consultation and after an almost carefree analysis of their situation, the two decided they had had enough and would at once turn back.

"We looked around for a route of descent," Farquhar continued, "and then, instead of climbing down, we both began to climb up. It was one of those spontaneous impulses that sometimes occur at critical moments. We found tolerable handholds and footholds and in a few minutes were safely above our ledge. Although the climbing was difficult, we did not stop until we reached the summit. . . . Not a trace of any previous ascent was to be found. With a shout we greeted the summit as its first visitors."

Along with other specialists in mountaineering came the rock climbers with their *pitons*, chisels, expansion bolts and nylon rope, to help conquer the unconquerable. By the 1950's there were few unscaled heights remaining in the Sierra and experts were concentrating on new routes up old favorites. The northeast side of Half Dome was one of these. Time and again the vertical backside of this famed monolith had been studied for handholds, fissures, chimneys, any irregularities; and prospective climbers had given up. The possibility of scaling it had long been discounted. The cliff rose a full 2,000 feet from its base and apparently there was no feasible route up it.

In 1954 a quartet worked over it for several days. They concluded that the upper and lower reaches could probably be climbed, but between them was an impossible traverse covered with a massive flake system and virtually fissureless. Another major attempt was made the following year, when 450 feet of the cliff were scaled before the team withdrew.

But Jerry Gallwas, Mike Sherrick and Royal Robbins weren't ready to take a negative. On June 23rd, 1957, they climbed 150 feet up the face, fixed a rope over the route, then descended and bivouacked to reconsider. Five days later they were at it again and this time they climbed 900 feet, to the edge of the crucial traverse.

Gaining a few yards and getting only halfway across it took another full day, and that was spent largely in placing *pitons* and expansion bolts. It involved a spectacular swing traverse in which one climber had to become the bob on a self-propelled pendulum. Suspended from a *piton*, he had to swing out on his rope far enough to reach a distant hold where another anchor could be placed—and this repeated again and again.

A third day took them the full width of the traverse, and, to facilitate retreat, a fixed rope was left in place. Then, like spiders on a rampart, they started climbing a network of cracks that occasionally resolved into a chimney. By dusk that day they were 1,500 feet above the base.

"Even enthusiasts must admit a certain amount of calculated risk in a climb of this kind," Robbins admitted coolly. "We recognized that the difficulties of removing an injured climber from the face would be insurmountable, so our whole emphasis was on climbing as safely as possible."

Playing it safe called for teamwork of the most demanding order; reading another's mind, anticipating his every move, never for a moment relaxing group guard. Three had to perform as one. Day after day the tension on the giddy heights built up. An unrelenting sun scorched the cliffs by day and penetrating chill crept over them at night. The hours of darkness were interminable. Lashed to narrow, sloping ledges, the climbers could count only on fitful moments of sleep. The suspense was never broken. It accumulated for five days. They admitted that they were fatigued, but could merely make cautious allowance for it and keep going.

Late on the fifth day spirits perked up, despite the weariness. Victory was within reach; they were 200 feet from the top. To expedite progress, the pack containing all gear not essential to climbing was jettisoned. It fell for a third of a mile without touching the wall.

Before darkness closed in, the team slowly crawled over the last shelf to the summit. Behind them on the precipice they had left a total of 275 *pitons* and twenty expansion bolts, all fixed in hard granite. Driving the *pitons* had been hard enough, but every one of the twenty holes for the bolts had to be laboriously chiseled out, chip by chip, while the mountaineers swung from a rope in mid-air or balanced tiptoe on a rock flaw, bodies pressed against the perpendicular wall.

That ascent of Half Dome ranks as one of the world's most incredible climbs, forbiddingly perilous—and not very beneficial to mankind as a whole. It solved none of the generation's problems, added nothing of note to theoretical or practical knowledge.

But, then, neither does an Olympic meet, a football classic or a regatta. If justification of the risks and the struggle has to be found, Sierrans would point to the heading of *le sport*. Theodore Solomons' preachment on morality notwithstanding, the mountain wall spoke defiance, and the challenge had to be answered with human defiance, skill and rare endurance. In the same spirit thousands of other mountaineers answer less demanding calls of the heights. The Sierra has much more to declare than the romance of spectacle and enchanting scenery. Besides, as John Muir pointed out, "The devil never gets above the timber line."

XIII

TERRIBLY DOWNRIGHT
UTTERANCES OF STORMS

For all the luminous serenity, for all the show of summer repose and solid permanence, the Sierra can be as temperamental
as an adolescent. No mood is held for long. The humors of the
mountains shift with the wind, the weather, the hour of day and
any other set of circumstances that nature may conjure up.
Though the range may be reasonably even-tempered in July

272

and August, there is nothing predictable about its caprice the rest of the year.

The mountains are at the mercy of two major sources of trouble and turbulence—chill tempests sweeping down from the Aleutians and warm gales blown in from the Hawaiian Islands. The violence of either is enough to stir up pandemonium; but occasionally the two stage a battle to the finish over the range and all hell breaks loose.

When the Sierra goes on a rampage, there is not much mere mortals can do but stand by and watch in awe. The omnipotence of the mountains is not to be disputed. From the towering shoulders may come thundering slides of rock, overwhelming masses of snow in the form of avalanches or oceanic volumes of water. Water is the worst.

Among all the displays of mountain temper, the floods that gush out of the canyons are the most damaging to earthlings and their chattels. Plunging from heights to foothills, a stream gathers body and momentum from every tributary en route, sweeps toward the lowlands, fills cramped channels long since choked with silt and spews the excess over the banks to submerge everything in sight. At the foot of the Sierra, and far out in the valleys, are fought the most harrowing battles against mountain petulance.

The wars against water are as old as the history of California. Spanish missionaries told of terrible floods in 1770. Indians saw Sacramento Valley turn into an inland lake in 1805; their villages were swamped and hundreds of tribesmen lost. Disaster struck in 1815, 1825, 1846, 1849-50, 1852. In 1861 water rolled three feet over the banks of the American River at Sacramento and lay twice as deep in adjacent troughs; so great was the force of the flood that San Francisco Bay teemed with fresh-water fish. The San Joaquin Valley was hardest hit in 1867; on Christmas Eve the town of Millerton was all but wiped out; trees were brought down the rivers in such quantity that the sawmill at Skaggs Bridge was supplied with enough logs to keep in operation for a full year.

Marysville, a sprawling city of over 5,000, at the confluence of the Yuba and Feather Rivers, was the victim in 1875. On Monday, January 18th, the local *Appeal* expressed a note of anxiety when attention was called to the fact that it had been raining off and on, sometimes heavily, for almost a week—one of those warm Hawaiian storms. "The threatening weather of the past few days," observed the newspaper, "culminated on Sunday night into another rainstorm, which continued at intervals through yesterday, and last evening turned into a heavy storm, the water coming down in torrents. The effects upon our rivers will depend upon its duration and how much snow is coming with the rain from the mountains."

The storm proved all too durable, and the rivers, fed by melting mountain snows, continued to swell. Marysville was scared. Original settlers in 1849 had built the town on the edge of a seventy-foot drop into the bed of the Yuba—a channel apparently deep enough to keep the streets high and dry in any flood season, yet three years later the booming city was completely inundated. In 1853 a worse flood struck, and after the water receded, the grade of the entire business district, including whole blocks of buildings, was raised twelve feet—at enormous cost.

But even that extra twelve feet of elevation served as little protection two decades later, for the scourings from upstream hydraulic mining had completely filled the seventy-foot river bed, and the safety of the city now depended on seven miles of narrow levees that reached around its circumference. Sections of the metropolis were actually below the normal level of the Yuba.

On Tuesday, January 19th, 1875, the levees, indeed, looked like a scant protective wall. Surging waters in both the Yuba and the Feather were rising at the rate of a foot an hour, and it was still raining. At seven o'clock in the morning the gauge at the railroad bridge read nine feet above high-water mark. Everyone knew that run-off from the mountains was largely responsible. The Sierra was again in a state of high dudgeon.

The fire bell sounded the first general alarm about midmorning. Water from the river had worked into an old abandoned sewer line and was discharging into the city with the force of a penstock. With the help of professional engineers, that maelstrom was stemmed and capped within two hours, but no one ventured any reassurance that leaks just as serious wouldn't burst at other points.

The water continued to rise. Late in the morning a hundred men were set to work re-enforcing a stretch of levee where a lashing wind was driving small waves over the top. They raised the height two feet and staved off disaster in that sector. To add to the general dismay, the skies turned night-black and the steady drizzle resolved into a crashing thunderstorm with a deluge that came down in wind-driven sheets. Then the clouds broke and the rain stopped altogether.

For those with enough curiosity to size up the seriousness of the situation from a levee top, the rampaging river made a blood-chilling sight. Bobbing along on the crest of the current was an almost solid pudding of cordwood and trees, logs and lumber, boxes, fencing, shakes, haystacks, doors, barrels, hogsheads, packing crates and chicken coops, and the water was already high enough to cast up refuse onto the embankment. It was too late for a mass evacuation; bridges were gone, trains stalled, fields on every side were quagmires.

By noon the Yuba had risen higher than any maximum ever known before. Water was seeping under the levees at countless points. It found hidden channels and bubbled up unexpectedly in basements, on lawns, in gutters. Mouths of gopher holes turned into gurgling fountains. Providentially the rain had discontinued, but a warm wind of gale force was blowing —a wind so fierce that it was peeling heavy planks off the top of timber stacks at a Marysville lumberyard and flinging them about like cardboard.

Teams of volunteers labored all afternoon on the levees, but more and more it looked like a hopeless struggle. The plains were a vast lake three feet deep, and water was backing up from the Feather River slough. Darkness came on early, and with it work at the levees was abandoned—abandoned with the terrible knowledge that a break could occur at any moment. Except for candlelight and kerosene lamps, Marysville that night was a blacked-out city, for the gasworks were already under water.

Just before seven o'clock the firebell clanged another general alarm. Watchmen had spotted a major levee rupture. Scores of men rushed to the site to stop the flow with rocks, scrap iron, mattresses, sandbags. Working up to their hips in the sludge, they hurled back the very flotsam that was being spewed at them from the Yuba. The breach was plugged and it held, but it was all too evident that the water-logged embankment was doomed. The gauge at the railroad bridge measured a flood height of fourteen and a half feet.

An hour later came the kind of disaster that everyone most feared. Waves surged in over a slump in the levee just north of the hospital. At the risk of their lives, volunteers tried to hold it; one man after another was caught in the swirl as the soggy clay gave way, and had to be rescued. There was no stopping this one. The banks crumbled and seemed to dissolve. Water billowed into the city at the speed of a millrace, carrying everything in its path—bridges, fences, outhouses.

A barn caught in the wash crashed against the railroad bridge over Slaughterhouse Slough, and both disappeared in the darkness. In minutes the brown tide swept over the city, rolling down the streets and rising to a depth of from three to five feet. The inundation was complete. No building was spared, for the foundations of few reached above street level. In the business district were structures with upper floors, where people could take refuge, but the single-story homes offered no such sanctuary.

A liveryman rescued his trapped family by swimming to his roof, ripping off a patch of shingles and hauling his wife and children through the improvised escape hatch to the ridge. A family of nine climbed to the top of their upright piano and somehow found room on it to perch through the night. Wading waist-deep in the tide, merchants piled their goods onto counters, shelves and tiers of boxes; then had to make space on a shelf for themselves to escape the rising water.

In the whole city there were not more than six rowboats, and they all seemed to belong to mercenaries who demanded five dollars per rescue; the most desperate didn't happen to have a fiver in their wet pockets and were left to flounder as best they could. When a raft carrying a six-year-old boy capsized, no boatman came to the rescue; the youngster disappeared. Nor was there an answer to the frantic cries of another lad who clung for nine hours to the top of a kitchen door.

Mayor Hawley's cow, tethered in the back yard, broke from her moorings and sought refuge in his residence; she crowded through the front door and drowned in his parlor. When the water in the county jail got up to the three-foot level, the sheriff took pity on his one prisoner and let him swim for his life.

Although water was everywhere, firemen were hard put to use it in killing the conflagrations that kept breaking out. The fire horses had been led to higher ground and the steamer was anchored in five feet of water. A private home burned to the water line, unattended. No one even bothered to sound the alarm. As water seeped into the storage rooms of Lee's Lime House, lime started to slake; the building burst into flames from the heat and went up in a crackling blaze.

More sinister was the fire at Ross Grocery Store in the heart of the city. There, kerosene from storage tanks in the basement worked to the surface on the flooded first floor, and an upset candle accidentally ignited it. From windows and balconies the cry of "Fire!" echoed block to block. If the blaze got through the roof where it could be wafted by the wind, half the city could go. Marysville's harassed citizens began to measure the choice between death by fire and death by drowning. Clouds of black smoke poured from the building in the light of an eerie glow.

The stubborn fire was fought from boats and rafts, by a ring of volunteers standing chest-deep in water, by firemen braving the heat and fumes on the second floor and roof. The only way to keep it from spreading was to let the oil burn off inside the building. It ate through the second floor and charred every exposed board and beam in the structure, but it was kept confined by townsmen furiously splashing water on the walls, floors and roof from every kind of container they could lay hands on. It was a full hour before the last of the orange flame flickered out and the torturing suspense was over.

About midnight the flood reached its crest—fifteen feet. An hour later it began to recede. At daybreak Wednesday morning, Marysville was a city half submerged, its roofs protruding above an inland sea on a level with the Feather and Yuba rivers. A riptide still swept down the main streets from the levee break on the north side.

During the day the gigantic flash flood fell back more quickly than it had come. By late afternoon on Wednesday people could come down from their roofs and balconies, and begin to clean up. Except for the layer of slippery silt, the streets were almost normal. But it was a major disaster. Many merchants suffered total stock losses and hundreds of families had few possessions that could be salvaged.

The Marysville calamity was only a sample of the kind of fury the Sierra could unleash in a savage tantrum. The sole hope for the city in its perennial war against mountain floods was to build higher and mightier dikes, so that the Yuba could by-pass it in a channel incongruously higher than the level of the streets.

Weatherwise John Muir was a close observer of that 1875 storm, and he had a ready explanation for it all: "The cause of this notable flood was simply a sudden and copious fall of warm rain and warm wind upon the basins of the Yuba and Feather rivers at a time when they contained a considerable quantity of snow. Both the rain and that portion of snow which the rain and the wind melt are sponged up and held back until the combined mass becomes sludge, which at length—suddenly dissolving—descends all together to the trunk of the rivers, where, heaping and swelling, flood over flood, they debouch upon the plain with violence and suddenness."

During the height of the great storm, while panic-stricken Marysville inhabitants were fighting for their lives and homes,

Muir was back in the mountains, calmly strolling in the rain, enraptured by the display of violence.

"It is a pity that so few people were fortunate enough to fairly meet with and enjoy this noble storm in its home among the mountains," he deplored. "It will doubtless be remembered far more for the drifted bridges and houses that chanced to be in its way than for its beauty or for the thousand, thousand blessings it brought. The pines had long slept in sunshine; they are now awake, and with one accord waved time to the beatings of the storm. The winds swept along the music curves of many a hill and dale, streaming through the pines, cascading over rocks and blending all their tones and chords in one grand harmony.

"Never have I beheld water falling from the sky in denser or more passionate streams. The heavy wind beat forward the spray in suffocating drifts. Go where I would, on ridges or in hollows, water still flashed and gurgled around my ankles. Dry Creek was a booming river, its current brown with mining mud washed down from many a claim, and mottled with sluice boxes, fence rails and ponderous logs that had long lain above its reach. On the slim footbridge stretching across from bank to bank, I was glad to linger, gazing and listening, while the storm was in its finest mood—the gray driving rain stream above, the brown savage flood river beneath.

"The storm language of the river was hardly less enchanting than that of the forest wind; the sublime overboom of the main current, the swash and gurgle of eddies, the keen clash of firm wave masses breaking against rocks, and the smooth hush of shallow currentlets feeling their way through the willows of the margin; and amid all this throng of sounds, I could hear the smothered bumping and rumbling of boulders down on the bottom, as they were shoving and rolling forward against one another. The glad, strong creek rose high above its banks. Alders and willows were standing waist-deep, while supple branches bending over the flood dipped lightly and rose again as if stroking the wild waters in play.

"Leaving the bridge and pushing on through the storm-swept forest, all the ground seemed in motion. Toward midday, cloud, wind and rain seemed to have reached their highest pitch of grandeur. The storm was fully developed; it was in full bloom, and formed, from my commanding outlook on the hill-top, one of the most glorious spectacles I ever beheld. As far as eye could reach—above, beneath, around—the dusty wind-beaten rain filled the air like one vast waterfall, bending the pines like weeds, pouring over all like an ocean current.

"I watched the gestures of the pines while the storm was at its height, and it was easy to see that they were not at all distressed. Several large sugar pines stood near the thicket in which I was sheltered, bowing solemnly and tossing their giant arms as if interpreting the very words of the storm while accepting its wildest onsets with a passionate exhilaration. How terribly downright must seem the utterances of storms and earthquakes to those accustomed to the soft hypocrisies of society!"

Few storm-battered Californians could afford the luxury of Muir's detachment. The utterances were too downright, too destructive, too recurrent to be heard with any glow of appreciation by valley dwellers. The Sierra knew no favoritism in distributing its largess. Any of the gentle streams tumbling down from the mountains could be transformed overnight into ravaging rivers—the Feather, the Yuba, the American, the Sacramento, the Mokelumne, the Calaveras, the Stanislaus, the Tuolumne, the Merced, San Joaquin, Chowchilla, Fresno, Kings, the Kern, the Truckee; and most of them had north forks, south forks, middle forks and a hundred tributaries. No town built close to the banks could be free from the outbursts of Sierra temper.

Marysville would be singled out for harassment one year; another season the brunt was taken by Modesto, or Auburn, Stockton, Sonora, Oroville or Sacramento. There were hundreds of communities and each seemed to wait its turn stoically, though the day of devastation might be postponed for decades, for half a century or longer. It was as though some vengeful Zeus, enthroned in the High Sierra, at a whim pointed an angry finger toward a particular community and then suddenly turned the waters loose. Adjacent towns always suffered too, but the pent-up wrath of the mountain gods seemed to be vented on one place in particular.

The old mining town of Downieville, high in the foothills, waited for its catastrophic visitation for ninety years—until 1937. Bisected by the North Fork of the Yuba, at a point just below the broad mouths of half a dozen creeks, Downieville was a natural for a watery assault. The town had lost stature and population since the gold rush days and was reduced to a minority of some 600 inhabitants, but it was still the seat of Sierra County, an important, proud, picturesque mountain village.

On Friday night, December 10th, 1937, it resembled a fantastic log jam, with timber, trees, beds, parlor furniture sandwiched between crushed front porches, sheds and barn roofs. The rain that brought disaster was labeled by old-timers "the heaviest downfall in the history of the County—beyond anything within living memory." It had poured torrentially for three days. All the rivers flowing out of the range were swollen and some thirty other towns were sorely stricken, but none quite like Downieville.

Early in the afternoon of the 10th, the snow in the uplands that had been soaking up water reached the saturation point and turned into fluid all at once. Whole mountainsides of sludge were dumped into the Yuba basin to form a long, rolling comber. Downieville was struck before the wave had a chance to spread or dissipate. The river rose four feet in an hour.

With the flood came every loose log, felled tree, building and bridge that trespassed the stream's ancient right of way. The mass was flung against a new highway bridge that had just been built to connect the two sections of town. Before the monstrous push of water, the collected waste was hurled into the streets. In a shrieking that could be heard above the roar of the deluge, the bridge collapsed. The stream bed was too shallow to contain the cargo of smashed lumber and uprooted trees, so the clutter was forced ashore. There were battering-rams to flail houses, and waves of flotsam, moving with the power of a glacier, to crush other buildings.

Luckily most of Downieville's back yards had emergency exits to the hills. Five hundred fled to higher ground. Not a life was lost. But from the hillsides, refugees watched surging currents eat away the streets and undercut embankments to create landslides. They saw battered houses riding the crest of the flood, tables, chairs, cupboards—even a hot-water tank wrenched so recently from its heater that it was still coughing steam. Before the afternoon of horror was over, exactly four major buildings remained standing, or undamaged beyond repair.

More than a day passed before the first relief crews could reach the distressed village, and then it was necessary to cross Goodyear Creek by bucket and cable strung between trees. The skies had cleared and the thermometer at the 3,000-foot altitude was dropping, but the water was still high.

"Sorely stricken by floods, the like of which seldom, if ever, have been seen in the Sierra," read one of the first eyewitness dispatches to come from the devastated town, "the people of California's Mother Lode country today faced a bitter winter. The mountains are a veritable sponge. The roads are coated with water, houses are gone or damaged, clothing has been swept away and communication with the outside is all but impossible. Add to that, freezing weather which is to be expected with the clearing skies, or deep snow atop the mud, and the plight of the people of the hills is indeed desperate.

"The Yuba river sweeps through here, still a maddened monster of yellow foaming silt, after carrying away most of the houses and leaving others standing crazily tilted, with a loss estimated at $500,000. Along the banks is a wake of piled-up trees, dislodged rocks, driftwood and suffering. Every crevice holds a stream of water. Thousands of those streams drop down to the river in almost mile-high waterfalls, like fairy threads woven among the green trees. Then they splash against the roads or into the river with silvery mists and rainbow hues.

"Again the water gurgles out of the banks at the side of the roads, crystal-clear springs, but they come from sodden masses of earth that loosely hang in place and threaten to cover the roads at any moment. For long stretches the roads have been covered with slimy silt and driftwood. At other spots the raging torrents have eaten under the banks of roads, causing cave-ins and threatening destruction. Dread of what is to come grips the people of Downieville. The Sierra is in sorry shape."

That was a limited engagement with the mountains. Eighteen years later all northern and central California seemed to be awash. During the century that Americans had been keeping a weather eye on the Sierra, meteorology had developed into a science, and by 1955 the diviners had erudite explanations for what was happening on the heights—explanation, but little solace: the high-altitude, jet-air stream that normally flowed from the Pacific and crossed northern California had unaccountably moved 1,000 miles to the South, a displaced river of moist, subtropical Hawaiian air, three miles deep and 400 miles across.

Urged on by gale winds, the jet stream dumped water over the length and breadth of the State, then rushed eastward to focus itself like a wavering blowtorch on the Sierra summits. Torrents lashed the mountains. Under the impact of wind and rain, almost the entire six-foot snow pack stored over thousands of square miles dissolved, and, as white water, came roaring down the San Joaquin, the Sacramento, the Feather, the Truckee and all the other rivers, to add to the surplus with which the lowlands were already saturated.

Few towns and cities bordering a river were exempt from invasion. But again it was the Yuba that acted up most dramatically. This time the floods came ironically as a Christmas present. Since the onslaught of 1875, Marysville had experienced many other incursions, and its population of 12,500 was now securely garrisoned behind monumental levees seventy feet wide. Yet on the afternoon of December 23rd, 1955, water was a scant two feet below the top of the barrier and still rising. Marysville was ordered evacuated.

Bumper to bumper 3,500 cars streamed across the bridge

connecting Marysville with its twin metropolis, Yuba City, on the west side of the Feather. Except for the obstinate few who insisted on remaining to hold the fort, Marysville was a deserted city within two hours. Burdened with brightly wrapped Christmas presents and the choicest family possessions, the evacuees accepted the holiday hospitality of Yuba City.

But Marysville wasn't to be the target of Sierra wrath after all. Hardly had the fugitives settled into their emergency quarters when the levees guarding Yuba City began to collapse, and the inhabitants of both cities had to move on. It looked like a mass migration—to Colusa, to Woodland, to Camp Beale, to Sacramento. On the day before Christmas an unbroken queue of cars stretched for twenty-eight miles between Yuba City and Colusa.

These were not the only population centers affected. Sutter City was ordered evacuated. Three thousand people fled from Stockton and 20,000 more were alerted, in case the San Joaquin burst its banks. Hundreds of towns were in trouble. On the other side of the mountains, the Truckee River was on a rampage too. Reno's streets were barricaded with sandbags, and tons of water were pouring through the business district— while loud-speakers at peak volume helped to drown out the roar of waters with a bombardment of Christmas carols.

On Christmas day 10,000 Californians were homeless, the death toll had risen to over sixty, estimated destruction to $200,000,000; nearly 1,000,000 acres were under water, and wide blocks of two states were officially listed as major disaster areas on orders from Washington. Among all the Sierra provocations, it was the most expensive yet known. In six days thirty inches of rain had fallen generally over northern California, and some localities measured forty.

In all likelihood, the air-jet stream had wandered off course many times before, undetected, bringing rainfall and a mountain run-off fully as heavy as the 1955 sample. Compared to floods the Indians and Spanish experienced, the mid-century deluge may have been relatively moderate. But with millions of people crowding the river banks and assembling perishable property of inestimable value, the valleys were becoming more and more vulnerable to colossal destruction, and despite all the efforts of flood control agencies, Californians and Nevadans could look forward to periodic dampenings that would be increasingly costly. It was foreordained when the Pacific and the Sierra Nevada long ago entered into a climatic conspiracy.

Joined in the conspiracy, too, are all the other destructive elemental forces—frost, heat, expansion and contraction, wind, earthquakes and fire storms like the violent ones of 1961 when as many as 170 conflagrations were simultaneously racing over the Sierra and other sections of California. Any of the destroyers can produce terrifying cataclysms, but the collapse of a cliff or summit pinnacle—wedged off balance by the slow working of earth forces—can be the most spectacular.

In ages past, unwitnessed by man, whole mountain tops have crashed into valleys in stupendous displays that sent streamers of dust high into the heavens. The immense talus slopes in the Kings River region bear witness to the events. Old Tom Mountain, one of the prominent peaks on the east scarp, lost its top. The debris fell thousands of feet to form a rock dump at the toe of the slope and carve a scar that is still visible. Rock avalanches of varying magnitude are constantly occurring—more frequently heard than seen. .

No natural disruption could be more awesome than the sight of a Niagara of rock cascading from a mile-high summit, but no one is ever likely to view it, for the cataclysm itself is obscured by its own cloud of dust. Spectators were present, however, for a minor dislodgment at Yosemite Valley in 1949.

"With a thunderous roar and amid a mushrooming cloud of dust, tons of rock cascaded from the south wall of Yosemite Valley in the vicinity of Sentinel Rock at 1:40 P.M. Sunday afternoon, October 23rd," reported a park naturalist. "So thick, indeed, was this cloud that it blotted out the sun in the general area and made it impossible to determine for a time just what had happened. Only as this cloud moved up the valley, rising almost to the top of the walls, was the magnitude of the slide revealed.

"High on the south wall of the valley, within a hundred or so feet of the top, and across the ravine of Sentinel Fall, a large section of the shoulder of a cliff had broken off, leaving a scar of perhaps several acres of loose and weathered rock. The tremendous concussion caused by the slide started a second one from the west shoulder of Sentinel Rock, itself, about 1,000 feet from the top.

"Mature trees were splintered or sheared off by the descending rock, while still others stood stark beneath the cliff, shorn of all branches. Dust lay an eighth of an inch thick over the rocks and ground for a quarter of a mile."

By chance a group on horseback happened to see the start of the spectacle before it was hidden by the dust. "We stared hypnotized, our horses tense and trembling," recounted one of the riders. "We could see great boulders shearing the branches from trees along the cliff wall; the noise increased, the low rumble was terrifying. Suddenly the foremost part of the slide hit bottom and dense clouds of dust and debris arose.

"It seemed as if a huge tidal wave of dust was advancing toward us. Within seconds we were completely enveloped, unable to see the trees next to us and obscured from each other. The dust became fiery red, filled with flying sparks caused by the intense friction. There and then we decided to get out before we were goners. Simultaneously, we all wheeled our horses and raced back to the Old Village, the billowing dust in hot pursuit."

More subtle, more insidious and even more lethal is the billowing dust of Sierra snow avalanches, for they slip off the foreheads of mountains with no thundering crash and roar. A muffled thud and a whisper are the only sounds that are likely to herald the coming of a snow slide. It gives no sporting chance of escape to anyone in its way, for a dry-powder avalanche can descend a forty-degree slope at a clip of 200 miles an hour. The convulsion is over in a trice.

In that moment of descent the thousands of tons of snow may carry away a forest or a village, sweep the chaos into a valley and far up the side of an adjacent mountain. But the greatest destruction is caused by the whirlwind and vacuum which the sudden displacement of snow creates, rather than by the weight of snow itself. Local eddies, fiercer than hurricane blasts, may flatten buildings or acres of forest completely removed from the path, and a human being, unscathed by the roll of snow, may be suffocated in the clouds of compressed crystals.

The Sierra is as natural a haunt for avalanches as for glaciers. For many years the range was counted as the snowiest on the continent. In a definitive monograph published by the *Monthly Weather Review* as late as 1915, the Sierra Nevada was credited with the national heavyweight snow championship. "California," asserted the report, "usually thought of as a land of fruit, sunshine and flowers, also has within its borders the region of greatest snowfall in the United States."

But weather analysts in the Cascades, on Mount Rainier, in the Olympics and the Coast Range of British Columbia and Alaska have since deprived the Sierra of its standing. Nevertheless, it still is entitled to the world's record for a single year's snowfall. That was established at Tamarack, California, 8,000 feet up on the west slope, in 1907, and it has yet to be surpassed. Between September 1906 and June 1907, more than 73 feet fell at Tamarack—an accumulation which, if it had fallen on Manhattan, would have buried every six-story structure in the city and reached the window ledges on the seventh floor of the Empire State Building.

Snow pack is another of the Sierra excesses—like the rain and the wind, a by-product of the close alliance with the Pacific. Even the 1907 accumulation edged out other records in the range only by a small margin, for Joseph Le Conte chalked up 775 inches at Summit for the season ending in 1880; 776 in 1890; 685 in 1895. Such monumental quotas of snow makes slides inevitable; it is too much for a steep slope to hold.

Down it comes at a velocity of a mere fifteen or twenty miles an hour when an unseasonable rain or thaw has added its weight, or at the 200-mile-an-hour clip when a few feet of new powder have built up on a slippery crust. Hundreds of shorn gullies and stripped slopes—often interspaced with fingerlike ridges of forest—are scattered through the range to memorial ize the avalanches that have swept down the flanks in past centuries, while the sites of more recent slides are marked at the foot of a bare incline by tangles of decaying trees embedded in depths of packed slide snow that may not melt for a decade.

Gold miners in the fifties, who attempted to weather the long winters near their diggings, were among the first to be exposed to the terrors of cascading snow. In 1852, Sierra "City" was a misnomer; it was a village of tents, shacks, log houses and a few frame buildings, including a baker's shop and the usual run of saloons and gambling houses. Its principal claim to distinction was based on gold, scenery and altitude. The diggings were incredibly productive; the jagged Sierra Buttes rose to a sheer height of 8,600 feet above the settlement; and the "city" itself was at an altitude of 4,100 feet.

Snow came early and piled up to unheard-of depths. Tents collapsed under the weight of it, and then the roofs of houses. As best they could, frozen Argonauts straggled to the valley, leaving behind a stricken town. Five stubborn die-hards remained, and they were too preoccupied with routine problems of survival to be watching when the Buttes suddenly discarded their top layer of drifts. The snow came down in a smothering swirl to wipe out the last vestiges of the village. Only three of the five surfaced.

The Sierra City tragedy was a prelude to the afflictions of the railroad builders during the next decade. Engineer John R. Gilliss told of one storm that lasted almost continuously from February 18th, 1867 to March 2nd, adding ten feet to the crippling mass of snow that already buried the construction camps at Donner Pass.

"These storms were grand," related Gilliss. "About the second or third day the wind would become a gale and would plough up the new-fallen snow and heap it in huge drifts. Thirty feet from our windows was a large warehouse; this was often hidden completely. On the cliff above, the cedar trees were deeply cut, many branches the thickness of a man's arm being cut off entirely by the drifting snowflakes. No man can face these storms when they are in earnest.

"Snowslides or avalanches were frequent. The storm winds, being always from the southwest, form drifts or snow wreaths on the northeast crest of the hills. When these become too heavy they break off, and in falling start the loose snow below, sliding on the old crust. Near the close of one storm a log house, containing some fifteen or sixteen men in all, was crushed and buried at daybreak. The bulk of the slide passed over the house, so that it was covered only fifteen feet deep. By six o'clock that night the men were dug out. Only three were killed. The bunks were close to the log walls and kept the rest from being crushed. The snow packed around the men so closely that only two could move about. Most of the men were conscious, although fourteen hours under the snow.

"This event startled us, for at the top of the cliff in front of the camp was a snow wreath forty or fifty feet long, projecting twenty feet, and of the same thickness. We were uncertain when it would come down and where it would stop, so a keg of powder was put down behind it next morning and fired. A white column shot up a hundred feet, and then the whole hillside below was in motion; it came down a frozen cascade, covered with glittering snow dust for spray. It was a rare sight, for snow slides are so rapid and noiseless that comparatively few are seen. They were so frequent across the trail leading to tunnel Number Nine that it had to be abandoned for some months. At tunnel ten, some fifteen or twenty Chinamen were killed by a slide . . . two road repairers were buried too and their bodies not found until spring."

Avalanches continued to be a menace to the Central Pacific long after the line was completed, as well as to highway travelers and mountain villagers, but not until throngs of skiers began making tracks on the high slopes a half century later did they become a subject of popular concern.

"There is a great menacing problem that we skiers must take seriously before it is too late," warned a pioneer of the hickories. "Hanging over our heads on almost every ski area in the

West is the constant threat of an avalanche." To give point to
the warning, he cited a list of recent casualties, and recalled
that the whole surface of Rustler Mountain had spilled into the
valley at six o'clock one weekend evening a few minutes after
the last of the ski crowd had quit the runs.

A miss, too close for comfort, almost brought disaster to a
line of half a dozen skiers on Mount Lincoln in 1949. "A muffled *crummph* from the snow beside me was the only warning,"
attested the fifth man to navigate safely the steep side of an
open bowl, a few feet ahead of "Barney," the Sixth. "Glancing
over my shoulder, I saw the surface that had been smooth a
moment before churning and sliding down. 'Look out, Barney!' I shouted.

"The moving snow swept around his legs. My eyes riveted on
him. The snow was flowing past the tails of my skis, while I remained in the zig of our climbing track. As I watched Barney
sitting in the sliding snow, questions flashed through my mind:
'How far would he go? Four skiers were obviously safe, but
would we have to dig Barney out? Could he manage to keep
his head up, and would the snow sweep over him?'

"After a few long seconds, he came to rest about forty feet
below the track and stood up. He was okay. As he started to
climb toward us, we could relax and look around. Barney, fifteen feet behind me, had been caught in the fringe of a small
avalanche, now motionless and silent. The slide filled the whole
bowl that drops off steeply from the east end of Mount Lincoln and drains into Cold Stream. It was from two to three hundred yards wide and probably more than four hundred yards
to the fall line. The escarpment arch at the top seemed all of
eight feet at its maximum.

"We had no desire to check closer. The big chunks of snow
in the middle of the slide could still topple and bury us; many
were jeep-sized, mixed with countless smaller blocks. . . . A
fine crack in the smooth snow beside my skis curved back and
up toward the slide area.

"The complete absence of trees in the bowl was evidence of
previous slides. Our uptrack had followed a route often taken

by skiers in climbing the peak. The avalanche had started from the breakup of a wind slab that extended across the bowl, bridging softer snow underneath. Superficially there was no sign of a wind slab. The surface was not crusty and there was no noticeable overhanging cornice. The weight of several skiers, turning and stamping on the uptrail had been enough to crack the edge of the slab at an anchor point, so that the whole slab fractured."

As avalanches go, that was diminutive. A typical full-blown one ripped down the north face of Ralston Ridge, above Echo Lake on March 24th, 1948. It came in the middle of a two-day storm that brought fifty-mile-an-hour winds and an accumulation of over three feet of snow in the first day, on top of an icy crust. So blinding was the storm and so high-pitched was the wind that people within a short distance of the avalanche were unaware of it until the sky cleared next day and they saw the litter of houses and trees strewn across Echo Lake.

An assortment of buildings was carried away by the slide, but more of them, well back from its course, were demolished by the powerful eddy of wind it stirred up. A cabin was blown from its foundations; a garage, twenty-five feet from the avalanche track, left upside down; an eight-foot water tank was blasted from its base; three summer cottages were shattered so thoroughly by the wind that only narrow tongues of wreckage, stretching for 125 yards, remained.

A bugle was found hanging high in a tree above the site of a lodge that had been totally demolished, and a phonograph, lifted by the wind, was left standing upright and undamaged a hundred yards from a wrecked shelter. The wall of one house facing the slide was intact, but the roof and opposite wall were lodged in a grove a hundred feet away. Freak cyclonic winds vaulted stands of pine, leaving them unscathed, but stripping trees beyond clean of their lower branches.

Only one cabin in the corridor of the avalanche had been occupied that weekend; with his wife, four children and a guest, John J. Gregg of Berkeley had packed in two days before the storm, and their arrival had been noted by the Jean Lan-

dres, good friends who lived across the lake. No occupant of
the Gregg cabin stood a chance of survival; against their snug
shelter the full blast of the slide was aimed.

Jean Landre had once lived in the Alps and knew from experience something of the devastation that could be dealt by
an avalanche. It was with a familiar chill of horror that he discovered next morning what had happened. There was the tell-
tale path of the slide, broken trees, the mountainous heaps of
snow and refuse spread far out onto the lake surface, and on
the slope beyond three missing cottages—including the
Gregg's.

Mr. and Mrs. Landre quickly donned their skis and slid
down to the lake. They inspected the confusion of litter and
packed snow and then climbed to the site of the Gregg cabin.
Nowhere was there a sign of life. Sadly they made their way to
the foot of the lake to report the tragedy: an entire family had
been wiped out, all buried under 1,500,000 cubic feet of snow.
It would be impossible to recover the bodies until the snow
melted.

But the Landres were wrong. There were no casualties.

"A gale that would snow us in for days was obviously brew-
ing," Gregg later explained. "I spent an hour trying to decide
whether I should risk getting the family out before the storm
broke or play it safe and stay in that nice, secure cabin. We
had no premonition of danger. Leaving before we were snow
bound and heading back to Berkeley seemed the most sensible
thing to do, though not halfway down the lake when we were
bucking a real blizzard and sticking to the shore line to keep
from getting lost, I regretted my foolish decision."

After the first spring thaw, the Greggs returned to recover
what they could of their belongings. Protruding from the snowbank was their outboard motor—in perfect condition; fragments of bathroom porcelain were strewn hither and yon on
the ice, yet a fragile glass container half full of kerosene was
picked up intact. Though splinters from their cabin roof and
sidings littered the lake, the floor and substructure back on the
slope were in no way damaged. And in a corner where the

kitchen had once been, lay a mousetrap exactly as it had been placed—not even sprung.

In the same area a ski party of four had an even closer call on New Year's Day of 1955. Nosing into a soggy storm of mixed drizzle and snow, the skiers set out from their lodge above Echo Lake at 9:30 A.M. for the summit of Mount Ralston. The surface was anything but ideal, for the heavy wet snow was being packed by a strong wind on top of a deep layer of dry powder.

Their route was a gradual climbing traverse up the lower slopes of the valley wall to the large *cirque* on the northern face of the mountain. They knew that great avalanches had occurred at Echo Lake in the past and were not unaware of the danger, but the trail passed over no prominent slide routes. Once, while crossing a small patch of debris, they distinctly heard the dull crunch of settling snow, yet it was nothing more than would be expected, considering the weather.

Before proceeding on to a high rocky knob above a long open slope, they paused to discuss the possibility of a slide, but any thought of a real hazard was dismissed, in view of the relatively small expanse. The incline was concave, varying from fifteen degrees at the bottom to sixty at the top. Skiing tip to tail, they had started across the slope in a climbing traverse when it suddenly happened. There was the usual ominous thud; then everywhere at once surface cracks began to open.

"Here she goes," someone shouted. They felt themselves side-slipping as the swirling blanket plummeted down. No moment of grace was given for consideration of possible escape. It was like a great hand of doom angrily brushing across the side of the mountain. In the confusion of slipping, blinding snow, four men were flung about like bundles of rags, swept toward the bottom of the slope and out of sight. It was all over in less than six seconds.

"I remember thinking that this couldn't be happening to me," one of them reminisced later. "When the slide stopped, I knew I was buried, but I had my left hand and arm free enough to clear the snow from my nose and mouth. For a few seconds, I could move the upper part of my body enough to get breathing clearance for my chest, then the snow consolidated so that any movement except with the free hand was impossible.

"I had the idea that my left arm was above the surface and that I was throwing handfuls of snow out of the hole above my face. As I shook off my mitt to give my hand more freedom and uncovered my eyes, it became apparent that I was really in trouble. There was a solid ceiling of snow above my head, and my free arm was only in an air pocket below the surface. I could see light through the snow, but could not even reach the roof over me.

"The snow held me as firmly as if it was cement. As I realized that there was no hope of extricating myself, I gave up all movement and called for help in the hope that at least one of us was still on the surface and uninjured. My answer was nothing but silence and a low moaning in front of me. Someone had been badly hurt and the others must also be buried. Our situation was therefore desperate.

"I thought I was able to analyze my own situation pretty clearly. I was warmly dressed and in a comfortable position, lying on my right side with my head slightly higher than my feet. My feet were together and parallel. Since I could see light, it seemed that I would get enough air to be in no immediate danger of suffocation. If outside help did arrive, I felt sure that I could survive for at least twelve hours. However, my only chance for ultimate survival was that another group of skiers would follow our route and pass close enough to hear my calls. But would the falling snow blot out our tracks? Would they hear me if they did come?

"This is it, I thought, a painless way to die, but not quite the right time for it. I prayed and contemplated the fact that I was probably going to freeze to death in a few hours. Problems that had seemed quite important a couple of days before suddenly seemed very trivial. Yet it didn't seem possible that this was I who was buried here. These things happened to other people in far-away places. Every few seconds I would call for help, with no effect."

Yet help did come, miraculously and swiftly. Within half an hour after the slide had settled, by sheer luck another group of skiers, after an exchange of quips about the best route up the mountain, decided to keep to the half-obliterated tracks made earlier in the morning. By the time they reached the slide area, it was already covered with fresh snow, but one of the four had landed at the foot of the slope with his face just clear of the surface—though otherwise locked in the viselike squeeze of compressed snow. His call for help was answered, and within an hour the last of the snow-bound captives was freed.

Weather casters, mountain rangers, ski *meisters* and climatology experts may predict some of the furies of the Sierra, and whether the element is rain, rock, ice or snow, they can forewarn trippers who are likely to stray into the path of a mountain tantrum. But, at best, outguessing the wiles of the range is touch and go. Man has hardly begun to make peace with the gods of the California heights.

XIV

THIS, MUIR, IS THE VERY
POETRY OF MOTION

How to make a pair of "skies"?

"Any light wood that wears smooth will do. The dimensions can be varied to suit the fancy of the owner," advised the Sierra Club for the benefit of do-it-yourself craftsmen in 1903. Preferable width—4½ inches; a good length—10 or 12 feet.

"The point should be thoroughly steamed," continued the

directive, "then bent around a graceful form and allowed to cool. Leave the end square and a little thick, so that in going uphill, in case the ski slips back, it would form a check or buttress. This, however, is not essential. The most particular point is to get the proper balance. The front part should rise a little when lifted by the toe in the strap."

As for the strap, well, that was made of firm, stiff leather—"say light sole leather, three inches broad and set in flush on either side of the skies. There should be sufficient room to let your toe well in, even though you have some wrapping around it to keep it warm." The cleat for the heel to catch on was important too. "Chances are you will not get this cleat up near enough to the toe strap, as the toe works farther under the strap when it stretches."

On the other hand, the cleat might be abandoned altogether, if the skier wanted to go along with the advocates of a new-fangled binding. In that case, "take a common shawl strap, double the buckle end over and screw it down on the skie a few inches in front of the toe. This strap should be brought back with one turn around the ankle, crossed over and buckled in, to hold the foot from slipping out of the skie, and still allowing the heel to have proper up-and-down motion."

Presto! The skier, dressed in a long, heavy overcoat, knee boots, a stocking cap and gaudy, trailing scarf, was ready for the slopes.

Oh, no. He couldn't take off until he had that other indispensible piece of equipment—"a 10- to 12-foot pole, very light and reasonably strong, with a small push disc at one end."

On the elongated, homemade gliders, dragging a twelve-foot staff to serve as rudder and propeller, the winter sportsman of 1903 headed for the hills.

The turn of the century marked the incubation of a veritable cult of Sierra ski fanatics. Not that they represented any school, system or technique of skiing—far from it. The idea of "control" never crossed their minds. Their sole interest was having fun in the snow, sliding straight down a hill at breakneck speed, standing bolt upright, and leaning on the pole only to retain balance. Form didn't count, as long as the skis weren't allowed to escape. The grace and sporting spirit with which one recovered from his headers was more important than stance. A real devotee was expected to be something of a vaudevillist, for entertaining fellow sportsmen was half the fun.

Back in the run-down mining villages there were, to be sure, veteran racers who did have a kind of form. They held the pole out in front like a tightrope walker, and to break wind resistance, leaned far forward and got into an uncomfortable, vulgar squatting position on bent knees; but these old pros were more interested in winning prizes than in sheer enjoyment. They were a carry-over from another generation, disregarded by the newcomers.

Leading exponent for the new cult was the inescapable John Muir. He had rediscovered the exhilaration and excitement of an old form of kinesthesia, and wasn't going to be content until his friends and followers had taken their constitutional on the slopes. Singly and in groups he persuaded them to saw out a pair of skis—which most people still called snowshoes—and join him in the deep snow.

"One of the eldest of my companions ventured with me on the steep slopes," Muir prated deliciously after a winter weekend at Lake Tahoe. "This was his first experience on snowshoes, and the several descents he made were the most remarkable specimens of falling locomotion that I ever had the fortune to witness. In shooting down steep declivities, the long, sled-runnerlike shoes have to be kept parallel, with firmly braced limbs. My friend, however, heedless of advice launched himself in wild abandon, bouncing and diving, his limbs and shoes in chaotic entanglement; now in the snow, now in the air, whirling over and over in giddy rolls and somersaults that would have shamed the most extravagant performances of a circus acrobat.

"How original and inimitable he was! Wonderfully refreshing and exhilarating his queer capers must have been; for on coming to rest, with his runaway members divorced and lost, he would quietly gather himself, pick out the snow from his neck and ears, and say with preternatural solemnity, 'This, Muir, is the very poetry of motion.' "

All this poetic expression of motion was not the beginning of California skiing—either as a form of recreation or of utilitarian locomotion. It was only a popular, short-lived revival, for skiing had been the major sport of the Sierra for half a century, under misleading titles like "snowshoeing," "snow-skating," "sheeing," "skieing." Regardless of what it was called, skiing in the high mountains was as old as gold digging. There everybody skied—men, women and children; and they didn't brag about their prowess; they took it for granted, attached no more significance to it than to riding, rowing or ripping down a log chute.

In the early days they had to ski to get around in winter. It was a practical necessity. Teams had sprung up naturally among the more proficient. There had been local ski associations and intervillage meets since the fifties—years before Berlin, New Hampshire, in 1882, organized "the first town ski club in the United States"; even before Oslo, Norway held "the first officially recorded ski competition in 1862."

Popular among the California Indians was a circular hoop, about a foot in diameter, cross-laced with a mesh of twisted bark, but they may also have had some form of ski, for early explorers repeatedly referred to Indians on snowshoes "skimming along like birds"—antics that could scarcely be performed on their webbed gear. And from New England and the Midwest came the Canadian snowshoe, a longer, oval adaptation, frequently with a tail.

The Sierrans adopted both of these, but they favored the Norwegian showshoe. Explained engineer John Gilliss in 1872, speaking for Central Pacific railroad crews: "We started with Canadian snowshoes, but soon abandoned them for the Norwegian, each a strip of light wood, ten to twelve feet long, a broad strap in the middle to put the foot under, and a balancing pole to steady, push and break with. The latter will be seen all-important, as a speed of twenty-five to thirty miles an hour is often attained on a hillside slope."

Fifteen years earlier, in 1862, William Brewer, geologist-explorer, made a similar observation: "In winter the only way of getting about is on snowshoes; not the great, broad Canadian ones that we see at home, but the Norwegian ones—a strip of light, elastic wood, slightly turned up at the front end, with an arrangement near the center to fasten to the foot. With these, people travel anywhere, no matter how deep the snow is, and downhill they go with frightful velocity. At a race on snowshoes at an upper town last winter, the papers announced that the time made by the winner was half a mile in thirty-seven seconds. And many men tell of going a mile in less than two minutes."

To the editor of Hutchings' *California Magazine* the Sierra skis of 1854 and 1855 were *skates*—"entirely unlike the snowshoes of the North American Indian or the people of the Canadas—peculiarly adapted to the rugged features of our mountains and the damp, compact snows that annually accumulate upon them. The skate consists of a single piece of strong, stiff wood.

"In making progress, the skate is raised from the snow when it is desired to make a shorter turn than would otherwise be possible. On uphill or level surfaces, the skates are placed parallel to each other and pushed forward alternately with ease— about the length of an ordinary step—but the impetus given causes them to slide farther than this, while upon descending surfaces, they run with great ease and rapidity; and when the declivity is very great, making it necessary to check the motion by throwing the weight of the skater upon the double-handed staff, forced into the snow upon one side."

Those were the years when the real schuss champions of the West were made—forgotten greats like Yank Brown, Charley Littick, Tommy Todd, John Hillman, Jake Gould and Mattie Judge. They were the Alf Engens, Dick Durrances, Ralph Millers and William Olsons of their day, and just as notable, though the champs of the toe strap never were accorded any national sports-page fame or honored with registration in the ski annuals.

Winners of great races were lugged around on the shoulders of teammates for a while and their skis displayed for a season in the town hall or on the porch of the country store. They were feted locally, and their victories declared in inconspicuous news paragraphs. The awards of a couple of hundred dollars were equitably shared with members of the club, as were the hams, shanks of bacon, the sacks of flour and sugar bestowed on them by merchants. They were idols in the Sierra, and their names perhaps savored for a night by reporters and the saloon crowd in San Francisco, but they were totally unknown elsewhere, for few people east of the Great Basin knew anything about the miracles that could be performed on Norwegian snowshoes.

The impresario who gave California the greatest head start in the sport was a Norwegian named Jon Torsteinson Rui, a strapping six-footer who arrived in the gold country with a delegation of Illinois prospectors in 1851, at the age of twenty-four. At panning he didn't amount to much, but as an artist and indoctrinator with those long boards, he was a whiz. After a few frustrating months searching for gold at Coon Hollow and Kelsey's Diggings, he gave up and followed other hard-luck boys to Putah Creek in Sacramento Valley, where he tried his hand at ranching. There, late in 1855, he spotted an advertisement in the Sacramento *Union* that caught his fancy: "People Lost to the World: Uncle Sam Needs a Mail Carrier."

The man Uncle Sam wanted was a hardy Leatherstocking to tote mail sacks over the mountains from Placerville to Carson Valley and make deliveries at places in between—a ninety-mile route through the ruggedest country served by the United States postal department. To test the mettle of the lone carrier was a continuous line of hazards—wolf packs, Indians, blizzards, forty-foot snowdrifts and row on row of mountain peaks. Two other postmen, traveling on Canadian snowshoes, had already tackled the assignment and resigned.

The Norwegian figured that a foreigner with a name like Jon Torsteinson Rui would not stand a chance of landing the job, and he knew very well that covering the distance on web snowshoes was next to impossible. So he adopted the alias of John A. Thompson, and from a green oak log fashioned a pair of skis, the like of which he remembered in Norway as a boy. Armed with the boards and a good American name, he diffidently presented himself for an interview.

Jon had failed to take into account the desperation of the postal authorities. They were ready to hire any honest-looking applicant. He was promptly sworn into the service before he had time to change his mind.

The postman shouldered a hundred-pound sack of mail, tucked his Bible in with the letters, and was off for Carson Valley and Genoa on the other side of the mountains. People in Placerville shook their heads and laid bets that they'd never see him again. They cheerfully paid off when he showed up hale and hearty five days later. On his fleet oak skis he had made the ninety miles to Genoa in three days flat, and returned in two.

Jon Rui at once became "Snowshoe" Thompson, and the hero of the Northern Sierra. For two winters he made the grueling run regularly twice a month, and occasionally worked in an extra trip when the mail was heavy. After 1858, a more orthodox carrier service to Carson Valley was instituted, but he continued to pinch-hit in emergencies or bad weather, and for almost two decades served on routes to remote Sierra regions.

From November to June, "Snowshoe" was the sole contact between snowed-in mountain villages and the outside world. His clientele depended on him for medicine, lightweight supplies and reports on ore assays, as well as for letters, messages, and perhaps a newspaper per town. Everything expected of a Saint Bernard in the Alps he performed with a chivalrous devotion, expecting no reward and getting little, except the adoration of the people on his route.

He was their life line to civilization. He brought cheer, wit and a spark of gaiety to the outlanders. He was a Santa Claus, a comedian and a ministering angel in one. James Sisson had been lying on the floor of his remote cabin for twelve days with frozen feet and only a little raw flour to keep him alive, when

Thompson rapped on his door the day before Christmas in 1857. Delivery of the United States Mail could be postponed for a few days in such exigencies.

The carrier doubled back to the valley, overnight sawed and shaped six pair of skis for a rescue squad, returned to Sisson's cabin and helped deliver the patient to a doctor in Carson City before proceeding on his route. Sisson's feet had to be amputated, so on the next trip over the mountains from Placerville, Thompson added to his burden the chloroform for the operation.

He spurned the thought of ever carrying a gun or a compass. If a pack of wolves defied him, he put on speed and pointed his skis directly into their midst, and they slunk away. Gifted with an uncanny sense of direction, he claimed it was impossible for him to get lost. He read his bearings in the stars, the posture of trees, the shade of moss and lichen, the drift of snow, the flow of streams, the tracks of animals. Often every last landmark that identified the site of a village was buried under the snow, yet he had an instinct for homing exactly on his destination.

He made a stirring picture shooting down the ridge above a town at reckless speed, his staff sending up a spray of snow as he braked to a halt. The broad grin on his bronzed, leathery face showed that he had good news and a packet of letters. Or as a special favor to an isolated family on his route, he made personal deliveries.

" 'Snowshoe' Thompson passed us daily, carrying the mail between Meadow Lake City and Cisco," one of his beneficiaries remembered with a touch of reverence. "After each storm he would carefully make his track in the soft snow. Starting at the top of Red Mountain, he would glide along the mountainside on a consistent grade. A frosty night would freeze the track, which would thereupon guide him as the steel rails do the locomotive. We would watch him sail down this four-mile course at a great speed, cross the ice-frozen river, throw our mail toward the house and glide out of sight up and over a hill by the momentum gathered in the descent."

Yet for all the affection lavished on him, Thompson was never able to collect his salary from Uncle Sam. Miners paid him well, recipients of verbal messages, medicine and favors reimbursed him handsomely, and gratuities were generous, but a postman on snowshoes didn't fit into any pay category known to the United States Government, and in the end, all he had to show for his labor and the risks he took was a bundle of promissory notes from California postmasters, totaling some $6,000. None of them was ever honored.

But while bringing mail to the Sierra hinterland, he also brought skiing—Norwegian snowshoeing. Young and old developed a great hankering to get about in the snow with the same ease, grace and speed as the popular postman, and whether coming or going, he always found time to drop a few hints on shaping a pair of boards or doing a little coaching. Before the end of the snow season of 1856 there were scores of aspiring skiers along his ninety-mile run, and within another year he was coaching men and youngsters in practically all the mountain towns. The sport was well under way.

It was the fun as much as the practicality that appealed. Two skiers in a community made competition; with a dozen there had to be downhill and cross-country races. Where snow had been a depressing encumbrance, it suddenly became an attraction that relieved the dull winter monotony. Gliding downgrade while standing erect was a trick that caught on like contagion itself. Every town soon had champions ready to challenge the champions of neighboring towns.

Sportsmen developed a jealous pride in their home-planed boards. They were painted and decorated on top, shined and sanded on the bottom. Pell-mell speed in sweeping straight down a hill was what mattered in winning a race, and variation in wet and dry snow could spoil the record of the best champion. Quandary mothered invention. None of the downhill enthusiasts—not even "Snowshoe" Thompson—had ever heard of treating the bottom surface to prevent snow from sticking and to make the runners more slippery, but the wily Sierrans tried it anyway—oil, salve, wax, grease, any likely substance they could lay their hands on.

The formula that proved a success with one club became a guarded secret, divulged to competitors on penalty of ostracism; and some wonderfully mysterious concoctions were devised. "Dope" it was called, regardless of the content. And for a long time the question of using dope was a moral as well as an ethical issue. It caused no end of rankling. Until competitors could develop their own secret compounds, applying the stuff to skis was nothing more nor less than a form of unconscionable cheating. Nobody could tell any longer whether a race was won fairly on skill or through deceitful reliance on chemistry.

Thompson was furious when he discovered what the boys were doing. He denounced dope and its users alike. To him it was "scientific racing" against "dope racing." But as soon as he was persuaded to try a little on his own boards, he was quickly converted and no longer interested in "scientific racing."

"The bottom, beside being highly polished, is made still more glossy by burning into it tar, pitch and beeswax," acknowledged an exponent who had done a little surreptitious prying. "Not satisfied with this, the snowshoers make a mixture or compound called 'dope,' which they rub over the last coat in order to make the shoe glide more smoothly. 'Dope' is regarded as the main thing in a test of speed, and many snowshoers are famous for the wondrous 'dope' they have made.

"The principal ingredient used is spermaceti, but almost everything found in country drugstores has, at one time or another, been experimented with. 'Dope' that is good for dry snow will generally cause wet snow to adhere to the bottoms of the shoes. Every kind of drug in the drugstores is given a trial, and every kind of mixture imaginable is made in order to find out some compound that will make fast 'dope.' There is a well-organized snowshoe club in most of the towns, and it is generally in charge of some old settler who has a good-sized bag of different kinds of 'dope' he has made from time to time, the ingredients and the proportions in which they are mixed being known only to himself."

Still another highly questionable practice evolved when sportsmen began having their equipment professionally manufactured, rather than making it themselves. This was clearly mercenary. John Madden, a clever cabinetmaker at Gibsonville, Sierra County, saw a real future in winter footgear for rich miners and plunged head over heels into the business. "Shoes famous far and near for their beautiful shape and speed," his barkers labeled them; and Madden's craftsmanship was indeed so superior that it needed little advertising, once champions began riding on his product. The only complaint was the cost: $10 for ten-footers, $15 for anything longer.

But casual examination showed that they were well worth the price. Moreover, he was adding a new feature—a long tapering groove running the entire length of the underside. "This groove is an equal distance from each edge of the bottom," he explained with the preciseness of a scientist and an expert salesman, "one and a half inches in width, one-half inch in depth at the heel and gradually tapering toward the toe. Its object is to cause the shoes to take a straight course and not slide from side to side. In manufacturing the higher grade of snowshoes, great care is taken in order that this groove may be perfectly straight and not vary the least particle in its gradual taper."

Madden's creations ranged in length from eight feet for children up to fourteen and fifteen feet for adults, and he was accommodating enough to vary the width "to suit the rider's feet." He also experimented with graduated thickness, so that the middle section of the board was as much as an inch and a half thick, compared to a quarter of an inch at the toe and three-quarters at the heel. For a small extra sum he would also supply "snowshoe moccasins—to prevent the snowshoes from slipping backward while climbing a steep hill—long narrow sacks made so as to just fit over the rear half of the shoes and tie at the strap." Madden had thought of almost everything, but he still stuck to toe straps.

DOPE IS KING! DOPE IS KING! clarioned the posters in anticipation of the sporting climax of a long winter. SNOWSHOE RACING AT THE LA PORTE RACE TRACK. THURSDAY, FRIDAY, and SATURDAY,

MARCH 3RD, 4TH AND 5TH. $300! IN PRIZES! $300! EACH DAY'S RACE
FOLLOWED BY A *GRAND BALL*.

The course was the steepest natural chute in the region, an
open slope close to a half-mile long, a sheer drop of some 1,200
feet at the start, ending with a long, gradual decline. Competitors shot down it at better than a mile a minute. Precaution was
tossed to the wind; they didn't go singly. It was more like a
track meet, with heats of four or, if the hillside was broad
enough, all the entrants from all the towns lined up at the top
of the run with scarcely elbow room between them. They
zipped down the slope together, each holding as straight a
course as possible, praying that the man in the lead wouldn't
take a spill in the wrong track, skis completely out of control,
and nothing but a toe strap and steering pole to give direction.
Only one rule mattered: "The first man through the winning
poles on his shoes, or on one shoe, wins."

"There cannot possibly be a more exciting contest," pro-
claimed a spectator. "Here, instead of depending upon the
efforts of some dumb animal, you are watching the efforts of an
intelligent human being in his attempt to gain supremacy.
From good authority we know that they have attained a speed
of over two hundred feet a second. Upon reaching the bottom
of the declivity, the riders often report that they have not had
time to breathe between the start and the finish.

"They are started off by the tap of a drum, and are privileged
to use their pole or 'stav' as much as they wish in order to accel-
erate their speed. When the signal is given, they raise themselves by means of the pole and give one grand shove. Some
strike the pole to the snow five or six times before they assume
the proper position which is by stooping as low as they can with
the pole held out directly in front, thus acting as a wedge to
cut the air apart. When they reach the bottom, the winner is
carried upon the shoulders of his admirers and a general feasting ensues."

Possibly the watch or measuring wand of the "good authority" had been thrown out of kilter by the high altitude, for
the rate of 200 feet a second would work out to approximately

136 miles an hour—a speed that no modern skier is known to have clocked. However, the speeds attained in the days of "Snowshoe" Thompson aren't to be discredited. Eighty-eight miles an hour was once reliably recorded on a 55 per cent grade of sleety crust, and that wasn't closely matched until 87 miles per hour was electrically timed more than half a century later on the Flying Kilometer Course in the Alps.

In any case, the boys at La Porte earned their awards of $300, and the townsfolk who anted up for the purses got their money's worth in suspense and the rip-roaring celebration that followed. Once the race was over, the excitement was dissolved in alcohol. In fact, it flowed so freely for three days and nights that the third Grand Ball was a rather drowsy debauch. Fifty years before winter carnivals came into vogue on college campuses, the pattern had been set by Sierra towns like La Porte, Cisco, Meadow Lake City, Howland Flat and Alturas.

It was the consistently deep snow as well as the derring-do on snowshoes that gave these mountain villages a real aura. In December, upper windows might show above the white waste; in January, a few roof ridges stood out among the drifts; but by February of a severe winter, everything was buried except the chimneys. When attic windows became inaccessible as a front door, long, slanting tunnels were dug under the drifts to the door. In such a desert of white, finding one's own house, or the mouth of the tunnel leading to it, posed a problem. Householders made a practice of erecting at their tunnel entrances tall poles with distinctive bandannas fluttering from the tip. The colored handkerchiefs and the chimneys in sunken hollows frequently were all that marked the site of a town in mid-March.

Where houses in a village were close together, a network of tunnels ran from door to door, to the grocery store, the saloons and the schoolhouse. Many chimneys had to be spliced to raise them above the snow level. A Meadow Lake resident, in 1865, complained that the forty-foot flagstaff in the central plaza was out of sight.

During the bitter winter of 1867, when a Cisco family ran out of food, the children were sent four miles to Meadow Lake to replenish the larder. But on arriving at the place where they knew Meadow Lake City should be, they couldn't find a trace of it, as one of them recalled in adulthood: "There was no city. Its people were celebrating a ski race half a mile down a mountainside and out over the frozen and snow-covered lake.

"We stopped a while to partake of this excitement and then hunted for the town. It was entirely obliterated. Puffs of smoke came out of the snow, but there was no sign of a chimney or the roof of a house. A man came up from below, a short distance from where we stood. He was peeling an apple, casting the peelings away. When he reached us, we were informed that a snow stairway leading down to the street was designated by two blue flags about a hundred yards distant from where we stood.

"Thanking the kindly gentleman, we proceeded, gathering and devouring the apple peelings on the way. Arriving at the flags, we went down about twenty steps which had been chopped out of the frozen snow. Then we crossed the street through tunnels carved through the snow, procured our provisions and returned home. The trips to the city grew into a weekly occurrence throughout the long and heavy winter. The snow entirely engulfed our house, necessitating the digging out of light wells down to the windows and a shaft to the front door after each snowstorm. For wood we cut green tamarack trees. The fireplaces were kept going continuously. When the snow thawed, our firewood tree stumps stood eighteen feet above the ground."

It didn't take more than a season or two for villagers to learn to prepare in advance for the inevitable. They stocked up in the fall for snow-bound confinement of six or seven months. If a man owned a horse, the animal was taken to the blacksmith in November and fitted with eight-by-ten-inch iron plates hinged to the front of the hoofs. "A horse, in order to be of any use must, like his driver, be an expert skier," advised a Plumas County resident.

Except for such transportation as a horse on showshoes afforded, mountain folk expected to hole up for the winter, and did—until skis brought them out into the fresh air and occasional sunshine. The social transformation created by "Snowshoe" Thompson and his boards was complete. Men of all ages took to them. The children joined in the fun; and a few daring women. Generally the female was considered out of place on the slopes, but she defied censure, insisted on her rights, and eventually the most conservative of males allowed that she was entitled to participation as long as she "dressed proper."

Yet despite all the hullabaloo about a fast, exciting winter sport among the mountain people, few valley residents were induced to show any interest in it. Until the late nineties, skiing was as foreign to San Francisco, Sacramento or Los Angeles as Scottish curling or Polynesian surf riding. It was an indigenous folk sport limited to isolated Sierra communities. For decades the best skiers in the nation were gliding down California mountains, but outside their own bailiwick they were unknowns. They received no general recognition for their prowess in the home state or anywhere else, and though their refinement of uncontrolled skiing was far ahead of any other development of the sport in America, in the end they contributed not so much as a lasting foible in popular technique.

In part, the remoteness was responsible; in part, the transitory character of the mountain population. Nothing in the mining towns was stable. When they were deserted, the ski teams broke up. The champions and their art passed into an oblivion as total as that of the towns.

Here and there the annual tournaments were continued until the turn of the century, and outsiders occasionally were tempted to capitalize on the spectacle. A quixotic promoter named C. F. McGlashan, for example, in the late 1890's had visions of converting Truckee into a gay winter-sports center. High above the town he erected a baroque tower-museum and flooded it with newfangled electric light. He built a terrifying toboggan slide, an ice palace that enclosed an acre of skating rink, and talked about wonderful ski slopes.

But the layout was designed for city people. They came from San Francisco to cut figures on the ice, to careen and scream down the toboggan chute and write poetry about the glorious scenery. Skiing? No. That was a hillbilly sport.

When John Muir and his clan discovered the thrills of Norwegian snowshoeing, it was like starting all over again—strictly an amateur experiment. And even the revival he helped to promote was of short duration. It was the beginning of a long period of blowing hot and cold over California winter sports. Every few years someone else would rediscover the fun of streaking down a mountain on pine boards and would try to tell the public about it, but very few were listening.

"One of the most wholesome and encouraging signs of the times and the most triumphant proof of the conquest of the human body over the Frost King," orated a typical convert in 1913, "is the increasing vogue and popularity of winter sports and winter outdoor games of all sorts, even during the chilliest and most inclement days of the year. The most delightful and exhilarating sports of the whole year are those which can be indulged in only in times of frost and snow." Then followed the usual plug for "skeeing."

The Sierra Club took up the cause again in 1915. "Put on your skis," urged the proselyte, "and go up to the mountain top. There pause. Gather yourself together in a crouching position, just as a bird does before it leaps into the air; then straighten out with equal scorn of your moorings, with life and freedom tingling from your toes to the sparkle of your eyes, and you too will fly over that white world, alighting gradually and uprightly—we hope.

"It takes quite a few pilgrimages to the skiing grounds to pass beyond that period of disfiguring the snow, and to glide with all ease and abandon down any sort of slope. To take bumps and dodge trees, you must approach them without fear, with the realization that they are to be considered, but with all the self-assurance and determination that you can muster, and that they have no terrors for you. . . . Come away from the rush and stress of life and follow on skis the flight of a mountain bluebird."

When one of these pilgrims from the city stepped down from the train at Summit in 1915, 1918 or 1920, carrying his ten-foot boards—still with toe straps—and a pair of the new European-style bamboo poles, more than likely he would be greeted in the station room by a wrinkled old codger, who spat on the floor and queried: "Going snowshoeing?"

"Er, yes, *skiing.*"

"Them sticks ain't no good. What you want is a big pole. Why, back in 'sixty-five—"

But the straps were on the way out. The skis were getting shorter and narrower. Where the West hadn't succeeded in influencing the East, ski techniques developed in the Alps, the White Mountains and the Adirondacks were being imported to the home of the American ski pioneers. A short, heavy boot with hard toe and a rigid binding that allowed only for lifting the heel were being advocated. Control rather than wild speed was the thing.

A crouch with forward lean, reminiscent of the style in the La Porte races, was in vogue, but instead of being called "La Porte," it was the "Arlberg" technique, attributed to an Austrian, Hannes Schneider. With the innovations came a whole new fancy language—*schuss,* snowplow, checks, *langlauf, slalom,* Christy and a hundred other terms. Alas, a ski was a ski, a snowshoe a snowshoe, and people looked blank when old-timers referred to Norwegian snowshoes.

During the thirties the new language arrived in the Sierra by snow train and in roadsters with bundles of skis protruding from the rumble seats. Slopes that had rarely been visited in winter before were dimpled with athletes—at Tuolumne Meadows, Lake Tahoe, Lincoln Saddle, Ward Peak, Bear Valley; and Yosemite became a year-round outdoor sports center.

A slalom meet was held at Badger Pass in 1933. The following year the Sierra Club built a ski lodge—Clair Tappaan. New chapters were added to the history of the range when modern explorers with lightweight equipment followed "Snow-

shoe" Thompson's tracks across the mountains, or made
monthlong cross-country jaunts over the shoulders of the big
mountains and along the high crests.

The tactics of ski troops during the first World War caught
the imagination of the public and helped bring on the burst of
interest in the twenties. Widespread activities of the Civilian
Conservation Corps kept it alive during the thirties. The training of mountain forces in World War II and their dramatic military exploits added still livelier momentum to a winter-sports
movement. From the 10th Mountain Division were graduated
enough experts to coach college teams and supply ski *meisters*
for new centers all over the country. Plenty of opportunity had
been given them to size up terrain from the Laurentians to the
Cascades, and among all the nation's mountain ranges, the
Sierra was hard to beat.

By 1946 the scattering of enthusiasts had multiplied to hundreds of thousands, and they were no longer content to shoot
down a hill in free, dangerous abandon. They wanted to learn
a technique and do it right. Moreover, they were in a hurry.
Spending half a day laboriously ascending a mountain for the
sake of a fifteen-minute descent had lost its appeal. Tows and
lifts to the top were demanded.

It took a lot of money to clear, grade and equip a ski center,
but promoters with the right kind of capital thought they saw
a new type of white gold in the Sierra. In a few short years California skiing changed from a tentative, experimental form of
adventure for a few stouthearted outdoorsmen to a big organized business catering to eager multitudes.

Roads into the mountains that had been open only to summer traffic became year-round highways, and along them
scores of ski ranches sprang up. Leading to the slopes and
bowls were rope tows, chair lifts, T-bars, Pomalifts, weasels and
magic carpets. The mobilization of five thousand weekend skiers at a single area was a common sight; group or private instruction for any category of beginner and intermediate was
available; and the snow conditions of places like Plumas-
Eureka Ski Bowl, Siberia Bowl, Sugar Bowl, Mount Rose Bowl,

Edelweiss, Phillips Pow-Wow Lodge, Echo Summit, Heavenly Valley, Peddler Hill, Dodge Ridge, Alpine Meadows, Yosemite and Sequoia National Parks were published with the regularity of stock-exchange reports.

Typical of the new developments in 1949 was a relatively obscure area known as Squaw Valley in the Tahoe National Forest, some five miles northeast of Lake Tahoe. In years past the Valley had been cursed with some of the heaviest snowfalls of the range. Now the curse was suddenly regarded as a blessing. It had open slopes and bowls, a variety of terrain to accommodate all kinds of skiers; it was an ideal spot for year-round recreation.

A great deal of colorful history was also packed into Squaw Valley. At its entrance once stood the town of Knoxville, a community of a thousand people drawn there by news of a great gold strike. The excitement over gold quickly played out, but prospectors left behind an assortment of abandoned mine shafts, diggings and dots on the map such as Powderhorn, Hell Hole, Lost Lake, Whisky Creek, Diamond Crossing, Five Lakes, Rubicon, Bear Pen Canyon.

Countless California-bound wagon trains had pushed through the Valley and on up over the summit of the Sierra to drop down to the headwaters of the American River by way of the Old Immigrant Trail. In more recent years Squaw Valley had served as a take-off point for pack trips into the high country and for ski groups who wanted to get away from the crowds. Escapists had built lodges on privately owned plots in the area, and one resident, Wayne Poulsen, who had acquired a wide expanse of mountain land, dreamed of building up a small, conservative skiing center for those who shrank from milling throngs.

But Poulsen's vision wasn't scaled large enough to suit a New York attorney, Alexander C. Cushing, who moved into the Valley in 1949. Backed by substantial capital and a well-organized company, Cushing was ready to spend real money on converting Squaw into the grandest ski area in the West.

In six months $400,000 was poured into a handsome ski lodge

with accommodations for 150, a two-and-a-half-mile hard-sur-
faced road, a 1,000-car parking area, and on the face of 9,000-
foot Squaw Peak a giant double-chair lift—the world's largest
—with a capacity of 600 passengers an hour. In the spring of
1949 Squaw Valley had a virgin look; that look was gone by
fall. Cushing's establishment was ready to open for business
on November 23rd.

That was only the beginning. The early-season crowds
weren't quite up to the proprietor's expectations. What Squaw
Valley needed was publicity. Places like Reno, Nevada, and
Anchorage, Alaska, were putting in bids for the 1960 Olympics,
and getting free advertising of their facilities. Why shouldn't
he throw Squaw's feather into the ring? Admittedly he didn't
have the setup to accommodate half a million spectators, such
as might turn out for the winter games, but at least he could
get a few good press notices.

Late in December he sent off an eight-page résumé on the
glories of Squaw Valley, to the United States Olympic Committee, and immediately things began happening with cyclonic
speed. Back came a letter clearly indicating that the committee
was quite taken with the idea of putting the show on in California and requesting him to appear in New York on January
7th to present his case in more detail.

It dawned on Cushing that he had started something bigger
than a publicity stunt, something he couldn't pull out of as
easily as he had wedged in. This was a multimillion-dollar proposition. The entrepreneur dashed to San Francisco for consul-
tations on finance; then to Governor Goodwin Knight. The
Governor balked at making any commitment in State aid, but
compliantly agreed at least to contribute toward the success of
the Winter Olympics if they were staged at Squaw Valley.
Armed with that all too indefinite promise, Cushing flew East
to his conference, and in a few days learned that his domain
had been selected over Aspen, Colorado; Sun Valley, Idaho;
Reno, and even Anchorage. The eyes of the sports world were
focused vaguely on Squaw Valley, for people had trouble finding it on the map.

The unknown little spot in the Sierra was the choice of the United States Committee; the final choice had to be made by sixty-three delegates from other nations at a meeting of the International Committee in Saint Moritz, Switzerland. Cushing was in too deep for any possible out. Back in California, with the help of an architect, he worked up an impressive model of what Squaw Valley would look like in 1960.

The model went on exhibition at Saint Moritz a few months later, and Cushing virtually went on trial before the international jury. No one gave him a Chinaman's chance of winning the competition. He faced the committee practically alone, while others had delegations of aides and agents. Unknown Squaw Valley was running against resorts that had been famous for generations—Saint Moritz itself, Germany's Garmisch-Partenkirchen, Austria's Innsbruck.

Behind the scenes, the Europeans generally agreed that Innsbruck should get the vote, for Saint Moritz and Garmisch had previously played host. It was Innsbruck's turn, and the Austrians were so confident of having their celebrated winter paradise chosen that representatives were already making space reservations. With all the lobbying and acrimonious debate, delegates predicted the voting would go on for hours. Squaw Valley was selected on the second ballot.

Anywhere else, a decade would have been a short time to elevate an obscure wilderness valley into a renowned sports plaza, but not in the Sierra, where gold cities of 5,000 people had sprung up in a summer. Yet a miracle in fund raising had to happen, and it did.

Altogether the conversion job cost close to $20,000,000 in State funds, federal subsidies, corporation contributions and private gifts. It wasn't just a problem of constructing athletic facilities, attractive buildings and the accessories for a world pageant; the promoters had to begin from scratch. Acres of land had to be cleared, bulldozed and graded; miles of four-lane highway built; even a sewage system big enough to serve a fair-sized city laid.

Plans called for incidentals like two churches, a complex of dormitories outfitted with everything from reading lamps to Finnish steam baths, a twenty-eight-bed hospital and nine first-aid stations, waxing huts, an eighty-foot "Tower of Nations," parking space for 10,000 cars, a bank, post office, movie theatre, a telephone system with 1,200 phones and 60,000,000 feet of wire.

The phones were working on the morning of February 18th, 1960. The Olympic gates opened at seven o'clock, and in the thick of a blinding mountain blizzard, where visibility was reduced to forty feet, the snarled traffic started to stream in. Snow that everyone now thought of as a blessing was once more a curse. Eight inches of it came down during the morning. But early in the afternoon, as though someone's prayer had proved effective, the clouds parted and the sun came through to spotlight the most monumental scene of pageantry the Sierra had ever known.

To the strains of the United States Marine Band, 740 athletes from thirty nations paraded around the central quadrangle of the Ice Arena, led by the banner of Greece, birthplace of the Olympic contests 2,736 years before. Above the marchers exploded burst after burst of rocketed flag clusters. There were booming guns, fireworks and waves of band music. The Canadians were togged out in mackinaws with broad white, green, red and black stripes; the Danes in heavy yellow parkas; the Norwegians in tweed coats; the United States team in red, white and blue raincoats; the Soviets in somber gray belted overcoats and fedora hats; the striking contrasts of color extended the length of the procession.

Seven hundred and forty athletes lined up in facing ranks on opposite sides of the eight-story sports arena and in front of the "Tribune of Honor" for the round of welcoming addresses.

"I now declare open the Olympic Games of Squaw Valley, celebrating the Eighth Olympic Winter Games," pronounced Vice-President Nixon.

Thirty-eight hundred students from fifty-two California high schools, in chorus and band music, gave a rousing rendition of the Olympic hymn. Ceremoniously the Olympic flag was unfurled and eight rounds of gunfire boomed and echoed against the gleaming mountains. From a battery of cages 2,000 white "doves of peace" fluttered into the sky and took off in the direction of Reno.

Then in a hushed, theatrical moment, the Olympic torch swooped ski-borne down the slope of Little Papoose Mountain in the hands of Andrea Mead Lawrence, retired Olympic ski-ing champion. The "sacred Olympic flame" in a great brazier at the base of the "Tower of Nations" was lighted, the Olympic oath recited, the "Star-Spangled Banner" played. In a stunning aerial display a shower of national flags attached to parachutes was rocketed aloft and thousands of colored balloons re-leased. Almost immediately the sun disappeared and the big flakes from the interrupted blizzard started falling.

Altogether the show was a little gaudy and overdramatic, but it was exactly right. A setting of such magnitude called for all the splash that could be invented; anything less showy would have been too puny to make an impression at all.

It was as though the world had at last come to pay tribute to the range and its forgotten Norwegian snowshoers of a cen-tury before. Moreover, the demonstrators wanted to do their jubilating in the extravagant, garish, flamboyant manner—the only manner completely in keeping with the spectacle which had garnished the long history of the mountains. That Olympic ceremony was perhaps the grandest hour in Sierra annals.

XV

BUT THE GREATEST OF THESE
IS WATER

Everyone was thirsting for water—Sierra water. In California it was either flood or dire shortage. Destructive deluges came rolling off the mountains in winter, to be followed by searing summer drought. Never dependable was the water supply in the valleys. For four or five years the rains and runoff would be adequate to permit inland dry farming, with fair

319

crops and fat cattle; then for no accountable reason would come a succession of dry years when arroyo beds became dust bowls, the barley yellowed before heading, orchards withered, cattle died.

The debris from surging floods of 1861-62 had scarcely been cleaned up when a terrible drought developed—two years of it. Hills that were normally green from November to May remained a dusty golden. Immense herds of longhorn cattle, which had been a mainstay of California agricultural economy during the Mexican regime, and into the American take-over, were all but wiped out. Carcasses by the thousands littered the valleys from Fresno to San Diego. Those two years spelled the end of the California cattle barons and brought doubt about the whole future of agriculture in the Southwest—until some more effective system of water distribution could be worked out.

State statutes and court rulings on use of water resources didn't help matters. The only consistently successful farmers were those who could bring water to their crops. Irrigation was essential whether one hoped to harvest Bartlett pears, wheat or spinach. Yet water rights didn't necessarily go with the land. The law of "appropriation" prevailed. To the first comer who seized, posted and registered a claim to rights on a stream belonged prior privileges. Even riparian rights were subject to dispute. Though a creek flowed through a rancher's property, a lumberman ten miles upstream might have legally appropriated and diverted the water for his flumes and mill, and as a dry season approached, the rancher would discover that his creek bed was parched and his crop doomed. Court appeals were futile.

Complained one victim: "Today we wake up to find that we have no water laws, that we can give a title to land, but that there is no authority, state or national, which can place above litigation the title to the water which alone gives value to the land. Some communities spend more money in litigation than in development. Settlement in the United States is following the waterline. The settlers are looking not for land, but for water. Water in arid America is the difference between a home and no home; it is the difference between *range* worth fifty cents an acre and land worth one hundred, two thousand to five thousand dollars per acre; it is the difference between the highest type of civilization and a barbarism with lizards and coyotes. Timber, land and water—these three—but the greatest of these is water."

Charles Crocker, construction boss of the Central Pacific, had a solution. That Herculean job had left his massive frame a little the worse for wear, and reduced him to a skeleton of some 225 pounds, but he still had a reserve of energy and his old capacity for self-commendation. After a brief period of recuperating, he came back with a bounce to build more railroads and to plunge into an enterprise that interested him even more—irrigation.

Charley had a wonderful idea; he wanted to revolutionize California ranching by attaching water rights to land rights. He was convinced that there were absolutely no limits to the future of his adopted State if only water could be more evenly distributed—delivered where it was most needed. To him, water famine made no sense in a country where countless rivers and creeks drained an excessive waste into tidelands and the Pacific.

Merced, gateway to Yosemite, was chosen for his Utopian experiment. Farmers in the area had already organized a sort of water co-operative there, but the venture wasn't backed by quite enough capital, quite enough engineering skill, quite enough administrative know-how. Crocker could supply all three. To help him along was the ready admission from the farmers that their ditch was no good; they had failed. Yet they did have a valuable franchise—by appropriation—and it was for sale. Charley bought it.

Striking up a partnership with a respected Merced citizen named Huffman, the old hand at bringing order out of chaos went into the irrigation-building business. Compared to rail construction, the project was an insignificant undertaking, involving an investment of a mere two or three million, employment of less than 1,000 of his "pets," and assembling a stable of some 500 mules, but he went at it as if he were building another transcontinental line.

Through tunnels and diversion ditches, the sparkling waters that tumbled down the falls of Yosemite Park were to be brought from Snelling, twenty miles north of Merced, and put to work making a new Eden in the foothills and converting desert worth eighty cents an acre into farm land worth $200. What he could do for a few thousand acres at Merced, others could do for millions.

In the inimitable, rambling discourse that was characteristic of Crocker, he told his own story: "We went on and bored a big tunnel, nearly a mile long. I could drive through it with a four-horse team after it was finished. Then we bored another tunnel nearly as long and fully as large. It took a great deal of money and a great deal more time than we expected; it was just about five years in building.

"The country is a rich country, and in favorable seasons has been a good wheat-producing country and a good fruit region; but the fruit needs some water to make it a first-rate one when there is a dry season. The land is as good as any in California, and its capacity with the water is going to be immense—simply immense. . . . Merced will be a great city of the future. The water right is attached to the land; that is to say, we sell the land for so much an acre, and the purchaser pays us one dollar an acre per year to maintain the ditch and keep the water going to him constantly. We guarantee to provide him water and he guarantees to pay us one dollar a year. The water right is attached to the land and belongs to him and is sold with it.

"The whole valley will be supplied with water from the Sierras. . . . There is no question about it; this will be the greatest state in the Union in less than twenty years from now —it will beat any state in the Union. If I live twenty years more, I expect to see fully ten million people here, and they are going to be happy, prosperous people; they are going to be rich—those who are frugal and save and economize, and work up to the best of their powers. Look at the wine interests! Look at the coopers that are wanted to make casks to hold this wine; look at the shipping that is required to carry it over the world; the raisins, oranges, fruit of all kinds; and the nuts—every kind of nut will grow in this soil; they will raise almost anything that is raised in the universe. . . .

"There are seasons in the year when that river runs booming down and we can store this water until it is wanted in the plains. I think the day will come when Huffman and I will be regarded as men who have done more for the country than the railroad builders. This is the only work that I have done, except building the railroad, for the benefit of the State. We started the movement and it is going to take."

The Crocker-Huffman creation was no ordinary ditch; it was a canal, 100 feet wide, carrying a veritable river down the twenty miles from Snelling to a huge reservoir of 640 acres outside Merced. Crocker never did things by halves; besides the canal, he created Yosemite Lake—"as pure as snow water; bright, clear, clean water." And the man who started the flow delighted most in repeating the comment of a distinguished visitor who came to survey the works just before they were completed: "Why, you people will each have three faucets in your houses and will ask guests, 'Will you have Bridal Veil, Yosemite or Cascade?—just whichever you choose.' "

Undoubtedly Crocker was a pioneer in attaching the guarantee of adequate water to the sale of land, but the Merced enterprise was far from being the first public irrigation project in California. Community water systems had been in operation for over a century. The missions started them: San Diego in 1770, San Juan Capistrano in 1776, San Fernando in 1779. A domestic water-supply system was established in Los Angeles soon after the pueblo was built in 1781. And the early American settlers were no less progressive.

Within a year after the gold-covetous throngs began pouring into California, valley ranchers and mountain miners alike were greedily channeling water from its natural course to homesteads and diggings. Through parched lands south of Bakersfield a canal was built on the sprawling El Tejon ranch in 1851, and two years later was irrigating almost 2,000 acres of wheat. A ditch running from Mill Creek on the Kaweah River was watering similar plantings of grain and garden in 1853. On the south bend of the Merced, farmer Harvey Ostrander was so successful with an experiment in raising alfalfa under irrigation in 1854 that he went into vineyards and fruit the following year.

In Sacramento Valley, General John Bidwell, a member of the first overland party to cross the Sierra, settled down at Chico, brought in water from Butte Creek and eventually planted an orchard with 400 varieties of fruit, ranging from apples and olives to grapes and mangoes. He pioneered with raisin growing and olive-oil production. By 1875 he had a fruit orchard of 1,200 trees and 15,000 vines thriving on Sierra water.

The biggest projects were in the San Joaquin Valley. Extending north from Fresno Slough for seventy miles was the San Joaquin and Kings River Canal, financed by a Massachusetts strategist, John Bensley. It cost $1,300,000 and alone carried enough water to irrigate 120,000 acres. Moses Church, an ambitious New Yorker from Chatauqua, took up a few thousand acres along Kings River near Centerville, secured the usual franchise to divert waters, and then—while waging a seven-year battle with cattle kings and riparian claimants—pushed forward a waterway until he could boast that he had "nearly a thousand miles of main and lateral canals with their ditches and feeders, thereby materially advancing the industrial, commercial and financial developments of the state a thousandfold."

Year by year the valley acres under irrigation increased from some 60,000 in 1870 to nearly 300,000 in 1880. Except along the coast and in the north and south extremities of the State, the summer supply of water all came from the high Sierra snow pack; and deep wells, drilled in a dry spot far out of sight of the peaks, or miles from a mountain river, were undoubtedly fed from the same source. Though few of the irrigation ventures were designed like Charles Crocker's, to furnish a municipal water supply as well as to guarantee an ample flow to regional landowners, irrigation had made a great deal of head-way long before the Merced project was started.

The greatest stimulus for building valley ditches came from the gold miners. They set the example, established the legal precedents and demonstrated just about all the practical means and methods of conveying water from the mountains. As extraction of gold progressed from pan to cradle, to "Long Tom," to sluice, to gouging and finally to hydraulic mining, increasing quantities of water were required. At dry diggings water often had to be brought for scores of miles in wooden flumes and open ditches. On reaching the diggings, it was channeled into smaller streams, and these made to serve two or three Long Tom's apiece. Most of the problems and principles of water distribution that applied to irrigation existed at the mines, and the same kind of squabbles were fought there too.

There were wrangles, riots and bloodshed—perpetual clashes over stream franchises, prior use, riparian codes, flume rights-of-way, excessive charges and downstream silting. As much as 10 per cent of the gold scoured from the hills was paid out in charges for water. At Timbuctoo, capitalists invested $600,000 in a thirty-mile ditch—all on a mad-brained gamble. It happened to pay off, and when miners heard that the Shylock financiers were drawing 40 per cent dividends on their investment, they were ready to take up arms.

At Columbia the miners struck the Tuolumne County Water Company, refusing to pay the daily charge of six dollars per "Tom." Four dollars was enough. They would give up mining rather than pay a cent more. The sluices were abandoned and the expensive water was allowed to run off down the valley unused, while the Argonauts attended mass meetings and prepared for battle.

In a vituperative resolution they declared that "the miners of this community have for a long time been oppressed by the exorbitant exactions of that monster monoply, the Tuolumne County Water Company, whose controlling spirits have been fattened by the sweat of the brow of the careworn workingmen;" that "we have in vain appealed to them on various occasions for a reduction in the price of water without a hope or prospect of success from that corporation, which is without a body to be kicked or a soul to be damned, and whose cupidity knows no bounds"; that "a vast majority of the claims pay so poorly that many of us cannot pay the honest demands of merchants, boardinghouse keepers and others, and as many of us are reduced to nearly a starving point, and have families at home in equally bad condition. . . ."

D. O. Mills, a Sacramento banker, had sunk close to $300,000 in the Tuolumne County Water Company and built a ditch and flume that extended for thirty miles back to the South Fork of the Stanislaus. He intended to make a killing on it, though it was reliably reported that he was getting only 2 per cent on his investment. For three years the miners took pity on Mills and cheerfully forfeited the six-dollar extortion. Then it leaked out that the 2 per cent represented the monthly, not the annual, returns; he was making well over 25 per cent. Not only that, he was selling the same water a dozen times over, for it merely ran from one tailrace into a ditch lower down, where Mills's agent collected again; and so on for miles.

The Tuolumne County Water Company had more than 1,000 clients. Rough computation of the miners on their part, revealed that they had contributed something like $5,000,000 in three years. The honeymoon with the water company was over. The strike was on. Hillsides around Columbia began to look like cemeteries, as hundreds of wooden crosses appeared with the common inscription: $4.00 FOR WATER AND NO MORE. Even then Mills refused to budge. The strike wasn't broken until the miners had withdrawn every dollar they had deposited in Mills's branch bank at Columbia and invested the money in a ditch of their own. But by the time the water company finally decided it could afford to make the two-dollar reduction, the miners were more interested in building their own ditch than in paying tribute to an old enemy.

The Tuolumne Water Company held rights to the South Fork of the Stanislaus, so the rebels went thirty miles farther back into the mountains to the North Fork. Theirs was to be a ditch far superior to Mills's. It took three and a half years to finish the project, including a six-by-seven-foot tunnel that had to be drilled through a mountain for more than half a mile; but the men owned it—a full eighty miles of aqueduct, worth $1,500,000, a conduit twice as long as the Tuolumne Company's and delivering twice as much water.

In the gaudiest holiday Columbia ever conceived, the completion of the Columbia and Stanislaus Water Company's masterwork was celebrated on November 28th, 1858. But in the end no one could claim a victory. So powerful were the streams flowing down the new flumes that within a year the store of gold that people had assumed to be inexhaustible was washed out and the miners were ready to sell their stock to Mills for ten cents on a dollar.

No less cantankerous were the feuds stirred up in downstream communities by the flow of silt and sludge from the mines. Rivers that had run into the valleys sparkling clear in 1848 were fouled, murky streams of mud by 1858. Not only were the river beds layered with tailings, but the banks were also deep with mire. Channels were filled and any freshet sent a river over its banks.

"Tornado, flood, earthquake and volcano combined could hardly make greater havoc, spread wider ruin and wreck than are to be seen everywhere in the path of the larger gold-washing operations," observed editor Samuel Bowles. "None of the interior streams of California, though naturally as pure as crystal, escape the change to a thick yellow mud. The Sacramento is worse than the Missouri. Many of the streams are turned out of their original channels, either directly for mining purposes, or in consequence of the great masses of soil and gravel that come down from the gold washings above.

"Thousands of acres of fine land along their banks are ruined forever by the deposits of this character. There are no rights which mining respects in California. It is the one supreme interest. The farmer may have his whole estate turned to a barren waste by a flood of sand and gravel from some hydraulic mining upstream; more, if a fine orchard or garden stands in the way, orchard and garden must go. The tornout, dugout areas, washed to pieces and then washed over side hills, are the very devil's chaos. The country is full of them among the mining districts of the Sierra Nevada foothills, and they are truly a terrible blot upon the face of nature."

At Cherokee in the northern Sierra foothills, the Spring Valley Mining Company opened operations in 1871, after laying a hundred miles of ditch costing $750,000 and building vast storage lakes in the mountains. That company was a typical hydraulic colossus, equipped with water guns that made city fire-fighting apparatus look toylike. Under lethal pressure the water was sent boiling into soil banks at such velocity that it could undercut a mountainside.

Water shooting down the flumes was fed into thirty-inch pipes and an inverted siphon two and a half miles long. That in turn fed the hoses—sixteen of them, with nozzle openings up to eight inches in diameter. The Spring Valley Company worked day and night for twelve years demolishing the landscape, and in all those years the sixteen giants were shut down only once for a brief hour—during the funeral of President Garfield.

Eventually it was estimated that the incomprehensible total of 1,550,000,000 cubic yards of gravel had been washed into California streams by assorted hydraulic operations. In 1880 the State Engineer found that 43,596 acres of agricultural land in the Sacramento Valley alone had been depreciated by $2,597,634. Yet not until 1893 was free hydraulic mining outlawed—or restricted to the few companies which could convince a State Debris Commission that they would dispose of their waste without washing it downstream.

By then the damage had been done. The dockets of State courts were crowded with lawsuits. Already Californians had acquired a reputation for provoking more litigation over water than most of the other states combined, and between the claims of big mining companies and big ranchers, the little man was overlooked. "We can litigate and litigate," wailed one distressed citizen, "but litigation cannot lead to justice. The man with the longest purse who can hire the most lawyers and employ the largest army of witnesses will win in the end, and that is equivalent to government by force rather than by law."

As the gold fields petered out, hordes of disconsolate miners descended upon the valleys to engage in the only other occupation they knew—farming. They wanted small plots of a few dozen acres. Plenty of land was for sale, but the water rights had already been grabbed and dry land was no good. Someone figured out that registered claims for the San Joaquin amounted to 172 times the normal flow of the river. A single claimant maintained that he held rights to its entire flow "from its surface to the center of the earth," yet there were hundreds of ridiculous conflicting appropriations like that of a Los Angeles patron who had signed up for "three thousand miner's inches under a four-inch pressure to take out in a pipe an inch and a half in diameter."

The situation on other rivers was almost as confused. Forty thousand dollars was being spent annually on litigation of property along the Kings River, where a homesteader observed that "there are places where private arsenals are maintained to facilitate the peaceful distribution of the water supply." In the Sacramento Valley a test lawsuit—the Gold Run Case—ran on for months, building up 12,549 pages of testimony and a carload of exhibits, including a map 100 feet long.

The State legislature was fully cognizant of the turmoil and periodically enacted laws calculated to pacify the antagonists, but no amount of legislation could entirely untangle the snarl. Presumably California had adopted the Common Law of England, and under that jurisprudence, prior right to a stream went to the possessors of property adjoining it—the riparian owners. Courts generally favored them. Nevertheless, new legislation of 1872 clearly upheld the old appropriation system: "The right to use of running water flowing in a river or stream, or down a canyon or ravine, may be acquired by appropriation. . . . As between appropriators, the first one in time is first in right."

The latecomers seemed to be out of luck. They found it hard to acknowledge that the arid West called for a system of water distribution entirely different from what existed elsewhere. In contentious propaganda, Easterners were constantly lobbying for closer adherence to the Common Law of England on which they had been brought up; and for a time in the early eighties it looked as though they were gaining ground.

To counter them, a vigorous organization, with an extravagant title, sprang up in 1884—the Association of the Anti-Riparian Irrigation Organization of the State of California. "Attempts are now being made to resurrect the English common-law doctrine of riparian rights from the grave to which the will of the people long since consigned it, and to impress it upon the jurisdiction of the State," warned its articles of faith.

"Such attempts, if successful, mean the desolation of thousands of homes; mean the desert shall invade vineyard, orchard and field; that the grape shall parch upon the vine, the fruit wither on the tree and the meadow be cursed with drought; mean that silence shall fall upon our busy colonies, and their people shall flee from the thirsty and unwatered lands; mean that the cities built upon commerce, which irrigation has created, shall decay; and that in all this region the pillars of civilization shall fall, and the unprofitable flocks and herds shall graze the scant herbage where once there was a land of corn and wine, flowing with milk and honey."

Then, raising his pitch to the full soprano of a psalmist, the composer of the articles prophesied: "If this attempt to forbid the useful appropriation of water is defeated by a righteous public opinion crystallized into law, the homes now planted in the midst of fruitful acres will remain the shelter of a happy people . . . and irrigation will advance the frontier of verdure and flowers and fruits, until the desert is conquested and has exchanged its hot sands for happy garlands; its vagrant herds for valiant people; and the bleak plains grown purple with the vintage and golden with the harvest, and the pleasures and profits and peace and plenty that come out of the useful rivers, will make this the Promised Land to millions of free people. . . ."

Due to the influence of the Anti-Riparians and a great many other organizations, the pillars of California civilization remained standing, the principle of "useful appropriation of water" was kept more or less inviolable, and people in the dry valleys continued to tap Sierra streams indiscriminately to develop a Promised Land for the millions. But as the years passed they were abetted by a growing bureaucracy to referee the squabbles: a State Engineer, a Water Commission, a Conservation Commission, a Debris Commission, a Federal Reclamation Service, a Water and Forest Association, along with other local, State and federal committees, courts and investigation boards. Gradually some semblance of order and justice began to be observed in the distribution of water.

The statute of 1872 had specified that appropriations be "for some useful or beneficial purpose." It was a golden rule accepted with a minimum of chafing by both water seekers and water owners. In 1887 was born another reasonable law, authorizing a new unit of local government—the Irrigation District—which was granted the right to organize and operate a water system under an elective board of directors. It was an ingenious device for curbing riparians as well as private appropriators—an elaboration of Charles Crocker's scheme. Within five years some fifty districts had been created, and that number steadily increased until there were over a hundred. As evidence of the general worth of the plan, irrigation in the State increased during the next decades at an average rate of almost 100,000 acres a year.

But the private wars over water supply appeared trivial when big thirsty cities began to eye the Sierra sources. San Francisco wormed into the act in the middle sixties. The Bay city was getting its water from creeks and canyons on the peninsula several miles to the south—good water and an adequate quantity in a normal season, but engineers and alarmists were predicting disaster for San Francisco if a long drought ever struck, and sooner or later, at the rate the metropolis was growing, a more dependable supply would have to be found farther afield. Clear Lake in the Coast Range, some eighty miles to the north, was one possibility; and the Sierra, twice as far away, offered a number of choices.

An indomitable engineer with more tenacity than tact, A. W. Von Schmidt, decided he was just the man to solve San Francisco's problem. He would tap the depths of Lake Tahoe and bring the most wonderful water in the world to the tables and bathtubs of Nob Hill. The Lake Tahoe Water Company and its machinations were a reality before the citizens of either California or Nevada were much the wiser. Details of Von Schmidt's plan were sprung on the public in August, 1866. For $8,000,000 he would build a dam at the one outlet of the lake, raise its level, bore a huge tunnel through the mountains, and by a circuitous route deliver the blue waters at the Golden Gate—20,000,000 gallons a day.

San Franciscans, far from jumping to the bait, greeted the prospect with indifference. No drought appeared imminent. They were satisfied with the water flowing from Pilarcitos and San Andreas Creeks. Why should they pay $8,000,000 for a system they wouldn't own after it was built? Moreover, Nevada claimed ownership of about a third of Lake Tahoe. How would the neighbor state respond to such robbery?

The response from Nevada was quick and vehement. One newspaper suggested that the water company had better recruit an army before it started stealing water it didn't own. With greater restraint, the Nevada Attorney General replied: "As an investment of eight million is contemplated, it might be well for the capitalists to inquire at the beginning whether the projectors of the scheme have any right to draw water from the lake. The Truckee River is now the only outlet to Lake Tahoe. Along its course, mills have been created whose owners have a right to use of its water by appropriation, and the owners of scores and hundreds of fine ranches along its banks have, under the common law, the right to the full flow of the stream in its natural channel, undiminished. It can hardly be expected that those thus interested in the water power of the Truckee will quietly allow the reservoir to be tapped and the water supply taken away for the benefit of the western slope of the Sierra."

Von Schmidt wasn't easily intimidated. "There is no intention whatever, in any way or manner to injure our sister State of Nevada," he apologized smoothly. "Any enterprise which will greatly benefit the people on this side of the mountains must redound to the benefit of those on the other. There is water enough and to spare for both sides. One third of the lake is east of the line dividing Nevada and California; the other two thirds are in California, as well as its outlet. The fact that California takes some of the water will not prevent Nevada also from receiving what she requires. It will be time enough for her to complain when she finds that she will be injured by the loss of water. In any event, she cannot undertake to claim more than one third to which she is entitled. And why should she assume to prevent California from taking the two thirds to which she is unquestionably entitled? Or does Nevada claim the right to take the whole lake and river? Why should not California match her other excellencies and glories with the grandest aqueduct in the world?"

But San Francisco wasn't interested just yet in having the grandest—and most expensive—aqueduct in the world. Neither the Mayor nor the Board of Supervisors took to the idea of being placed at the mercy of a private corporation for a water supply, and there were other creeks farther down the peninsula that should be explored first. "Even if Lake Tahoe were the only available source," expounded the Mayor acidly, in an official rejection, "it would be far preferable for the city to bring in the water and own and control the works. I am satisfied that we have enough water of excellent quality on this peninsula, if properly collected and stored, to supply the city for many years."

The persistent Von Schmidt couldn't take *no* for an answer —not with all that lake water, "the purest of any in the world," going to waste. In ordinary seasons, he maintained, 800,-

000,000 gallons of it were discharged in a single day, and three times that much in flood season. A daily 20,000,000 gallons of it were just the tonic San Francisco needed. By raising the lake six feet, he figured, the runoff would be 82,000,000 gallons a day, without causing any interference with the regular flow.

Regardless of San Francisco's preference for creek water, he built the dam at the lake outlet and another a few miles downstream on the Truckee, asserting that his rights to the water had been confirmed by an Act of Congress. And in 1875 he was back at the city fathers with a still better plan. His conduit would take Tahoe water through a five-mile tunnel under the mountains to Soda Springs; then in a ditch to mining towns like Iowa Hill, Michigan Bluffs, Yankee Jims and Forest Hill, down to a reservoir at Auburn. From there it would travel in wrought-iron pipe to Sacramento and Vallejo, through a tunnel under Carquinez Straits, on to Oakland, and finally across the Bay to San Francisco. For those who had doubts about his ability to install plumbing under the Bay, he explained that he would float the pipe out in short lengths, make flexible joints, lay the pipe between rows of piles; then sink the line. Total distance from Tahoe to San Francisco, 163 miles; total delivery per day, 500,000,000 gallons; total cost, $10,000,000; total expected profit each year, $1,000,000.

"I know of no other enterprise," raved Von Schmidt, "which will pay a better or surer rate of interest on the amount of capital invested or that will be of greater blessing to the greatest majority of the people of California than the utilizing of this unfailing and abundant supply of pure water."

It was the greatest bargain San Francisco ever turned down. But fortunately Lake Tahoe was saved for the tourists, and the Grand Canyon of the Tuolumne was later desecrated instead.

Meanwhile, the little Pueblo of the Angels was growing into quite a metropolis, but it was parched and dust dry. Either the city had to get more water somewhere or stop growing. The Los Angeles River was hopelessly inadequate and the ground water level was steadily going down and down. Artesian wells that had flowed prodigiously in the seventies were being pumped, and pumped dry in the nineties. San Fernando Valley looked like a backward, beggarly country, dotted everywhere with plebeian windmills.

In the balmy climate almost any tree would grow, given a little moisture and encouragement, but there wasn't a dependable rainfall even in winter. So scarce was water that no park in the entire city could be kept respectably green; the limited water supply couldn't be used for purely decorative purposes.

Mayor Fred Eaton worried a great deal about water and the future of Los Angeles during his term of office in 1899, and he kept on worrying afterward. The superintendent of the city water system, William Mulholland, worried too, for it was his job to keep water in the household faucets, and he frequently failed. Eaton studied the maps carefully, toured the southern quarter of the State, and concluded that the nearest reliable source was the Sierra in Owens Valley on the east side of the mountains, 240 miles away.

Much too far, said Mulholland. Moreover, he knew that there would be small chance of getting water at Owens Valley by appropriation, riparian claim, condemnation or any other means short of war. A stream the size of Owens River was guarded jealously against intruders from outside, and water prospectors were likely to be tailed with a gun.

But the citizens of Independence didn't give a suspicious thought to Fred Eaton when he began poking around, posing as a rancher, buying up land and establishing his son Harold in the cattle business. To them he was a wealthy old crackpot, gone daffy on stock raising, a "locoed millionaire." In fact, his coming was regarded by most as a visitation of Providence, for he was pouring money into Independence like a benefactor who didn't know when to stop. People took advantage of his openhandedness on every side, yet he didn't seem to catch on.

The land along Owens River had limited value, anyway. Farmers had staked out claims, erected buildings and imported cattle only to find that much of the area was practically useless because of all the lava and soda in the soil. Many were glad to get rid of their holdings, and charged reasonable prices for them at first. Gradually the prices doubled, but that didn't faze Eaton. The man was land-mad, would pay any price, and stock the slopes with good cattle too.

In early 1903 he encountered his first real obstruction—from government engineers. The National Reclamation Act of 1902 had authorized federal construction of irrigation projects in the West, and someone in Washington had inconsiderately selected Owens Valley for a key experiment. But Eaton was also an engineer; he could talk their language, and soon had them agreeably yielding to whatever he wanted.

The only cattleman who held out was Thomas B. Rickey. Rickey's Ranch was the biggest single piece of private property on the river and one of the best—50,000 acres. Retaining it was a matter of pride to Rickey. He had stumbled into the valley in 1895, a poor man, and by dint of hard work developed a ranch that anyone could be proud of. Eaton kept after him and from time to time raised his offer. The rancher was unmoved, until finally in May 1905, Eaton presented an option for exactly $500,000. That was too good to turn down. Rickey took it, never guessing that the 50,000 acres were the last major obstacle to Eaton's securing water rights for the city of Los Angeles, 240 miles away.

Even then the cagey ex-Mayor waited for three months before letting the public in on his secret. He conceived of the water system as a private venture and wanted to take his time about assembling the necessary capital. But at that point Superintendent Mulholland, convinced at last that Eaton was right, stepped in, appealed to his public spirit and persuaded him that the project should be financed by the city itself, not by individuals.

The sensational news finally leaked out on July 28th, 1905. TITANIC PROJECT TO GIVE CITY A RIVER, screamed the Los Angeles *Times*. "Agents representing Los Angeles city have secured options on about forty miles of frontage on the Owens River, north of Owens Lake. Fred Eaton, ex-Mayor of Los Angeles, and the Superintendent of the Los Angeles waterworks were in the valley in an automobile the early part of the week. They closed the last outstanding options. The price paid for many of the ranches is three or four times what the owners ever expected to sell them for. Everybody in the valley has money and everybody is happy. The deal is riveted.

"The cable that held the San Fernando Valley vassel for ten centuries to the arid demon is about to be severed by the magic scimitar of modern engineering skill. Back to the headwaters of the Los Angeles River will be turned the flow of a thousand mountain streams that ages ago were tributaries of the current that swept past the site of the ancient pueblo of Los Anglees to the ocean. The problem of Los Angeles' water supply has been solved for the next 100 years, even though her population increase to 2,000,000.

"Thirty thousand inches of the purest snow water is to be taken from the bed of the Owens River in Inyo County, right in the heart of the Sierra Nevada Mountains and conveyed for a distance of 240 miles over arid plains and through the heart of mountain ranges to be emptied into mighty reservoirs. The enterprise is one of titanic proportions; the reality transcends the flights of imagination.

"For four years we must wait; it will require that length of time to bore the thirty miles of tunnels through the mountain ranges. Then will Los Angeles indeed become the Promised Land. More precious than milk and honey will be the flow of the pure mountain water—aye, more precious than gold and diamonds.

"Working in secret, bound by a pledge, which through all the months of preliminary surveys and negotiations, involving options on more than 100,000 acres of land, the officials of the water department have paved the way for the consummation of the greatest scheme for water development ever attempted on the American continent.

"Purchase of the private land meant buying outright a valley in which are located over 2,000 people. It probably means the wiping out of the town of Independence. Digging the tunnels and building the canals will mean a cost of approximately $23,000,000, but it is an enterprise in which the end will justify the expenditure, were it thrice the sum. Water is the treasure of the Southwest. Where the canals flow there is wealth before which the fabled treasures of Ind are but bits of cut and colored glass.

"Los Angeles will have a supply of water greater than that of any other city of equal size in the world. San Fernando Valley can be converted into a veritable Garden of Eden. Vast acres of land now devoted to grazing and grain will be converted into orchards and gardens, the peer of any in the world. It is greater in value than the Rockefeller millions; greater than the combined wealth of a dozen European and oriental principalities."

The crowing was premature. When the citizens of Inyo County learned how badly they had been duped, lynching was too charitable an end for any representative of Los Angeles who dared show his face in Owens Valley. Eaton's cunning plot was labeled "the greatest water steal on record." How dared the *Times* suggest that the town of Independence would be wiped out!

If Owens Valley had not been so hopelessly outnumbered in population by San Fernando Valley, civil war would have been declared. The mountain communities had been taken in by the Federal Reclamation Service as well as by Los Angeles. Robbed of their water, they had no future. Appeal after appeal went to Washington, only to be ignored or brushed aside. Eaton and the Angelenos could never be forgiven, and the feud, with frequent outbursts of violence, was kept alive for half a century.

Disregarding the belligerence in Owens Valley, Mulholland boldly went ahead with the construction of the long aqueduct. Laying the water course under the mountains, up and down the precipitous sides of canyons and across miles of torrid desert was a feat almost as spectacular as taking the Central Pacific over the Sierra. Once Californians had been convinced that only rails and the steam engine could bring them economic salvation; now it was water. Delay of another year or two in its arrival would have been the ruin of Los Angeles. By the time it was turned on on November 5th, 1913, Mulholland had become "the Goethals of the West" and, as one orator at the celebration declared, water was "king in fact if not in name."

The water was delivered on schedule and at very nearly the original estimate in cost. The only gross error was in undercalculating the bloom it would bring to San Fernando Valley. Boom followed bloom. The forecasters hadn't taken into account how flourishing expansion could compound expansion. There were no multiplication tables in existence that could do the fantastic reckoning, and instead of a solution to the water problem that would last for 100 years, a desperate search for more water was under way in less than two decades.

Eaton's subterfuge at Owens Valley made mountain residents and conservationists wary about similar invasions from other cities, and when San Francisco finally began scouting the Sierra for water, the guardians were ready. In 1901 the city's Mayor had filed a claim to water rights along the Tuolumne River. The move was followed two years later by an official application to the federal government for the use of Hetch Hetchy Valley as a reservoir site.

Hetch Hetchy was one of the major valleys in Yosemite National Park and a small-scale counterpart of Yosemite Valley itself. Years before, John Muir had gone on record in claiming that less than 100 among 10,000 Yosemite visitors, "if set down suddenly in Hetch Hetchy, would entertain no slightest doubt of their being in Yosemite. They would find themselves among rocks, waterfalls, meadows and groves of Yosemite size and kind, grouped in Yosemite style; and amid such a vast assemblage of mountain forms that only acute observers, and those most familiar with Yosemite Valley, would be able to detect special differences."

Prostitution of such a national monument, even for the benefit of a great city like San Francisco, was unthinkable. The Secretary of the Interior turned down the request summarily. The plight faced by the Bay area was grim. Spurred to action by that rebuff, city overseers again began looking around; but no source seemed to be quite as satisfactory as Hetch Hetchy, where there was a natural site for a dam and where water could be backed up without flooding inhabited areas.

In Washington, administrations changed, and San Francisco's Board of Supervisors had the courage to try a second appeal in 1907. Special commissioners were appointed to make careful surveys, and shortly they came up with exactly the same answer as had the city engineers: Hetch Hetchy was unquestionably the most feasible reservoir site.

The Sierra Club and a dozen organizations of nature lovers sprang into action, as if Yosemite itself were on the auction block. Californians who had never heard of Hetch Hetchy before were told that its crystal river, sublime rocks and waterfalls, its gardens, groves and flowery meadows formed almost a duplicate of Yosemite. A giant rock face, nearly a half mile high, called "Kolana" by the Indians, corresponded to the Cathedral Rocks. On the opposite side was the counterpart of El Capitan, and over its brow dropped a fall more beautiful than Bridal Veil. To the east boomed and thundered "Wapama," a Niagara 1,700 feet high. Then in the main river, a short distance above the head of the valley, was a broad, massive fall and a chain of magnificent cascades, the like of which did not exist anywhere else in the park reserve. Hetch Hetchy, too, had its Half Dome. How could any respecter of nature permit these wonders to be swallowed behind an ugly concrete dam?

"In these ravaging, money-mad days," Muir angrily charged, "monopolizing San Francisco capitalists are trying, with a lot of sinful ingenuity, to get the government's permission to dam and destroy Hetch Hetchy Valley. . . . The few cunning drivers of the damming scheme are working in darkness like snakes in a low-lying meadow. . . . This use of the valley, so destructive and foreign to its proper use, has long been planned and prayed for, and is still being prayed for by the San Francisco Board of Supervisors, not because water as pure and abundant cannot be got from adjacent sources outside the

park—for it can—but seemingly only because of the compara-
tive cheapness of the dam required. . . . Nature's own wonderlands, like everything else worthwhile, have always been
subject to attack, mostly by despoiling gain seekers—mischief-
makers of every degree from Satan to supervisors . . . eagerly
trying to make everything dollarable.

"These temple destroyers, devotees of ravaging commercial-
ism, seem to have a perfect contempt for Nature, and instead
of lifting their eyes to the mountains, lift them to dams and
town skyscrapers. Dam Hetch Hetchy! As well dam for water
tanks the people's cathedrals and churches; for no holier temple has ever been consecrated to the heart of man."

In an eloquent petition to the Secretary of the Interior, the
Sierra Club "devoutly prayed" that the application of the
Board of Supervisors would be denied. The answer to the
prayer came on May 11th, 1908. "I am convinced," declared
the Secretary, "that the public interest will be much better conserved by granting the permit. Hetch Hetchy Valley is great
and beautiful in its natural scenic effects. . . . If it were
unique, sentiment for its preservation in an absolutely natural
state would be far greater. In the near vicinity, however, is the
Yosemite Valley itself. . . . The reservoir will not destroy
Hetch Hetchy. It will scarcely affect the canyon walls. The
prime change will be that instead of a beautiful but somewhat
unusable meadow floor, the valley will be a lake of rare beauty.
As against this partial loss to the scenic effect of the park, the
advantages to the public for the change are many and
great. . . ."

The battle was lost. Magnificent Hetch Hetchy Valley was
drowned, and the next generation of West Bay residents could
sprinkle lawns with water from Tuolumne. But the augurs who
envisioned an improvement on Sierra scenery eventually had
to acknowledge that they were very wrong.

"What is Hetch Hetchy now?" asked a Sierran, three decades after the valley was inundated. "Just another dammed
artificial lake. . . . Before it was flooded the flowing water and
the valley vegetation cooled it, and the trees gave shade and

relief from the heat reflected from the granite walls. Now with the grass and trees gone, there is nothing but a narrow body of monotonous water with an ugly shore line, typical of all reservoirs where the water level shifts, surrounded by stark stonewalls. It is hot and uninviting. The falls, as seen through trees from the floor of the valley were beautiful, but with the setting gone, they are about as interesting as the spillway of a dam. . . . The valley was made more accessible, but for every million who go to Yosemite Valley to stay, a mere thousand go to Hetch Hetchy to turn around and leave."

A battle was lost, but a cause was won. In the long campaign to save Hetch Hetchy a mighty army of nature defenders had been recruited. They saw all too clearly what despoilers had done to the Grand Canyon of the Tuolumne and weren't going to have it repeated elsewhere. In the future when compelling arguments were advanced for relandscaping mountain valleys to suit the interests of powerful corporations and dehydrated municipalities, a reference to Hetch Hetchy was enough to cause the most fluent solicitor to falter.

The contention over water grabs in the early 1900's was only a forewarning of more demonstrative controversy that would be heard later in the century. California was destined to become the most populous state in the Union—and the thirstiest. A host of latter-day overlanders cried for volumes of water such as no inhabitants of a semiarid land had ever demanded before—water for crop irrigation, for industry, for power, for back-yard pools and 5,000,000 bathrooms.

In 1928 the State had at last faced up to the fact that neither the ancient conception of riparian rights nor the idea of acquiring water by appropriation fairly met local conditions. By constitutional amendment water became a resource that could be used by its riparian owners only within the bounds of "reasonableness"; public welfare and public benefit had to be taken into consideration; water not used in one region could be conserved and diverted to areas where it was needed.

With this principle fixed, it was just another step to the introduction of a state-wide system of water collection and distribution, and the start of such a plan came three years later. Man-made rivers began to crisscross dry California valleys where no reliable streams had ever flowed before—the Delta-Mendota Canal, Madera Canal, Friant-Kern Canal, Contra Costa Canal.

From that modest beginning evolved a colossal program for conveying water from all accessible areas of surplus to all irrigable areas of deficiency within the State bounds—the California Water Plan. It would be carried out piecemeal. Construction might take a century, but eventually a network of canals and aqueducts would meander for thousands of miles from the Klamath River on the northern boundary to San Diego County in the south, and take into account every aspect of surplus and demand, from flood control and outboard boating to the corner hydrant.

On November 8th, 1960, 5,500,000 voters went to the polls to cast their ballots for or against "Proposition One"—as hot a political issue as the State had ever fermented. At stake in Proposition One was the go-ahead for the California Water Plan; a commitment to bond the State for $1,750,000,000, as a preliminary expenditure; and authorization of the first major construction unit, the Feather River Project, which called for a giant earth-filled dam and flood-control system that would impound some 4,000,000 acre feet of water.

In effect, it was communizing the water supply of the State, placing an estimated legal debt of over $400 on every family, committing future generations to a policy and an enormous obligation. And there was no unanimity about it. Residents of impecunious mountain towns wanted to know why they should pay the water bill for well-heeled Hollywood or Malibu—pay for carrying the flow of the Feather River 500 miles down the valleys and across the Tehachapi Mountains to Los Angeles and San Diego.

Why should urban merchants subsidize ranch irrigation in the San Joaquin Valley; or villagers dependent on drilled wells be taxed for a system that would never benefit them? That $1,750,000,000 was the largest bond issue ever presented to voters in a state referendum. The Feather River Project alone would cost more than the entire Tennessee Valley Authority and, by one estimate, take 103 years to pay off.

Nevertheless, California voted for it—by a narrow margin. The idea that Charley Crocker had promoted in a modest way ninety years earlier had taken hold exactly as he predicted. The voters had spoken; at long last they wanted the assurance that water would go with the land wherever it was and whoever owned it.

Most of the water would come from the Sierra. The whole future of California depended on the Sierra. After all, it wasn't gold nor lumber nor pasturage nor climate nor soil nor scenery that stood out as the most valuable natural resource of the mountains: it was water, priceless water. Without the Sierra Nevada, much of California would be a blighted desert. Those awful mountains that pioneers risked their lives to cross and conquer were in the end what gave the Promised Land its promise.

Acknowledgments

I am indebted to the following for assistance in the preparation of *The Sierra:* Mr. Bennett T. Gale and Dr. John A. Hussey of the National Park Service; Mr. Bruce M. Kilgore and Miss Elizabeth Lehman of the Sierra Club; Dr. George P. Hammond and the staff of the Bancroft Library, University of California; Mr. Allan R. Ottley of the California State Library; Mr. and Mrs. Ralph S. Minor, Jr.; Mr. John J. Gregg; Mr. Ralph Lee; and the publishers listed under "Quotation Sources" who kindly granted permission to quote from copyrighted works.

Quotation Sources

CHAPTER I. Pp. 12-16—Sierra earthquake: Sacramento *Bee,* March 26 to April 3, 1872; *Alta California,* March 31, 1872; *Inyo Independent,* March 30, 1872. P. 25—Lake Tahoe fire: Mark Twain, *Roughing It*° (Hartford: American Publishing Co., 1872), pp. 176-77. P. 26—Tahoe fires of 1960: Berkeley (California) *Gazette,*° August 22 to 26, 1960. P. 30—Morning of creation: Harriet Monroe, "An Appreciation," *Sierra Club Bulletin,* January 1916, pp. 26-27.

CHAPTER II. Pp. 35-38—Description of San Gabriel: Reprinted by permission of the publishers, The Arthur H. Clark Company, from H. C. Dale's, *The Ashley-Smith Explorations and the Discovery of the Central Route to the Pacific, 1822-1829* (Glendale: 1941) pp. 194-96, 208, 209, 222. P. 36—Letter to Plenipotentiary: A. F. Rolle (editor) "Jedediah Smith, New Documentation," *Mississippi Valley Historical Review,* September 1953, pp. 307-08. P. 40—Letter to Fray Narciso: Edmund Randolph, "Address on the History of California," (San Francisco: 1860.) P. 42—Muir on passes: John Muir, *The Mountains of California* (New York: Century Company, 1894), p. 78. Pp. 43-45—Leonard's record: J. C. Ewers, *Adventures of Zenas Leonard, Fur Trader* (Norman: University of Oklahoma Press, 1959), pp. 77-82.

CHAPTER III. P. 52-55—Colton's descriptions: Walter Colton, *Three Years in California* (1850—Palo Alto: Stanford University Press reprint, 1949) pp. 253, 301, 314. P. 56—Titans at work: C. H. Shinn, *Mining Camps* (New York: Scribners, 1885) pp. 144-48. P. 62—Elite scoundrels: J. D. Borthwick, *The Gold Hunters* (New York: Outing Publishing Co., 1917), pp. 217-18. P. 63—Carrying religion: Bayard Taylor, *Eldorado* (New York: Knopf, 1949). Pp. 63-64—Plume your wing: Colton,° op. cit., pp. 358-59. P. 65—Taylor quotes: William Taylor, *California Life Illustrated,* 1858, pp. 286, 290. Pp. 66-67—Bristol: Sherlock Bristol, *The Pioneer Preacher* (New York: F. H. Revell Co., 1887), pp. 168, 171-72. P. 67-68—Taylor's comment: William Taylor, op. cit., pp. 204-06. Pp. 68-69—Brewer's observations: W. H. Brewer, *Up and Down California* (Berkeley: University of California Press, 1949) pp. 420-21.

CHAPTER IV. Pp. 75-76—Caleb Greenwood: Edwin Bryant, *What I Saw in California* (New York: Appleton, 1849), pp. 354-56. P. 79—Royce adventures: Sarah Royce, *Frontier Lady* (New Haven, Yale University Press, 1932), pp. 64-69. Pp. 82-85—Borthwick's descriptions: J. D. Borthwick, op. cit., pp. 106-14. Pp. 85-86—Browne's descriptions: J. Ross Browne, *Peep at Washoe and Washoe Revisited* ° (Balboa Island, California: Paisano Press, 1950), pp. 24-25. Pp. 87-88—Melee: ibid. pp. 117-21. P. 91—Baggage: ibid., pp. 146-47. Pp. 92-93—Coach ride: ibid. pp. 165-66. P. 93—Bowles' recommendation: Samuel Bowles, *Across the Continent* (Springfield: Bowles and Co., 1865), p. 273.

CHAPTER V. P. 104—Gold Lake: Sacramento *Transcript,* June 19, 1850, (Courtesy California State Library). P. 107—Relic: *American Journal of Science and Arts,* Second Series, Volume XLIII, 1867, pp. 265-67. Pp. 109-10—Fish story: *Alta California,* January 10, 1878. Pp. 111-12—Holdup: Mark Twain, op. cit., pp. 564-66.

Acknowledgments and Quotation Sources

CHAPTER VI. Pp. 116-17—Christman on lynch law: Enos Christman, *One Man's Gold* °
(New York: Whittlesey House—McGraw Hill Book Co., 1930) pp. 202-03. Pp. 117-18—
British visitor: Borthwick, op. cit., pp. 217-19. Pp. 124-25—Bold attempt: *Alta California*,
August 14, 1856. Pp. 125-26—This Tom Bell: ibid. Pp. 126-27—Most Wanted: Sacramento *California American*, September 2, 1856. P. 129—Nevada City robbery: *Alta
California*, May 4, 1858. Pp. 130-31—Confederate robbery: ibid., July 3, 1864. P. 133—
Black Bart—Wanted: ibid., November 14, 1883. Pp. 137-38—Boles' capture: ibid.

CHAPTER VII. Pp. 141-42—Gutta-percha hunter: Borthwick, op. cit., pp. 176-77. P. 144
—Muir's bear: John Muir, *My First Summer in the Sierra*° (Boston: Houghton Mifflin Co.,
1911), p. 182. P. 145—Bloody Pass: ibid., p. 293. Pp. 145-47—Dave Brown: ibid. p. 36.
Pp. 149-50—Marryat's hunt: Frank Marryat, *Mountains and Molehills* (Palo Alto: Stanford
University Press, 1952), pp. 111-13. P. 153—Poster: Borthwick, op. cit., p. 276. P. 154
—Colton's bear fight: Colton, op. cit., pp. 217-18. P. 155—Bull and bear fight: Borthwick,
op. cit., 280-82.

CHAPTER VIII. Pp. 160-61—Details: Sacramento *Union*, June 6, 1864. P. 166—Crocker's
ridicule: Charles Crocker, "Crocker's Railroad Manuscript," ° Bancroft Library, University
of California, Berkeley. Pp. 166-68, 170—Crocker's statements: ibid. P. 170—Colfax
speech: Bowles, op. cit., p. 412. Pp. 176-77—Tramper's observations: Robert L. Harris,
"Pacific Railroad—Unopen," *Overland Monthly*, September 1869, pp. 224-52. P. 177—
Greatest work of the age: Henry George, "What the Railroad Will Bring Us," *Overland*,
October 1868, pp. 297-98.

CHAPTER IX. P. 180—Gould and Curry Mine: Brewer, op. cit., p. 555. P. 182—
Poet-realist: B. P. Avery, "Building the Iron Road," *Overland*, May 1869, pp. 476-77.
Pp. 184-85—Calendar: "Pioneer Days in the Tahoe Region," *Timberman*, August 1929,
pp. 178-79. Pp. 185-86—Chinese greaser: Val Shaw, "The Rape of the Redwood,"
Overland, March 1909, p. 740. Pp. 188-89—Truckee chutes: Sacramento *Daily Record*,
May 29, 1875. P. 189—Little aqueducts: "A Sawmill Railroad," *Hutchings California
Magazine*, August 1857, p. 62. Pp. 190-91—Rule No. 2: *Rules and Regulations of the
Sierra Flume and Lumber Co.* (Sacramento: 1876), p. 17. Pp. 191-93—Flume ride:
New York *Tribune*,° September 16, 1875. P. 194—Hay or wood: Robert L. Fulton,
Epic of the Overland (San Francisco: A. M. Robertson, 1924), p. 38. P. 194—Idyllic
Tahoe: Sacramento *Union*, August 23, 1863. Pp. 195-96—Gardner's story: "Pioneer Days
of the Tahoe Region," ° *Timberman*, August 1929, pp. 178-79. P. 197—*Overland* comment:
Taliesin Evans, "Western Woodlands," *Overland*, May 1871. P. 197—Muir's comment:
John Muir, "Lake Tahoe in Winter," *Sierra Club Bulletin*, May 1900, p. 124. P. 199—
Resolution: "West Side Flume and Lumber Company," *American Lumberman*, September 29, 1900, p. 30. Pp. 199-200—Brewer's comment: Brewer, op. cit., pp. 398-400.
P. 200—Big Trees: "Calaveras Big Trees," *Sierra Club Bulletin*, February 1901, p. 262.

CHAPTER X. P. 207—San Francisco critic: Socrates Hyacinth, "A Flock of Wool,"
Overland, February 1870, pp. 141-46. P. 212—Mutton stew: Joseph Le Conte, *A Journal
of Ramblings Through the High Sierra of California by the University Excursion Party*
(San Francisco: Sierra Club, 1960), pp. 72-73. P. 213—Confession: H. M. Gompertz,
"Up and Down Bubb's Creek," *Sierra Club Bulletin*, May 1897, p. 86. P. 216—Lambs:
R. B. Milne, "Shepherds and Sheepherding," *California Magazine*, March 1880, p. 326.
Pp. 216-18—Muir's comments on sheep: John Muir, *John of the Mountains*,° L. M. Wolfe,
editor (Boston: Houghton Mifflin, 1938), pp. 1-34; *My First Summer in the Sierra*, pp. 75,
85, 125, 152, 275. Pp. 218-19—Sheepmen as firebugs: Sacramento *Union*, Feb. 5, 1876.
P. 220—Query from *Century* editor: *Sierra Club Bulletin* (editorial), January 1918, pp.
322-23. Pp. 220-21—Dudley's observations: W. R. Dudley, "Forestry Notes," ibid.,
January 1899, pp. 292-93. P. 221—Mason's observations: Marsden Manson, "Observations
on the Denudation of Vegetation," ibid., June 1899, pp. 295-310.

CHAPTER XI. Pp. 227-28—Delano's endorsement: Sacramento *Union*, July 19, 1862 and
August 14, 1865. P. 229—Press comments: *Pacific Rural News*, June 9, 1877, p. 364.
Pp. 230-31—Strawberry: Browne, op. cit., pp. 36-42. P. 232—Grand Central: Sacramento
Daily Record, May 29, 1875. Pp. 233-35—Senate Bill: *Congressional Globe*,° 1864,
p. 2300. Pp. 236-37—Bunnell at Yosemite: L. H. Bunnell, *Discovery of Yosemite*°
(Chicago: 1880), pp. 54-61. P. 238—Tenaya: ibid., pp. 45-46. Pp. 239-40—Yohamite
Valley: *Hutchings California Magazine*,° July 1856, pp. 2-8. P. 242—Hutchings House:
J. M. Hutchings, *In the Heart of the Sierras* (Oakland: 1888), p. 127. P. 243—Bowles'
comment: Bowles, op. cit., pp. 223-24. Pp. 247-48—Muir on sequoias: John Muir,
"Save the Redwoods," *Sierra Club Bulletin*, January 1920, pp. 1-4. P. 248—Roosevelt's
address: "Notes and Correspondence," ibid., June 1911, p. 131.

Acknowledgments and Quotation Sources

347

CHAPTER XII. P. 251—King on Mount Whitney: Clarence King, *Mountaineering in the Sierra Nevada* (Boston: 1872), p. 277. P. 253—Public statement: *Inyo Independent,* November 15, 1873. Pp. 257-59—Keough's trip: "Over Kearsarge Pass in 1864," ° *Sierra Club Bulletin,* January 1918, pp. 340-42. Pp. 260-61—Brewer's description: Brewer, op. cit., pp. 410-11. P. 262—Le Conte's explanation: Le Conte, op. cit., preface. P. 263—Tourists: John Muir, *My First Summer in the Sierra,* p. 130. Pp. 264-66—Solomons' climb: T. S. Solomons, "An Ascent of Cathedral Peak," ° *Sierra Club Bulletin,* February 1901, pp. 236-41. P. 266—Colby's statement: "Notes and Correspondence," ibid., February 1901, p. 250. P. 267—View from Mount Whitney: E. T. Parsons, "Notable Mountaineering of the Sierra Club in 1903," ibid., January 1904, pp. 44-49. Pp. 268-69—Farquhar ascent: F. P. Farquhar, "First Ascent of the Middle Palisade," ° ibid., 1922, pp. 264-70. P. 270—Robbins' admission: Royal Robbins, "Half Dome—the Hard Way," ibid., December 1957, pp. 12-13.

CHAPTER XIII. Pp. 278-80—Muir's observations: John Muir, "Flood Storm in the Sierra," ° *Overland,* June 1875, pp. 489-95. Pp. 282-83—Dispatch from Downieville: San Francisco *Chronicle,* December 13, 1937. Pp. 285-86—Yosemite rock slide: "Mountaineering Notes," *Sierra Club Bulletin,* June 1950, pp. 125-26. P. 287—*Monthly Weather Review:* A. H. Palmer, "The Region of the Greatest Snowfall in the United States," *Monthly Weather Review,* May 1915, p. 217. Pp. 288-89—Gilliss' description: "Tunnels of the Pacific Railroad," American Society of Civil Engineers *Transactions,* XIII, 1872, pp. 157-59. Pp. 289-90—Menacing problem: *Sierra Club Bulletin,* November 1948, p. 5. Pp. 290-91—Lincoln avalanche: L. F. Clark, "Avalanche on Lincoln Mountain," ibid., February 1949, p. 9. Pp. 293-94—Mount Ralston avalanche: K. D. Adam, "California Avalanche," ibid., October 1955, pp. 62-68.

CHAPTER XIV. Pp. 296-97—Homemade skiis: L. L. Hawkins, How to Make Skies," ° *Sierra Club Bulletin,* June 1903, pp. 312-13. Pp. 298-99—Muir's trip on skis: John Muir, "Lake Tahoe in Winter," ibid., May 1900, p. 125. P. 299—Indian snowshoes: J. C. Frémont, Memoirs of My Life (New York: Bedford, Clark and Co., 1887), pp. 324, 331. P. 299—C. P. snowshoes: Gilliss, op. cit., pp. 154-55. P. 300—Brewer's observation: Brewer, op. cit., p. 435. P. 300—Skates: "Crossing the Sierras—Norwegian Snow Skates," *Hutchings California Magazine,* February 1857, p. 350. P. 303—Thompson at Cisco: C. M. Wooster, "Meadow Lake City and a Winter at Cisco in the Sixties," *California Historical Society Quarterly,* June 1937, pp. 152-53. P. 305—Dope: H. G. Squier, "Snowshoers of Plumas," ° *California Illustrated,* February 1894, pp. 318-24. P. 306—Groove: ibid. Pp. 306-07—La Porte race: ibid. P. 309—Meadow Lake City: Wooster, op. cit. P. 309—Horse skis: Squier, op. cit. P. 311—Conquest over Frost King: Woods Hutchinson, "Value of Winter Sports," *Sierra Club Bulletin,* January 1913, p. 53. Pp. 311-12—Pilgrimage: Hazel King, "Ski Running—An Impression," ibid., January 1915. pp. 271-73.

CHAPTER XV. Pp. 320-321—Complaint: R. R. Howard, "Grabbing of the Western Water Rights," *Pacific Monthly,* June 1908, pp. 667-73. Pp. 322-23—Crocker's story: Crocker, op. cit., pp. 59-63. Pp. 325-26—Resolution: S. T. Harding, *Water in California* (Palo Alto: N-P. Publications, 1960), p. 63. Pp. 327-28—Bowles' comment: Bowles, op. cit., pp. 308-09. Pp. 328-29—Wail: "Struggle for Water," *Land of Sunshine,* October 1901, p. 285. Pp. 330-331—Anti-Riparians: Harding, op. cit., p. 39. Pp. 332-33—Attorney General's reply: Sacramento *Daily Union:* October 9, 1866. P. 333—Mayor's reply: ibid., October 15, 1866. P. 334—Von Schmidt's rave: *Alta California,* May 15, 1875. Pp. 336-38—Titanic project: Los Angeles *Saturday Times and California Mirror,*° August 5, 1905. P. 339—Muir on Hetch Hetchy: John Muir, "Hetch Hetchy Valley," *Overland,* July 1873, pp. 45-46. Pp. 340-41—Muir's charge: "The Hetch-Hetchy Valley," *Sierra Club Bulletin,* January 1908, pp. 211-220. P. 341—Interior Secretary's edict: ibid., June 1908, p. 324. Pp. 341-42—Hetch Hetchy now: R. K. Cutter "Hetch Hetchy—Once is Too Often," ibid., June 1954, p. 11.

°Note: In order to present a more readable text, deletions of material not pertinent to a subject have occasionally been made without insertion of ellipses, and in some instances sentences have been juxtaposed for clarity or unity.

Index